# Foreigners' Rights in Japan

Boundaries between Stayers and Deportees

By
Kiyoto Tanno

# Foreigners' Rights in Japan

Boundaries between Stayers and Deportees

By
Kiyoto Tanno

TRANS
PACIFIC
PRESS

*Foreigners' Rights in Japan: Boundaries between Stayers and Deportees*
© 2024 by Kiyoto Tanno
Originally published in Japanese in 2023, *Gaikokujin no Jinken no Shakaigaku*
(Sociology of Foreigners' Rights in Japan) by Yoshida Shoten
This English edition published in 2024 by Trans Pacific Press Co., Ltd.

**Trans Pacific Press Co., Ltd.**
PO Box 8547
#19682
Boston, MA, 02114, United States
Phone: +1-6178610545
Email: info@transpacificpress.com
Web: http://www.transpacificpress.com

Copyedited by Miriam Riley, Armidale, NSW, Australia
Layout designed and set by Ryo Kuroda, Tsukuba-city, Ibaraki, Japan

**Distributors**

**USA, Canada and India**
Independent Publishers Group (IPG)
814 N. Franklin Street,
Chicago, IL 60610, USA
Email: frontdesk@ipgbook.com
Web: http://www.ipgbook.com

**Europe, Oceania, Middle East and Africa**
EUROSPAN
1 Bedford Row,
London, WC1R 4BU
United Kingdom
Email: info@eurospan.co.uk
Web: https://www.eurospangroup.com

**Japan**
MHM Limited
3-2-3F, Kanda-Ogawamachi, Chiyoda-ku,
Tokyo 101-0052
Email: sales@mhmlimited.co.jp
Web: http://www.mhmlimited.co.jp

**China**
China Publishers Services Ltd.
718, 7/F., Fortune Commercial Building,
362 Sha Tsui Road, Tsuen Wan, N.T.
Hong Kong
Email: edwin@cps-hk.com

**Southeast Asia**
Alkem Company Pte Ltd.
1, Sunview Road #01-27, Eco-Tech@Sunview
Singapore 627615
Email: enquiry@alkem.com.sg

Library of Congress Control Number: 2023924173

Cover image: Artwork by Mr. Tomoya Akamine in collaboration with Japanese residents and foreigners promoting multiculturalism and diversity, at the Homi Danchi apartments in Toyota City, Aichi.

All rights reserved. No reproduction of any part of this book may take place without the written permission of Trans Pacific Press.

ISBN 978-1-920850-20-3 (hardback)
ISBN 978-1-920850-21-0 (paperback)
ISBN 978-1-920850-22-7 (eBook)

# Contents

List of Figures ................................................................................................. vi
List of Tables .................................................................................................. vi
List of Photographs ....................................................................................... vi

Acknowledgments ........................................................................................ vii
Introduction: A Comparative Sociology of Human Rights Based on the
    Treatment of Foreigners ............................................................................ 1

1  A Socio-Legal Study of 'Fake Nikkei': Japan's Treatment of Foreign Workers ....... 23

2  The Sociology of Foreign Juvenile Delinquency ....................................... 51

3  LGBT Foreign Nationals and the Sociology of Deportation Orders in Japan:
    Protecting the Rights of a Minority within a Minority ............................ 69

4  The Sociology of LGBT Foreign Nationals and Post-Deportation Concerns ........ 97

5  The Sociology of the Hate-Speech Rally Ban: The Case of Kawasaki ................... 109

6  Japanese Management through the Lens of Foreign Labor:
    The Significance of Foreign Workers to Enterprises and the Community ......... 129

7  The Sociology of 'Foreigners' Human Rights' ......................................... 151

8  Re-examining 'Foreigners' Human Rights': Approaching 'Long-Term Residence'
    from the Historical Sociology of Residence Status ................................. 175

9  Discovering Justification for Special Permission to Stay:
    A Constitutional Order Approach ........................................................... 207

10  The Japanese System for Evaluating 'Foreigners' Human Rights':
    Shifting the Epistemological Perspective from 'Foreigners' Human Rights'
    to 'the Rights of Humans, Including Foreigners' ..................................... 229

Bibliography .................................................................................................. 259
Index .............................................................................................................. 273

# Figures

3.1 The number of special permissions to stay issued ....................................................... 84

# Tables

6.1 Statement of costs per Nikkei employee ..................................................................... 140

6.2 Running costs per technical intern/trainee for three years ..................................... 141

# Photographs

5.1 A hate rally in front of Nakaharaheiwa Park on June 5, 2016 ................................. 110

6.1 Brazilian workers assigned to product testing ........................................................... 136

# Acknowledgments

This book represents what I have learned from the case studies of lawsuits involving foreign nationals that I conducted with the help of ALT Law Firm over a seventeen-year period from 2005. I would like to express my gratitude to its attorneys, Gen'ichi Yamaguchi and Yuki Maruyama, and administrative procedures specialists, Madoka Majima and Ryōko Tateiwa, for allowing me to spend countless hours in their offices—I probably spent more hours there in some months than in my own office at Tokyo Metropolitan University.

During my initial attempt to put together an English edition (the first seven chapters of this book), I felt unsure about the standpoint from which I should present the issue. Professor Yoshio Sugimoto, the founder of Trans Pacific Press, guided me in the right direction. The original Japanese edition, *Gaikokujin no jinken no shakaigaku* (Sociology of foreigners' human rights in Japan), was published in 2018 with the help of many suggestions provided by Prof. Sugimoto in numerous workshops during his visits to Japan since 2013. The results of these workshops have also been published in English under the title of *Amorphous Dissent* (Horie, Tanaka and Tanno [eds.] 2020). I am grateful to him for accepting my request to include my latest unpublished studies in the English edition of my 2018 book.

I would like to extend my thanks to Shinya Yoshida of Yoshida Shoten who readily agreed to my idea of publishing an expanded English edition of my original Japanese book with three additional chapters. As a result, the English and Japanese editions are being published almost simultaneously and I am pleased to be able to present to the English-speaking world the most up-to-date information on the situation in Japan. Part of the Japanese edition is based on the English edition and this is a new experience for me. I am grateful to Shinya Yoshida as well as Yūko Uematsu of Trans Pacific Press for giving me this opportunity.

The original Japanese edition was published with the assistance of a Japan Society for the Promotion of Science Grant-in-Aid for Scientific Research (KAKENHI) for the publication of research results (17HP5179). The publication of this English edition was also made possible by KAKENHI subsidies (22HP6005). The studies discussed in some of the chapters in this book were supported by funding from the following sources: a Grant-in-

Aid for Scientific Research (B) (16H05715 and 17KT0063), the Mitsubishi Foundation (201920002) and the Japan Securities Scholarship Foundation contributed financially to work reported on in the Introduction; the Toyota Foundation (D11-R-0069) funded research in Chapter 1; a Grant-in-Aid for Challenging (Exploratory) Research (16K13148) funded studies in Chapter 3; the Toyota Foundation (D11-R-0069), a Grant-in-Aid for Scientific Research (B) (22402038) and a Grant-in-Aid for Challenging (Exploratory) Research (26590054) contributed to studies in Chapter 6; and the Mitsubishi Foundation (201920002) funded research in chapters 8 to 10. I would like to express my deepest appreciation to these research support organizations as their understanding and assistance have been indispensable for the conduct and publication of my work.

In addition, I gratefully acknowledge the assistance given to me during the process of bringing this book to publication by former director of Seikyū-sha Bae Jungdo, director of Seikyū-sha Tomohito Miura, attorney Emiko Miki, secretary-general of Seikyū-sha Chiyoko Hara, Hiroko Suzuki, Kim Bangja, Yōko Ōta, director of Kawasaki Fureaikan Choe Gangija, Drs. Takashi Sawada and Rie Imai of Minatomachi Medical Center, former head of Hamamatsu City Council Social Department Yoshiaki Ishizuka, director of NPO TORCIDA Kiyoe Itō, Marie Matsuoka of Hamamatsu Foundation for International Communications and Exchanges, Hiroki Furuhashi and Yurina Kageyama of Hamamatsu City Council International Department, Yūichi Sasao of Suiran Senior High School, Kumi Katō of Kawasaki Senior High School, Reiko Kurakata of Daishi Senior High School, attorneys Jun Shinagawa, Ryō Nakamura, Akito Ishisaki and Futaba Kaido, administrative procedures specialist Hisashi Mutō, my colleague Shin'ichirō Ishida, and my former colleague Professor Atsushi Kawahara of the Open University of Japan.

# Introduction

## A Comparative Sociology of Human Rights Based on the Treatment of Foreigners

Those who study the condition of foreigners in Japan come up against a bizarre reality, which compels them to question, in extremely simple terms, 'Are foreigners "human"?'. Of course, I mean 'human' here in a social sense, not in a biological sense.

T. H. Marshall, who is famous for his idea of the 'three elements of citizenship', describes the stages of the formation of citizenship-based democratic society in modern Western Europe:

1. establishing 'civil rights' to protect the individual's life, property and beliefs from the king's arbitrary acts under absolute monarchy;

2. securing 'political rights' for political participation through the French Revolution, the Chartist Movement and the labor movement; and

3. recognizing 'social rights' to enable people to lead a healthy and cultural life during the development of post-WWII welfare states.

Marshall argues that citizenship comprised of civil, political and social rights is necessary for people to be able to exist and act as citizens (Marshall and Bottomore 1987).

According to the fundamental understanding of citizenship in this type of political and social thought, foreigners in Japan do not have rights. Even under the Constitution of Japan, which declares 'the equality of the sexes' and 'respect for individuals' as key pillars, foreigners' freedom is only guaranteed within the scope of their residence status and is far removed from the human rights of Japanese nationals. Their freedom of choice in employment, residence and movement exists only within the limits of their residence qualifications. Consequently, individual freedom can be extremely restrictive depending on their status.

A typical example is the case of foreign technical intern trainees. They are not permitted to change their training sites (business premises where they work) or employer-provided accommodation. They are denied their freedom of choice in employment, residence and movement. If they want to continue working, they have to keep working under the initially offered conditions no matter how bad their employers are. It is no wonder that this program has been criticized as 'modern slavery'.

This book examines 'foreigners' human rights' by analyzing the reasoning mechanism operating at the most critical junctures in legal cases involving foreigners on the 'issuance of special permission to stay'. When the authority finds special reasons to allow a foreigner subjected to a deportation order to remain in Japan, it rescinds the order and issues special permission to stay granting residence status to the foreigner. This decision-making process can be regarded as the drawing of a demarcation line between acceptable foreigners and unacceptable ones by the state (in practice, decisions are made by the Minister of Justice or directors of regional immigration bureaus). This book examines several court cases concerning special permission to stay in detail with the focus on the existence of Japan's 'preferred foreigners' ideology behind this demarcation between 'acceptable' and 'unacceptable' categories of foreigners.

## Assessment of individual data in the issuance of special permission to stay

The decision-making process for special permission to stay is published as *Guidelines on Special Permission to Stay in Japan* on the website of the Immigration Bureau of the Ministry of Justice (hereafter referred to as 'Immigration Bureau').[1] Firstly, the Immigration Bureau's assessment method is similar to the analytical framework described by linguist Kenneth Pike.

Pike argues as follows.

> There are two basic standpoints from which a human observer can describe human behavior, each of them valuable for certain specific purposes. In the one, the etic approach to the data, an author is primarily concerned with generalized statements about the data, such

that he (a) classifies systematically all comparable data, of all cultures in the world, into a single system; (b) provides a set of criteria to classify any bit of such data; (c) organizes into types the elements so classified; (d) studies, identifies and describes any newly found data in reference to this system which has been created by the analyst before studying the particular culture within which the new data have been found.

In contrast to the etic approach an emic one is in essence valid for only one language (or one culture) at a time—or, more specifically, for only one minimum dialect at a time or for the relatively homogeneous and integrated behavior of people of one culture area or culturally defined class of people; it is an attempt to discover and to describe the pattern of that particular language or culture in reference to the way in which the various elements of that culture are related to each other in the functioning of that particular pattern, rather than an attempt to describe them in reference to a generalized classification derived in advance of the study of that particular culture. (Pike 1954: 8)

In simple terms, the etic approach understands the subject in reference to a collection of data based on some criteria while the emic approach understands the subject as an individual.

The *Guidelines* nominate the following as 'positive elements to be given particular consideration'.

1. When one or both of the applicant's parents are Japanese nationals or special permanent residents.

2. When the applicant supports (i.e., has custody of and raises) his/her own child born of the applicant.

3. When a marriage between the applicant and a Japanese national or special permanent resident has been legally established.

4. When the applicant is living with, having custody of and raising his/her own child, who is enrolled in an institution of primary or secondary education in Japan and has resided in Japan for a significant period of time.

5 When the applicant requires treatment in Japan for a serious illness, etc., or when the applicant cares for a family member who requires such treatment in Japan.

The *Guidelines* go on to list 'other positive elements':

1 When the applicant has appeared in person at a regional immigration bureau to report that he or she is residing in the country without legal status.

2 When a marriage between the applicant and a person who is a permanent or specified resident in Japan has been legally established.

3 When the applicant supports his/her own child with resident status in Japan as his/her dependent child.

4 When the applicant is a minor and unmarried child receiving the support of his/her parent with resident status in Japan.

5 When the applicant has resided in Japan for a considerable period of time and is deemed to be settled in Japan.

6 When there are humanitarian grounds or other special circumstances.

Then there are 'negative elements to be given particular consideration' in evaluating whether special permission to stay should be issued to the applicant.

1 When the applicant has been sentenced for a serious crime, etc.[2]

2 When the applicant has committed an offense related to the core concerns of national administration on immigration control or a highly antisocial offense.[3]

# Introduction

These are followed by 'other negative elements':

1. When the applicant has entered the country illegally by stowing away on a ship, or by using a false passport etc. or residential qualifications.

2. When the applicant has undergone procedures for deportation in the past.

3. When the applicant is deemed to have committed other violations of penal law or misconduct of a similar nature.

4. When the applicant has some other problems in the circumstances of his or her residence in Japan.

These factors affecting judgment on whether to grant special permission to stay in Japan are described by the *Guidelines* in an etic manner, including the degree of strength. However, the individual judgment is not made on the basis of a set of etic elements. The *Guidelines* state as follows after listing the above etic elements.

> An application for special permission to stay in Japan is given favorable consideration when, after the items listed above as positive and negative elements have been individually evaluated and given all due consideration, circumstances that should be regarded as positive elements clearly outweigh those that should be regarded as negative elements. Therefore, *an application for special permission to stay in Japan is not necessarily given favorable consideration just because a single positive element exists; conversely, the existence of a single negative element will not prevent an application from being given favorable consideration altogether.* (emphasis added)

Each application is judged as an individual case and special permission to stay is issued only when a rationale to permit residency is discovered. This means that the immigration authority grants special permission to stay when it finds a rationale to do so in an emic manner.

## A historiographical approach to data handling

If I were asked to nominate a book similar to this one, I would name *The Judge and the Historian* by Carlo Ginzburg (2002) without hesitation. Ginzburg's friend Adriano Sofri was arrested out of the blue on suspicion of involvement in the 1972 murder of police officer Luigi Calabresi in Milan eighteen years after the incident. Sofri was found guilty by the court. Ginzburg dissects the trials through a detailed examination of the court hearings of the defendant (Sofri) and witnesses, testimonies submitted as evidence and transcriptions of interrogations by the prosecutors and police.

There is no doubt that Ginzburg wrote this book with the intention of proving Sofri's innocence. However, he was not merely trying to explain all the details of a criminal case.

> ... the transcripts of the interrogations conducted during the preliminary inquest by Judge Antonio Lombardi, the ordinance-sentence calling for a trial that Lombardi drew up, the transcripts of the hearings of the Milan Court of Assizes, with Judge Manlio Minale presiding, the summations of Assistant District Attorney Ferdinando Pomarici, the summations of the lawyers for the defence, along with various ancillary material concerning Leonardo Marino and his alleged confederates. In all, some three thousand pages. I have already spoken of the unexpected (and therefore disconcerting) sensation of *familiarity that came over me as I read the testimony assembled by the investigating magistrate*. (Ginzburg 2002: 18–19; emphasis added)

For Ginzburg, this was what warranted investigation. His work ultimately uncovered the reality in which even defendants in today's court trials are pushed into a situation that is no different from medieval witch trials. In this sense, *The Judge and the Historian* is a critique of modern society by way of analysis of what goes on in trials rather than a study of legal precedents.

Introduction

Out of a similar interest to Ginzburg's, I have been studying court cases surrounding 'special permission to stay' in Japan (fought in the court over 'a stay of execution of a deportation order') and published my findings in 'Zairyū tokubetsu kyoka no hōshakaigaku' (A socio-legal study of special permission to stay; Tanno 2013: Chapter 11), 'Kokuseki hō no hōshakaigaku' (A socio-legal study of the Nationality Act; Tanno 2020a: Chapter 5), and 'Teijū kokuji no hōshakaigaku' (A socio-legal study of the public notice on long-term residence; Tanno 2020a: Chapter 6). These studies examined trial documents in order to shed light on the views of the Immigration Bureau as the administrative arm of the state, the views of the foreigners involved and those of their attorneys, and the judgments (the views of the judicial branch of the state) made by the court in light of these parties' views in court proceedings on the issue of special permission.

Studies on court cases involving foreigners conducted by social or labor movement activists tend to present them as a social issue or take the form of case studies. They either criticize the oppressive socioeconomic conditions under which foreigners work (e.g., Ishida, Kondō, Miki and Azusawa 1999; Gaikokujin kensyūsei mondai Nettowāku [ed.] 2000, 2006) or analyze specific court judgments (Gaikokujin rōdōsha Bengo dan [ed.] 1992; Kantō bengoshi Rengō kai 2012; Tokyo bengoshi kai Gaikokujin no Kenri ni kansuru Iinkai Gyōsei soshō Kenkyū bukai [ed.] 2013; Watanabe and Sugimoto [eds.] 2015).

On the other hand, I am interested in the court's decision-making process more than individual judgments themselves, including the following points.

1 What is the intention of the administrative branch of the state in dealing with foreigners?

2 What is the administrative and judicial authorities' understanding of arguments made by the foreigners concerned?

3 How does the court analyze and assess arguments made by the plaintiff and the defendant?

In other words, I would like to discover how Japan sees foreigners and what lies beneath Japanese society's view of such people.

A deportation order is issued according to the Immigration Control and Refugee Recognition Act (hereafter referred to as the Immigration Act) and entails the following procedures.

1. Immigration officers investigate an alleged violation (Articles 27–38).

2. The suspect is detained under a detention order issued by a supervising immigration inspector (Articles 39–44).

3. An immigration inspector examines whether any of the causes for deportation (Article 24) are applicable to the case (Article 45).

4. If an objection is raised, an oral hearing with a special inquiry officer is held (Article 48).

5. If an objection is raised, the foreign national's complaint is filed with the Minister of Justice (Article 49).

6. A written deportation order is issued by a supervising immigration inspector (Articles 49-6, 51 onward). (Jōzuka 2016: 3)

The process involves multiple officials, namely, immigration officers, supervising immigration inspectors, special inquiry officers and the Minister of Justice, within a single organization, the Immigration Bureau. While an attorney is allowed at the oral hearing, the investigation into and examination of an alleged violation are conducted without the attendance of a third party.[4]

The structure of investigation and examination adds further weight to the words of Marc Bloch, who argued that any piece of evidence of a social relationship is imperfect and therefore needs to be examined from various standpoints.

> To sum it all up in a word, the vocabulary of documents is, in its way, only another form of evidence. It is, no doubt, an extremely valuable

one, but, like all evidences, imperfect and hence subject to criticism. (Bloch 1953: 168)

Evidence gathering, investigation and examination in the deportation procedures are carried out by the immigration authority alone. The deportation procedures are undertaken based on the information collected by the administrative agency alone as opposed to a proceeding in an adversarial system such as a court hearing where rebuttal or other evidence can be presented.

Nevertheless, the Immigration Act allows the Minister of Justice or the director of a regional immigration bureau mandated by the minister to grant special permission to stay if they recognize that the subject's special circumstances warrant it. Special permission to stay can be granted before or after the commencement of the deportation procedures, or during or after a court proceeding for a stay of execution of a deportation order. If the immigration authority loses in court, the deportation order is rescinded and special permission to stay is granted as a matter of course. Therefore, 'after a court proceeding' here refers to when the immigration authority wins the court case.[5] It means that the immigration authority can grant special permission to stay at any time when they find 'special grounds'.[6]

## A sociological study of 'foreigners' human rights'

To start with the conclusion, this book aims to demonstrate that while 'foreigners' human rights' exist in Japan, 'foreigners in Japan do not have human rights'. This is evident also in the aspect of administrative practices surrounding court trials. In recent years, it has become a norm that 'stay of execution of a deportation order cases' (meaning lawsuits seeking special permission to stay)[7] are concluded in three courtroom sessions with the aid of pretrial conferences.

> In order to conduct more substantial and efficient hearings, the Tokyo District Court introduced a practice whereby the defense submits, before the first oral argument, evidential documents together with a statement explaining how they determined that they did not overstep or

abuse their discretionary power in around 2007. This practice has been largely established today.

It is now commonplace, following the presentation of these documents by the state (defendant) on the day of the first argument, for the court to request that the plaintiff submits a rebuttal brief and counter-evidence together with the plaintiff's and others' statements by the second oral hearing.

If the court reaches a decision after examining assertions and evidentiary documents submitted by both parties, it is possible for the court to conclude the proceedings on the day of the second hearing. For this reason, preparing for the first and second pretrial conferences is critical, especially the latter for the plaintiff. (Jōzuka 2016: 8)

The executing administrative agency is required to supply a statement of assertions (defense or pretrial brief) and evidentiary documents explaining their rationale for the contested decision and supporting evidence before the first or second hearing date. The plaintiff is required to examine these materials, determine grounds for their claim of illegality of the administrative action and submit any supporting evidence before the next hearing date (the second or third hearing). After that, the administrative agency may change any of the reasons for the decision if necessary. If that is not necessary, the groundwork for the trial is largely completed and the court may be able to conclude deliberation and render a judgment on the second or third hearing date depending on the case. (Jōzuka 2016: 9)

According to judge Makoto Jōzuka, this measure was introduced to avoid both attempts to protract the proceedings unnecessarily and vexatious suits that had been observed among cases involving foreign nationals. He then summarizes the key factors in the stay of execution of deportation order cases from the judge's viewpoint as follows: 'Because the examination and determination are ultimately made using the framework of the aforementioned McLean judgment, the plaintiff needs to argue and prove that "the [authority's] decision was not grounded in fact at all due to errors in material fact on which the decision was based" or that it "clearly lacked validity to a significant degree in light of commonly accepted ideas because the evaluation of facts evidently lacked reasonableness'" (Jōzuka 2016: 13).

On the other hand, 'special permission to stay in Japan' was eventually granted in the '"fake" Nikkei (Japanese-descendant)' case (see Chapter 1) and 'foreign juvenile delinquency' case (see Chapter 2) addressed in this book. The first case was brought on when the immigration authority decided that a foreign applicant had falsified documents and rejected his application for permission for extension of residence period even though he was a genuine Japanese descendant and had never falsified his documents. It was a false accusation case in relation to residence status.

When the plaintiff was found to be a genuine Japanese descendant, the original disposition to reject his extension application was rescinded and special permission to stay was granted. He was subsequently granted a fresh 'long-term resident' status for a period of twelve months. However, this immigration authority's mistake had already resulted in his inability to extend his visa and the loss of his job and accommodation. He had not been able to send any money to his family in Bolivia who had no other income. Moreover, he had received no explanation of why special permission to stay was issued. He would not have had any chance of finding this out had he not sued the government for compensation for economic losses. Where is the justice in this?

The same situation was found in the foreign juvenile delinquency case. Even the attorney for the youth did not know why his client was granted special permission to stay. However, there is no doubt that the crucial factor in the granting of special permission was the possibility of his rehabilitation based on strong documentary evidence submitted by the attorney demonstrating the youth's support network and how much he, his mother and younger sister were needed by Japanese society. These cases involving special permission to stay indicate that the swift judicial process advocated by Jōzuka is not conducive to proper evaluation of the possibility for rehabilitation and whether the applicant should be given a 'favor'.

By comparison, the foreign national in the 'LGBT foreigner' case (chapters 3 and 4) had built up a wide variety of social relationships in Japan after staying in that country for a long period (she had established the foundation of her life solely in Japan where she had resided for two decades after leaving Brazil at the age of nineteen). Yet, most of the social relationships she[8] formed and that supported her life in Japan at the time did not merit special consideration by the state. Her whole family had initially been employed in Japan as foreign workers, but her father and brothers had returned home. Even if she had found a Japanese cohabiting partner, this relationship would not have been treated as a legal marriage under Japanese law, which does not recognize same-sex marriages. She did not have any legal kin recognized by the Japanese government. Consequently, the number of materials demonstrating her local connections to support her residence in Japan in her lawsuit was far fewer than that in the fake Nikkei case and in the foreign juvenile delinquency case.

Upon scrutinizing these cases with the focus on criteria for judgment used in their trials, it became apparent to me that the same concept underpinned the 'hate rally ban case' in Kawasaki (Chapter 5) judged on the basis of the enforcement of the Act on the Promotion of Efforts to Eliminate Unfair Discriminatory Speech and Behavior against Persons with Countries of Origin other than Japan (hereafter called the Anti-Hate Speech Act)— the concept of 'family'. I use quotation marks here because the word has a particular meaning in this context. It is clear that the term as interpreted by the court emphasizes its formality rather than the fact of cohabitation as a family unit given that an LGBT foreigner's partner is not recognized as family.

The emphasis on 'family', albeit in limited scope, in dealing with foreigners is a relatively new phenomenon in Japan. The Alien Registration Order was proclaimed in 1947 shortly after WWII and the Immigration Control Order was decreed in 1951 as one of the ordinances issued in relation to the Potsdam Declaration. The latter law was enforced with people from former Japanese colonies in mind until the name was changed to the Immigration Control and Refugee Recognition Act upon Japan's ratification of the 1951 Refugee Convention. The Immigration Control Order was designed to operate in tandem with the Alien Registration Order. The former was to ascertain foreigners' place of residence while the latter was to control their cross-border movement. This mechanism clearly started with the 'Memorandum concerning entry and registration of non-Japanese nationals in Japan' (Supreme Commander for the Allied Powers Directives to the Japanese Government Index No. 852) issued on April 2, 1946.[9] The first clause states, 'Foreign nationals unattached to the Occupying Forces may be given permission to enter Japan from time to time. *It is anticipated that they will reside in Japan on a semipermanent basis*' (Saikō saibansho Jimu-sōkyoku Shōgai-ka 1950b: 359; emphasis added). GHQ knew shortly after the war that foreigners entering Japan would intend to stay for a long time. During the transition from the Immigration Control Order to the Immigration Control and Refugee Recognition Act, however, no attention was paid to family ties even in cases where foreigners violated the immigration law clearly due to the bond between parent and child or siblings. It is obvious that Japan did not attach importance to 'family unity' (Chapter 7).

## Selective immigration or alternative justice

The issue of how materials and data are rated, as raised by Bloch and Ginzburg, is of particular importance. A power relationship is always involved in the leaving of evidence (especially written official records and testimonies) to a certain degree and hence there is no evidence that is completely neutral to nor colored by power. If researchers fail to take into consideration the power relationship that has led to the evidence, they cannot exclude the possibility of distorting facts in their attempt to carry out research based on objective evidence. Moreover, the power relationship that has led to the evidence is undetectable in the evidence itself. They will not notice it unless they try to find it because an 'invisible hand' is at work there.

This 'invisible hand' is no different from one Adam Smith described in *The Wealth of Nations*. Smith's invisible hand represented the social division of labor. Each individual living in a society with a fully functioning social division of labor is merely a cog in the wheel of society.[10] Being a component, they do not have a complete understanding of their society as a whole but they can take part in the overall formation of a stable society by devoting themselves to their roles.[11]

Smith located the foundation of the social division of labor in the morals and ethics to which people mutually agreed to adhere in addition to law and demonstrated that these people had various forms of shared code with which they mutually agreed to comply. When they engage in activities individually under a shared code, these activities share certain directionality. From this viewpoint, the Immigration Act may confer wide discretionary authority on the Minister of Justice but there must be a certain degree of directionality in granting special permission to stay, even though it is judged on a case-by-case basis, because the immigration authority has published the guidelines for the granting of special permission to stay in multiple languages and carried out day-to-day administration according to *Ihan shinpan yōryō* (Manual of tribunal procedures for illegal residency) for law enforcement. It is unlikely that judgments on the granting of special permission to stay are made completely arbitrarily.

As mentioned earlier, it has been stated that special permission to stay is granted as a 'favor' when the Minister of Justice or the director of a regional immigration bureau mandated by the minister finds a reason for special consideration and that such a reason is considered on a case-by-case basis for there are no set criteria. Special permission to stay may or may not be granted even in similar cases. For this reason, some people regard special permission to stay as 'selective immigration' (Suzuki 2007). There is no question that it functions as a selective immigration tool given the importance of children's education in improving the chance of obtaining special permission to stay.

It is also possible to think that the state sees some kind of alternative justice in halting the execution of a deportation order and granting new residence status through this tool by finding some reasons to give special consideration to the circumstances of those who otherwise could not stay in Japan. Shin'ichirō Ishida uses a collective term 'alternative justice' for 'alternative approaches to the conventional judicial system' and argues that it is 'spreading all over the world' (Ishida 2011: 7). This way of thinking has developed in parallel with concepts such as alternative dispute resolution (ADR) and restorative justice. The approach has been confirmed as a particularly effective means to achieve a social consensus in relation to ethnic disputes escalating to armed conflicts in Africa and Southeast Asia, truth commissions on South Africa's apartheid regime, and the oppression of people by Latin American military governments, as well as regarding ethnic minority rights (Ishida [ed.] 2011).

Introduction

In *The Judge and the Historian*, Ginzburg points out that the judge in the Calabresi murder case used a 'suicidal judgment' method, so called because the judgment was 'written in such a patently illogical manner that it automatically left itself open to annulment on the grounds of formal faults' (i.e., as if it was expected to be overturned on appeal) (Ginzburg 2002: 191). Ginzburg questions whether this manner of conducting a trial should be judicially acceptable even if it is technically possible. The same can be said about special permission to stay. It is questionable why it is acceptable to the judicature that the Minister of Justice can grant special permission to stay regardless of the outcome of a lawsuit simply because the minister has the discretion to do so. If this system is to continue, it needs to be legitimized in a logical manner in some form. A review from the standpoint of alternative justice would be one of the effective approaches.

My argument so far shows that the granting of special permission to stay, which is determined by the question of whether the Minister of Justice can take pity on the foreigner complaining to the court (or the applicant filing an objection to a deportation order prior to a lawsuit) outside of the logic of law, takes into consideration not only the circumstances of the plaintiff's or the applicant's stay in Japan but also all aspects of the life of their family and household in Japan. This is one of the reasons for my attempt to address this issue from a sociological perspective. We can uncover the logic of 'demarcation' concerning special permission to stay only when we examine the foreigner's social existence itself. A precise picture of this line-drawing has been reported by a practicing legal professional (Yamaguchi 2007). In this book, I attempt to go beyond case-based fact-finding and examine how Japan as a nation sees foreigners based on the logic of demarcation by the administrative agency and its underlying perception of history (and society).

## A hidden logic recognizing foreigners' human rights

Chapter 8, 'Reconsideration of "foreigners' human rights"', Chapter 9, 'A discovery of the logic justifying special permission to stay', and Chapter 10, 'A Japanese-style "foreigners' human rights" evaluation system' relate to the plaintiff in the case discussed in chapters 3 and 4 who filed a 'petition for reconsideration' after dismissal by the Supreme Court on the grounds of a change in her circumstances (i.e., she formed a relationship of mutual support and cooperation with a new Japanese partner and settled in cohabitation). These chapters contain revised versions of my submissions to the Tokyo District Court (Chapter 8) and the Tokyo Hight Court (chapters 9 and 10).

By the time of these submissions, five years had passed since I wrote chapters 3 and 4 and I had deepened my understanding of 'foreigners' human rights' and become aware of the existence of a hidden logic behind this issue in Japan. Chapter 8 focuses on how foreigners' human rights have been defined in Japan's legal history, especially on shifts in logic before and after a change of those officials empowered to order 'deportation'. My research has found the following. In the prewar era, the authority to deport was conferred on prefectural governors and the emphasis of foreigners' residence management was on controlling and keeping records of the length and place of their residence with a relaxed attitude toward their employment-related movement. After Japan's defeat in WWII, foreigners' residence management transitioned to the status of a residence system (granted upon entry depending on their intended activities, including occupation) and the authority to order deportation was given to the Minister of Justice and the Immigration Bureau. Since this transition, the immigration authority has been using a comprehensive list of requirements, including those from the prewar era, the transitional phase and subsequent law revisions, in qualifying foreign nationals wishing to stay in Japan.

The Immigration Act stipulates that the foreigner's residence status dictates conditions for the person's social life, including living with family. Under this premise, the foreigner's right to the pursuit of happiness (i.e., scope of human rights) in Japan is dependent on the person's residence status. Reflexively, this means that we can determine the scope of a given foreigner's human rights by scrutinizing the historical background of the creation of the residence status applicable to that person. Assuming the emergence of 'idiosyncratic human rights peculiar to' each residence status, Chapter 8 approaches the 'human rights of "long-term residence" status' from a historical sociological standpoint.

Chapter 9 discusses where we may find grounds for the logic allowing the Minister of Justice and directors of regional immigration bureaus authorized by the minister to issue special permission to stay, cancel the existing deportation order and grant a new residence status when they believe that the foreign national ordered to leave the country under the law should be given a favor in the context of the constitutional order under the new constitution. I was interested in the constitutional litigation theory pioneered by constitutional law scholar Nobuyoshi Ashibe, especially the applicability of 'dual criteria for evaluation' (legally called the 'double standard of judicial review') emphasized by him to special permission to stay. I was surprised by not only the applicability of the dual-criteria evaluation approach but also a similarity in nature between administrative discretion exercised in immigration administration and the legislation of economic regulations (although this statement may be tautological as dual evaluation criteria is a highly effective legal theory for legislating economic regulations in the first place). While the dual-criteria approach is closely linked with the postwar constitutional review system, it has developed gradually through court cases on discretionary control, and was established under the new constitution prior to the McLean judgment rather than starting when the new constitution came into operation. The point at which dual criteria gained a foothold in Japan as an established legal principle is debatable. As far as immigration administration is concerned, the McLean judgment was the crucial factor for its establishment in my opinion.

Chapter 10 reveals not only that the dual-criteria principle is operating in evaluations of special permission to stay but also that the system of petition for reconsideration cannot be understood without it. A petition for reconsideration can be filed after a legal action over a deportation order has concluded. If the Minister of Justice agrees that the petitioner's subsequent change of circumstance warrants favorable consideration, the minister cancels the previous decision and grants special permission to stay. However, the petition for reconsideration is a de facto act and not a legally prescribed procedure as Prime Minister Shinzō Abe stated in the 185th extraordinary Diet session: 'It is my understanding that what is sometimes called "petition for reconsideration" is a de facto act by which foreign nationals who have received a deportation order, including those whose application for refugee status have been rejected, file a request to revoke the said disposition and to issue special residence permission and not a statutory procedure provided by the Immigration Control and Refugee Recognition Act (Cabinet Order No. 319 of 1951)'.

If a legally issued deportation order can be arbitrarily overturned by a non-judicial act, Japan can no longer be regarded as a nation governed by law. The petition for reconsideration must be grounded on law-based administration and therefore needs to be legitimized as an administrative act. This brought me to the realization that the petition for reconsideration can be positioned as a legitimate administrative act if we understand that the dual-criteria evaluation approach operating in the granting of special permission to stay is functioning in a more distilled form with this procedure. I would like to shed light on the hidden logic at work when administrative acts under the Immigration Act are justified.

## What are 'foreigners' human rights' in Japan?

The primary aim of this book is to examine the reality of the 'exercise of bare power' over foreign individuals in Japan. My personal view of 'foreigners' human rights' is irrelevant because a person's private view almost never leads to the exercise of power. In my view, the scope of 'foreigners' human rights' is shown by the 'exercise of bare power' in the line of thinking of government officials involved in immigration law enforcement, the state's assertions in immigration violation cases and final judgments handed down by court judges.

Because of my desire to demonstrate the process of the 'exercise of bare power', some of the chapters begin with the presentation of a complaint filed with the court, followed by other documents reflecting the sequence of submissions to the court, in order to clarify the logical process leading to the conclusion. Very few legal actions involve TV drama-style oral arguments in the courtroom. In reality, the parties submit documents by the set date and either party wishing to make a counterargument submits additional documents. The court hearing on the set date is for the judge to communicate if they require additional submissions for further deliberation or intend to conclude the trial. No exchange of oral arguments takes place in the courtroom and each hearing (even delivery of a judgment) normally ends in less than five minutes. In this situation, a trial is conducted purely through examination of evidential documents submitted by both parties. A virtual legal contest takes place when the parties are examining one another's submissions outside of the courtroom. This is very different from criminal trials by jury.

After conducting my research with this intent, I arrived at the conclusion in Chapter 10 that there were no 'foreigners' human rights' in Japan. This means that there are no 'foreigners' human rights' in Japan with specific referred content. In other words, I am unable to say what 'foreigners' human rights' are. This does not mean that I have given up my endeavor to address 'foreigners' human rights'.

In theorizing the universal law of gravitation, Isaac Newton considered that ontological questions such as 'What is the essence of universal gravitation?' and 'Why does gravitation exist?' should not be of concern to natural philosophy (physics), and that there was no need to puzzle over matters such as 'How does universal gravitation travel through space?' and 'What is the medium through which universal gravitation acts on objects?' (Yamamoto 2003b: 868). Newton's intention here was to explain the relationship arising between objects in gravitational phenomena in terms of the law of universal gravitation rather than to describe what gravitation and gravity were.

Similarly, what I see as 'foreigners' human rights' are dictated by relationships based on considerations made in evaluating foreign nationals or their social relations. In other words, foreigners' human rights in Japan do not belong to the foreigner as an individual but are identified and evaluated as the aggregate of human relationships between the foreign individual and other people. Consequently, the door to residence in Japan is opened if it is decided that removing the foreign individual from Japan will significantly damage the perceived totality of relationships around that person. The foreigners' human rights are human rights incorporated in a society and integrated with social relationships (i.e., 'rights of humans, including foreigners') rather than the individual's human rights.

## Notes

1. The *Guidelines* was released in October 2006 and revised in July 2009. Its English, Spanish, Portuguese, Tagalog, Korean, simplified Chinese and traditional Chinese versions can be found on the website of the Immigration Services Agency of Japan for non-Japanese speakers: https://www.moj.go.jp/isa
2. Receiving an unsuspended sentence for a vicious or serious crime or for involvement in smuggling or trafficking of illegal drugs or firearms are mentioned as examples.
3. Examples include receiving an unsuspended sentence for abetting illegal employment, crimes related to mass stow-away or illegal receipt or issue of passports, or having a history of committing an act that compromises the social order by abetting illegal or fraudulent residence in Japan, or personally engaging in prostitution or procuring prostitutes, human trafficking or significant infringement on human rights.
4. The investigation and the examination are carried out simply to determine if there are sufficient facts to warrant the issuing of a deportation order, not to look at all aspects of the foreign national's residence in Japan.
5. The case in Tanno (2013: Chapter 11) is a typical example. The plaintiff won the first trial in the Tokyo District Court and secured 'a stay of execution of a deportation order' and special permission stay. The ruling was overturned in the Tokyo High Court. Despite winning the appeal trial, however, the state did not execute the deportation order nor cancel the plaintiff's special permission to stay. The state appears to have appealed in order to avoid the lower court decision becoming the final judgment (a precedent).
6. This is why all evidence used in the series of legal procedures surrounding decisions on deportation and special permission to stay needs to be examined 'in light of "imperfections of evidence"' as pointed out by Bloch, and each piece of evidence has to be treated on the assumption that it is not neutral.
7. It is extremely difficult to challenge the legality of denial of special permission to stay because the Immigration Act gives the Minister of Justice considerable discretionary powers to grant or deny special permission to stay. On the other hand, decisions on a stay of execution of a deportation order are required to follow certain rules of law as detention in an immigration detention facility is in effect no different from imprisonment for a criminal offence and the ultimate deportation forcibly removes a person from their social space (equivalent to death in that the person no longer exists in Japan). In other words, while decisions on special permission to stay can be made on an individual basis, there is much higher pressure on the execution of a deportation order to treat like cases alike. For this reason, legal actions for a stay of execution of a deportation

# Introduction

order are often fought on the grounds of the equality principle under Article 14 of the Constitution of Japan.

8  While this foreign national is listed as male in her passport, female pronouns are used in this book as she is a transgender woman.

9  'Memorandum for registration of Chinese nationals' (GHQ Directives to the Japanese Government Index No. 1543) was issued on February 25, 1947, and the Alien Registration Order was proclaimed as Imperial Ordinance No. 207 on May 2, 1947 (the Enforcement Regulations of the Alien Registration Order was Ordinance of the Home Ministry No. 28, 1947). The Alien Registration Order is known as the last imperial ordinance.

10 Smith also talks about the 'invisible hand' in *The Theory of Moral Sentiments*: 'all of whom thus derive from his luxury and caprice, that share of the necessaries of life, which they would in vain have expected from his humanity or his justice. The produce of the soil maintains at all times nearly that number of inhabitants which it is capable of maintaining. The rich only select from the heap what is most precious and agreeable. They consume little more than the poor, and in spite of their natural selfishness and rapacity, though they mean only their own conveniency, though the sole end which they propose from the labours of all the thousands whom they employ, be the gratification of their own vain and insatiable desires, they divide with the poor the produce of all their improvements. They are led by an invisible hand to make nearly the same distribution of the necessaries of life, which would have been made, had the earth been divided into equal portions among all its inhabitants, and thus without intending it, without knowing it, advance the interest of the society, and afford means to the multiplication of the species' (Smith 1976: 184–185).

11 This is applicable to the deportation procedures and the issuance of special permission to stay following a stay of execution of a deportation order. The immigration officer, inspector, special inquiry officer, regional immigration bureau director and the Minister of Justice involved in the process are merely playing their roles according to the law.

# A Socio-Legal Study of 'Fake Nikkei': Japan's Treatment of Foreign Workers

## Introduction

After the global recession precipitated by the collapse of US financial services firm Lehman Brothers in 2008, a wave of non-regular employment termination called '*haken-giri*' (laying off temp workers) swept Japan from the autumn. When the wave reached foreign workers of Japanese descent, a majority of whom were in non-regular employment, the government set up a support program for the unemployed in this category wishing to return to their home country (hereafter called 'repatriation support program') and encouraged those who could not pay their own travel costs to return home. Up to 300,000 yen was given to unemployed workers of Japanese descent and up to 200,000 yen to dependent family members. In other words, the government offered a family of unemployed parents and two children one million yen from national coffers to incentivize them to leave Japan. It also announced in anticipation of a sluggish labor market that the beneficiaries of the repatriation support program would not be permitted to re-enter Japan for three years.

In March 2014, however, the Committee for Japan's Future, set up in the Cabinet Office, began discussions on expanding the utilization of foreign labor and the need to boost the immigration intake as part of the measures to counter depopulation due to the declining birthrate and super-aging society.[1] Debate over the foreign labor intake was suddenly reactivated when some of the concrete policy measures were put forward, including 'expanding the intake of technical interns in the construction industry and extending their period of stay from three to five years' and 'creating the domestic support immigrant labor (housekeeper immigrant) category'. The

Japanese government did a complete about-face from desperately turning back foreign workers to wanting to welcome them with open arms within a short period of five years.

Prime Minister Abe's cabinet proposed economic policies, collectively called 'Abenomics', involving the simultaneous implementation of three pillars—audacious monetary easing policy, aggressive and expeditious fiscal policy, and a growth strategy promoting private-sector investment—which brought about a certain level of economic recovery. This must have contributed to the resurgence of the argument for a greater foreign labor intake. When the same argument was heating up at the time of the revision of the Immigration Act in 1990, Japan was troubled by labor shortages in all job categories amid the bubble economy. This time, the idea of accepting more foreign workers in the face of depopulation was filling the pages of newspapers while reports on the problems of the low income of non-regular Japanese employees, especially young workers, and the existence of so-called 'black companies' (with exploitative employment conditions) were still common. Economic recovery was clearly happening in some industries, but it had not spread to the whole country. In this context, the new argument for accepting foreign labor has been advanced without paying much attention to how Japan received and treated immigrant workers in the past.

Foreign nationals of Japanese descent who were granted 'long-term residence' visa status under the 1990 revision of the Immigration Act were not subjected to any restrictions on the number of times they could extend their visa, accompany their family members or gain employment. Japanese descendants were given the more preferential conditions among Japan's foreign workers. Nevertheless, even they had been subjected to extremely inadequate treatment in the past. I would like to present an example of Japan's immigration administration in order to demonstrate these inadequacies in the treatment of foreign workers in this chapter.

The said example involves a Bolivian national of Japanese descent (hereafter referred to as 'A') who entered Japan with a 'long-term residence' status. The case (hereafter referred to as the 'fake Nikkei' case) started when his visa extension application was rejected because his Japanese ancestry was deemed 'fake' by the Immigration Bureau. He became an overstayer when his residence extension was denied, and his one-year 'long-term residence' status was forfeited. As a result, he was issued a written deportation order and taken into custody. He decided to fight for a stay of execution before the court because he was a genuine Japanese descendant. When the trial began, attorneys for A gathered additional materials proving his Japanese descent and submitted them to the court. The additional evidence played a crucial role in leading the Immigration Bureau to admit A's eligibility for 'long-term residence' status and grant a one-year extension of his resident visa before the conclusion of the trial.

In this 'fake Nikkei' case, A, the 'long-term resident' who was eligible for an extension of his residence period, was denied the visa and consequently became an overstayer against whom a deportation order was executed. He was put in an immigration detention facility, albeit temporarily, and lost his position at his place of employment. He alone suffered the negative consequences of this case even though he was never at fault. After dropping the court action, he made a state compensation claim with regard to the series of decisions made by the Immigration Bureau in an attempt to find out (1) why he was judged as a 'fake' Japanese descendant, and (2) why he was recognized as a Japanese descendant after being served a deportation order on the grounds of false identity (hereafter referred to as 'state redress case'). Thus, the case transitioned from a complaint against the denial of a visa extension application to a demand for state compensation. I will examine this course of events to ascertain the scope of the foreigners' rights recognized and accepted by Japan.

## Working in Japan and procedures for acquisition of residence status

The case happened while A, a Bolivian man of Japanese descent, was staying and working in Japan for the second time. He first came to Japan in 1991 and had to return to Bolivia in 1992 as he could not extend his single-year 'long-term residence' status at the end of the residence period. After returning home, he and his uncle worked as *seringueiros* (rubber harvesters) in rubber plantations near Riberalta in northern Bolivia. It was difficult for A to support his family with income from this work (around 500 dollars a month). In around 1997, work evaporated due to the deteriorating rubber market, so he moved to Santa Cruz with his family and found a job in a construction business. However, his income in Santa Cruz was even lower than that in Riberalta and made him consider returning to Japan to work again. He needed money for his children's schooling and had no prospect of earning enough in Bolivia to support his family.

In around 1998, A decided to work in Japan for the second time. As he became aware that he could apply for a certificate of eligibility for the acquisition of status of residence if he had family in Japan, he decided to proceed on his own without relying on an agent. He sent the required documents to his younger sister staying in Japan who then acquired a certificate of eligibility for him.[2] She mailed the certificate to Bolivia but it failed to reach him.

A relative informed A that his 1992 visa extension application had been rejected on the following grounds: 'your grandfather had been married in Japan before coming to Bolivia, then he married your grandmother in Bolivia, and therefore you should have provided proof that your father was really your grandfather's child'. Thinking that he would need a certificate confirming that his grandfather had acknowledged his father as his own child, A took a bus from Santa Cruz to Riberalta, presented copies of his and his father's birth certificates and his parents' marriage certificate to the town's civil registry and obtained the original certificates. He then went to the notary public office, presented his identification paper and obtained a copy of a sworn affidavit of his grandfather acknowledging his father as his own. He returned to Santa Cruz and had his and his father's birth certificates and his parents' marriage certificate from Riberalta notarized and registered in the city's registry called Jefatura Departamental. He also received a duplicate of each certificate for fifty boliviano (about 700 yen) per copy there.

Guillermo Nema, a lawyer and chairperson of Federación National de Asociaciones Boliviano-Japonesas, was asked by A to translate the certificates and notarized statements into the Japanese language. He paid a translation fee of thirty boliviano to Nema, who was the only person authorized by the Japanese Embassy to translate official documents,[3] sent these documents to a cousin in Japan and applied for a certificate of eligibility for residence status on July 24, 2001, with his uncle as the endorser in Japan. In August 2001, a certificate of eligibility for one-year of 'long-term residence' was issued and sent to Bolivia. He bought a plane ticket to Japan and arrived in Narita Airport on September 22, 2001.

He initially stayed at his younger brother's house in Chiba. When he started working in Chiba from December 2001, he rented an apartment with his brother as cosigner where he lived alone. He was employed by a business contractor and dispatched to a sash factory as an aluminum parts sorter, where he worked from 8am to 8pm. While his take-home pay varied depending on overtime hours, he generally earned around 250,000 yen per month. After paying a monthly rent of 43,000 yen plus utility and food expenses, he sent most of the remainder to his family in Bolivia. His monthly remittance averaged around US$1,000.

In May or June 2002, the end of his one-year 'long-term residence' period was approaching and A asked his wife in Santa Cruz to send him the same documents he had used in obtaining his current certificate of eligibility to use in the upcoming visa extension application. The mail took one month and reached him just one week before the visa was due to expire. He lodged an application for an extension of residence status, together with the documents from Bolivia, his grandfather's removed family register arranged by his brother, and his brother's letter of endorsement, with the Tokyo Regional Immigration Bureau Chiba Branch Office on September 18, 2002.[4] He had his passport stamped with the word 'APPLICATION' and went home. After his brother arranged for the creation of his father's family register, A submitted the father's family register certificate to the Immigration Bureau as an additional supporting document (the creation of his father's family register made him a second-generation Japanese descendant). Although he did not include the family register certificate in his application on September 18, the family register itself was created on September 2.

He received a summons postcard from the Immigration Bureau and attended the Chiba branch office with his brother on November 5, 2002. He was handed a 'DEPORTATION' document and immediately subjected to questioning by an immigration officer for nearly three hours. He was handcuffed at the end of questioning and notified of the reason: 'doubts about the authenticity of supporting documents (birth certificates etc.)'. Then, the Immigration Bureau issued and executed a detention order against

A. He was put on a bus and taken into custody in the immigration detention facility of the Tokyo Regional Immigration Bureau Building No. 2.

## The 'fake Nikkei' case according to the plaintiff's complaint

Now we have established the basic facts, let us ascertain what this case means according to the plaintiff's complaint. It begins by explaining that this case arose because 'the defendant denied the plaintiff's application for an extension of residence status on the grounds that the plaintiff, who is a genuine Japanese descendant, was a so-called "fake Nikkei" who submitted falsified documents, then it immediately commenced deportation procedures and executed a detention order against the plaintiff'. This indicates the plaintiff's intention to fight the case on two points:

1 'A' is a genuine Japanese descendant.

2 Given A's genuine Japanese ancestry, the decision to reject his application for an extension of residence status and the subsequent set of deportation procedures, including the issuance of a detention order, based on that decision were illegal.

To demonstrate the first point, the complaint presents the specifics of how A's grandfather went to Bolivia and set up a family there. The grandfather had six children, and three of them—the first son (A's father) and two younger sons—created a family register in Japan on September 2, 2002, and obtained Japanese nationality. Next, it explains that A's maternal grandfather (Japanese) married in Riberalta and had A's mother. Finally, the circumstances of A's parent's marriage and the birth of their twelve children were explained according to a genealogy chart.

By the way, the question arises upon verification of A's Japanese descent as to when the generation of a Japanese descendant is determined. The procedures of an application for an extension of residence period, under which A was rejected, relate to people who fall into the category of 'children of a person who was born to a Japanese national (excluding those who come under (ii) above)' in Table II appended to Article 7 of the Immigration Act. This was contained in Ministry of Justice Public Notice No. 132 issued on May 24, 1990, as one of the 'statuses listed under the Long-Term Resident category in Appended Table II pursuant to the provision of the Immigration Control and Refugee Recognition Act Article 7-1(ii)' (hereafter called 'public notice on long-term residence'). Because a family register for A's father had already been created by the time A applied for his visa extension, A was no longer a subject of the public notice on long-term residence. The public notice was applicable only to (I) the spouse of a child of a Japanese national (second-generation spouse), (II) the child of a child of a Japanese national (third generation), (III) the spouse of a child of a child of a Japanese national (third-generation spouse), and (IV) the unmarried, minor and dependent child of a child of a child of a Japanese national (fourth generation). If the father had not acquired Japanese nationality, A would have been a third-generation child of a child of a Japanese national to whom the public notice on long-term residence was applicable. Following the father's acquisition of Japanese nationality, however, A did not fit into any of the statuses under the public notice. This means that the disposition to reject his application for a visa extension and subsequent deportation procedures were illegal dispositions lacking factual support.

The complaint refers to the existence of similar cases represented by A's attorney in which the following genuine Japanese descendants were treated as 'fake Nikkei':

1   a third-generation Japanese-Columbian;

2   a third-generation Japanese-Bolivian from A's hometown of Riberalta;[5]

3   a third-generation Japanese Brazilian and spouse;

4   a third-generation Japanese Brazilian family of five.

In the first two cases, the clients switched their status to 'short-term stay', reapplied with newly gathered evidential material, and had their change of status to 'long-term residence' approved. The latter two cases went to court, but the Minister of Justice granted an extension of residence period as soon as the defense realized the irrefutability of their Japanese ancestry. The plaintiffs dropped their court actions as they saw no merit in continuing them.

Then, the complaint explains the difference between Japan and Latin American countries, including Bolivia, in terms of the legal system and its operation, customs, religion and all other aspects of life in general. Regarding the marriage system, in Bolivia, the civil marriage system through registration at a public office was established only in the second half of the twentieth century. Many people among the poor still do not register their marriage because identity registration is another side of the state's control over citizens and does not bring any benefit to their social welfare. Only a small segment of the population can afford to have a formal 'church wedding' as it costs as much as an average worker's annual income in some cases. Under these circumstances, an unregistered marriage is treated as a 'legitimate marriage' in various government procedures and social life.

In Latin American societies, especially Bolivia, the scope of legal terms such as 'marriage', 'legitimate child', 'paternity acknowledgment', 'marital separation' and 'divorce' as well as the format of various certificates differ from those in Japan. Also, administration of the original identification documents is sometimes transferred from one government body to another, which may change the certificate numbering system. In the abovementioned Case 2 involving a person from Riberalta, it appears that immigration officers (one of whom was also the chief inspector in A's case who determined that his documents had been falsified) were ignorant of this situation and assumed that the submitted documents had no originals. In Case 2, the Tokyo Immigration Bureau's inspector S at the time explained to the plaintiff's attorney and the complainant, 'Today, I had a discussion with senior immigration officials about your visa; your grandparents' marriage certificate issued in Bolivia in 1997 (certificate number 198543) was a forged document; our investigation in Bolivia found that the original certificate belonged to someone else, not your grandparents', in front of the submitted documents. This was the result of their blind faith in a Bolivian governmental body's response. The Immigration Bureau subsequently withdrew that determination in that case. Nevertheless, a similar situation happened in A's case. It signifies that the individual immigration officers involved and the chief inspector in charge of the earlier case were not warned about 'the danger of judging solely based on information from the home country'.

In A's case, it is highly likely that a local investigation was carried out in the wrong public office and caused confusion about original certificate numbers just as in the earlier case. The complaint verified the authenticity and legitimacy of submitted documents, presented A's military service book issued by Bolivia's Ministry of Defense in 1976, which is recognized as an important identification certificate in the country, and argued that A and his relatives in Japan were willing to undergo DNA testing.

## How did the Immigration Bureau determine A was 'fake Nikkei'?

The plaintiff filed a state redress claim as a 'joinder of additional claim' on March 3, 2003. The grounds for the claim were the analogical application of Article 29-3 of the Constitution stipulating just compensation for property legally taken by a public authority. They submitted four pre-trial briefs leading up to the filing of the claim whereas the immigration side submitted none.

The Immigration Bureau simply argued that A's claim was without merit because the rejection of his extension application had been rescinded on January 17, 2002 and special permission to stay was granted with one-year 'long-term residence' status on January 23. The defense also asserted that the Immigration Bureau was not at fault and not liable for further explanation because it had followed the set administrative procedures based on the information that birth and other certificates submitted by A were 'falsified documents' from the Bolivian government via Japan's Ministry of Foreign Affairs. On July 30, 2003, the Immigration Bureau finally disclosed the reason for rejecting A's extension application. This was more than eight months after the start of the legal action, which was by then a state redress suit.

The state alleged that A had no standing to claim compensation under the State Redress Act. The state's way of thinking about foreigners' rights is condensed in the explanation provided by the Immigration Bureau. It is especially evident in the opening passages of the state's pre-trial brief stating as follows.

> 1 Article 1-1 of the State Redress Act provides that "When a public employee who exercises the public authority of the State or of a public entity has, in the course of their duties, unlawfully caused loss or damage to another person intentionally or negligently, the State or public entity assumes the responsibility to compensate therefor". "Unlawful" in this paragraph refers to violations of legal obligations in the course of duty (code of conduct) with which a public employee must comply in relation to *individual citizens* having specific rights or interests protected under the law.

> 2 To assess unlawfulness under the said paragraph, consideration must be given to a comprehensive range of matters, including the nature and content of the administrative disposition in question such as whether it was a beneficial act or an infringing act, the purpose and mode of the public employee's involvement, the level and content of *the citizen's* involvement in the disposition, and the level and content of damage suffered, from the standpoint of fair division of responsibility, and *a determination should be made on whether the public employee violated their legal obligations in the course of duty (code of conduct) with which they should comply in relation to the citizen and thereby infringing on the citizen's rights protected under the law.* (emphasis added)

The state/Immigration Bureau as the executive arm is asserting that foreigners are not eligible to claim government compensation. They then make another assertion.

> 3 In application procedures for an extension of residence period, the applicant has the responsibility to establish "reasonable grounds" for granting an extension of residence period.

After stating these rules, the Immigration Bureau finally explained why A's application was rejected. The reason was inconceivable.

> Because the number of so-called fake Nikkei arrivals began to increase from the summer of 1991 and the number of applications using forged birth certificates and other documents also began to increase, the Immigration Bureau strengthened its intelligence gathering with regard to falsified documents and implemented more careful examination.
>
> On December 6, 1996, the Tokyo Regional Immigration Bureau discovered a Bolivian national who entered and lived in Japan as a third-generation Japanese descendant by fraudulently using the plaintiff's grandfather's family register and pursued an investigation through interviews with the grandfather's children and grandchildren living in Japan.

One of A's relatives made a statement 'suggesting that a number of people unrelated to A's grandfather might have entered Japan pretending to be A's grandfather's grandchildren and third-generation Japanese descendants' and that the Immigration Bureau 'became aware of the presence of someone pretending to be a third-generation Japanese descendant purporting to be the plaintiff's grandfather's grandchild in the country'.

To prove the appropriateness of its procedures, the Immigration Bureau then cites an inquiry it made to the Bolivian authority about the documents. By the time of A's application for a certificate of eligibility for residence status through his cousin in Japan on March 15, 1999, the Immigration Bureau had learned about 'the presence of someone pretending to be a third-generation Japanese descendant by falsifying their identity' using A's grandfather's family register. In addition, 'A's previous application for extension of residence period was rejected on August 25, 1992' on his first stay in Japan 'due to insufficient documentary evidence'. For this reason, the Tokyo Regional Immigration Bureau 'made an inquiry to the Bolivian government via the Ministry of Foreign Affairs in August 1999 about the authenticity of the birth certificates submitted by the plaintiff in order to verify his identity'. This inquiry took two years. Because the Immigration Bureau had not received a reply from the Bolivian government at the time of A's application for a certificate of eligibility in 1999, it 'tentatively treated the submitted documents as authentic and granted a certificate of eligibility for acquisition of "long-term residence" status for a period of one year in July 2001'. However, the Bolivian government replied on June 18, 2002, that 'the plaintiff's and his father's birth certificates and the plaintiff's parents' marriage certificate had been forged from the registered documents'. This is why the director of the Tokyo Regional Immigration Bureau rejected the application for the extension of residence status in question.

## Points of contention presented by A's attorney

Once the defense and the plaintiff exchanged their assertions, points of contention became clearer. A's attorney narrows down his list to the following four points. First, it is said that a decision on an extension of a foreigner's residence period and a change of residence status are left to the discretion of the Minister of Justice. The Immigration Bureau asserts the legitimacy of the decision based on this argument about ministerial discretion and that this is according to international customary law. However, international customary law can explain up to the point of delegating discretionary decision-making power to the Minister of Justice under legislative policies for the Immigration Act, but this does not automatically translate to wide discretionary powers in administration. The scope of the Minister of Justice's discretionary power is defined in interpretation of the Immigration Act in the first place. The foreigner's right to apply for a change or extension of residence status is recognized also in administrative interpretation. This is evident from the fact that change of residence status or extension of residence period has to be granted when such an application made by a foreigner meets the requirements of the law and that rejection of an application satisfying all requirements can be subjected to a lawsuit for revocation as an unlawful disposition. The issue in this case is a decision enforced by the director of one of the eight regional immigration bureaus within the Immigration Bureau under the Ministry of Justice rather than a discretionary decision made by the Minister of Justice and therefore it is completely different from the Minister of Justice's wide discretionary powers premised on the denial of the foreigner's right to residence.

Second, the primary responsibility with regard to documents submitted to support an extension of residence period rests with the applicant, as Article 21-3 of the Immigration Act states, 'When the application set forth in the preceding paragraph has been submitted, the Minister of Justice may grant permission only when he/she finds that there are reasonable grounds to grant the extension of the period of stay on the strength of the documents submitted by the foreign national'. Nonetheless, the foreigner's right to apply for a change of residence status and extension of residence period is not denied. Article 59-2 of the Immigration Act recognizes the existence of the power to conduct an inquiry by stating, 'The Minister of Justice may have an immigration inspector inquire into the facts, if necessary, in order to conduct dispositions relating to [...] revocation of the status of residence [...]'. By a similar logic, the Immigration Bureau uses material and information besides the documents submitted by the applicant when considering an application for a change of residence status, not because the applicant failed to submit the necessary documents.

Third, the decision not to grant an extension was made by the director of the Tokyo Regional Immigration Bureau based on his own investigation. The applicant had no way of knowing about the material that the Immigration Bureau had acquired through its own fact-finding investigation. When the Immigration Bureau bases a rejection decision on the material it has obtained itself in addition to the applicant's submission, it should give the applicant a chance to state their case, and when a foreign government takes a long time to reply to an inquiry, the Immigration Bureau should not blindly use the reply in making a decision. It is the natural duty that someone with decision-making authority owes to the application process to examine the trustworthiness of the information in the light of evidence and facts. According to the Ministry of Justice, paragraph 2 was added to Article 59-2 of the Immigration Act in its 2001 revision because 'in the examination pertaining to a foreign national's landing or stay, it is difficult to make an appropriate decision solely on the basis of submitted documents in some cases'. A similar provision in Article 61-2(3) (amended in 2007 to become Article 61-2-14) referred to cases 'where a proper recognition of refugee status may be impossible based on the documents submitted pursuant to Article 61-2(1) or where it is necessary to conduct dispositions pertaining to recognition or revocation of other refugees' also according to the Ministry of Justice. Article 59-2 is thought to have the same intent as this paragraph.

Fourth, the Immigration Bureau's awareness of the presence of 'fake Nikkei' at the time does not absolve it from its responsibility to conduct a thorough investigation. While the Immigration Bureau claims that 'fake Nikkei' arrivals began to increase from around 1991, it would have foreseen this phenomenon because the issuance of the public notice on long-term residence on May 24, 1990, gave foreign nationals of Japanese descent eligibility for residence status, which was to be assessed solely on the basis of submitted documents. The plaintiff did not know that his relative was suspected of being a 'fake Nikkei'. However, the Immigration Bureau should not have assumed that A's documents had been falsified even if his relative had some involvement in falsification. Moreover, the director of the Tokyo Regional Immigration Bureau simply cited the Bolivian government's reply as proof and failed to explain which part of A's submission was false. He then discarded the original communication from the Bolivian government.

After this lawsuit was filed, the director of the Tokyo Regional Immigration Bureau released A from detention on provisional release. He then promptly withdrew the previous dispositions, issued a special permission to stay and granted A 'long-term residence' status. This is hardly the conduct of someone who was convinced that the documents were false based on a long-term investigation. We cannot help but think that the director executed a string of dispositions without thorough analysis while he remained 'uncertain' about the documents' authenticity. The director did not have to accept the veracity of the reply from a foreign government. Especially in Latin American countries without an integrated identity registration system like Japan's family registration system, a married person registered in one province can sometimes get a certificate of unmarried status from another province, and an inquiry about the authenticity of identification papers via the central government can be treated only as a guide. The rejection of A's application was initiated when the Immigration Bureau determined that the submitted paperwork contained falsified documents after it received a reply from the Bolivian government. The plaintiff requested the defense to present the original copies of the alleged forged documents to explain exactly which part and in what way they were forged.

## The 'fake Nikkei' problem and procedures

The plaintiff was able to obtain 'long-term residence' status as a result of taking the matter to court. His complaint was based on the following logic. At the time of rejection of A's application for an extension of residence period by the director of the Tokyo Regional Immigration Bureau, (1) A was a child of a Japanese person, i.e., a second-generation Japanese, whose residence status should not have been assessed under the criteria set by the public notice on long-term residence; and (2) as A's application was assessed under criteria that were not applicable to him, the rejection of his application itself was unlawful. However, the Immigration Bureau's logic behind the subsequent granting of a one-year 'long-term residence' status was different from the logic in the plaintiff's argument. This is evident in the fact that the Immigration Bureau was able to confirm A's identity based on his military service book. It is possible to argue that, if A's Japanese descent status was confirmed and eligibility for residence was granted on the basis of his Bolivian military record, the criteria in the public notice on long-term residence would be applicable to him as he was a third-generation Japanese descendant at the point of time relevant to the military service book (prior to his father's acquisition of Japanese nationality).[6]

The very fact that these decisions were made based on his Bolivian military service book makes us wonder what the Bolivian government's reply actually said. Given that the Immigration Bureau used it as the reason for rejection, there are three possibilities.

1 The person listed in the document with the reference number supplied by the Immigration Bureau was not A.

2 There was no problem with the content of the document but the manner in which it was obtained was suspicious.

3 There were significant discrepancies between the documents submitted by A for his immigration checks and application for eligibility certificate and the original birth and other certificates.

In either case, the decision should have been reserved. As mentioned earlier, there had been a similar case against a person from A's hometown of Riberalta. The transfer of management of birth and other certificates from one public office to another had resulted in a change of the numbering system. The Immigration Bureau made an inquiry without knowing about this change and arrived at the assessment that the applicant was a 'fake Nikkei'.

In A's case, his birth certificate was submitted twice. The first one was issued in Riberalta Municipality, which was the place of registration, while the second one was issued in Trinidad Municipality, the capital of Beni Department.[7] A's identity documents were initially registered at public office No. 890, which was later recast as the first civil registry office due to a reorganization of government agencies. Given the earlier example, the director of the Tokyo Regional Immigration Bureau must have failed to distinguish between the place of issue and the place of registration and made an inquiry to the Bolivian government about 'documents registered at public office No. 890 in Trinidad' without knowing about the government reorganization. We can surmise that the Bolivian government took a long time to investigate the issue and eventually gave a vague reply for that reason. We can also argue that it is absurd to think that A would have obtained a forged birth certificate. Procuring a forged document in Bolivia is prohibitively expensive, considerably more than the average annual income. There was no incentive for A, who is a genuine Japanese descendant, to spend such a large sum of money on forging a certificate or procuring it through a broker.

In any case, A's one-year 'long-term residence' status meant that he would have had to have extended his period of stay in a year's time by submitting the documents that the Immigration Bureau had previously determined to be 'forged'. The Immigration Bureau argued that an application would have been rejected even if the applicant was a genuine second-generation Japanese descendant if the submitted documents were fake. A disposition made by the Immigration Bureau 'has a kind of superior validity when a government agency enforces it based on special authority awarded by law on the understanding that it complies with legally established criteria for the purpose of realizing the public interest under the principle of administration ruled by law, and is given tentative validity, which is legal enforceability whose effect cannot be denied by a private person unless it is invalidated by an administrative agency or a court authorized to do so' (Koshiyama 1983: 30–31). If the Immigration Bureau had have accepted the plaintiff's argument that the disposition should be withdrawn because A was a second-generation Japanese descendant to whom a different set of criteria for an extension of residence status should have been applied, then it would not have had to dwell on the authenticity of submitted documents. However, as the Immigration Bureau verified A's Japanese ancestry based on his military service book, it did not change its view that the documents submitted by A were false. The plaintiff had to prove the authenticity of the documents separately from how the court would make a judgment on his special permission to stay.

By joining forces with lawyer Guillermo Nema, who had translated A's documents, the plaintiff sent two registrars in Riberalta's first civil registry office, Beni Department, the copies of A's birth certificate, his father's birth certificate and parents' marriage certificate, which A submitted on January 19, 1999, and which the Japanese government claimed to be forgeries, and asked them to verify their authenticity. The plaintiff received a reply confirming that they 'investigated the presented copies of the documents and the birth register as well as the marriage register archived in the public office and found all of the original documents from which these copies had been made are true copies of the registered documents, hence, true and correct documents and not falsified documents as claimed by the defendant [the director of the Tokyo Regional Immigration Bureau]'. This reply was submitted to the court.

## The court's decision

The plaintiff lost the state redress claim suit. It is interesting to note that the court provided detailed discussions on the pros and cons of state redress for the defendants' decision to reject an extension of residence period and ensuing deportation procedures in the original case while delivering its decision on compensation for A's main complaint about lost employment opportunities in a few sentences. Even though the court reached the conclusion that 'the degree of error on the part of the Immigration Bureau (and the director of the Tokyo Regional Immigration Bureau) was not severe enough for an award of compensation', which is similar to its conclusion about economic loss, it devoted thirty pages of its judgment to this question. The court adopted the view that a foreign national could seek compensation from the state in some cases as against the Immigration Bureau's assertion that 'state redress is the right of Japanese citizens against actions of public officials and therefore foreign nationals have no right to claim it'.

The court judgment began by marshalling the plaintiff's and defendant's arguments. Then, it presented the court's opinion as to each party's argument. First, it stated that 'In this case, the plaintiff's visa extension application was rejected once, then the rejection was withdrawn and the permission was granted. *This should give rise to a strong suspicion that the rejection and the detention order executed on this premise were objectively unlawful*' (emphasis added). However, it then laid out a prerequisite for the unlawfulness of conduct under the State Redress Act by stating:

> It does not immediately lead to the assessment that these actions were also unlawful under the State Redress Act; they should be considered unlawful only when the director and the supervising inspector of the Tokyo Regional Immigration Bureau who executed these dispositions (hereafter referred to as "co-defendant officers") are found to have breached their professional legal obligations owed to the plaintiff.

The Immigration Bureau not only received information that someone among A's relatives was complicit in falsifying identity documents but also confirmed a fake Nikkei case as described by the informant. In view of these factors, the court accepted that a further examination of A's documents was reasonable by stating: 'As there might be an imposter among those who declared to be the descendants [of A's grandfather] upon entering Japan, there were reasonable grounds for their decision about the need for a thorough investigation'.

The court, however, voiced an objection to the Immigration Bureau's unquestioning acceptance of the Bolivian government's reply on which it based its decision to reject A's application:

While somewhat vague in some parts, it is possible to understand [that the Bolivian government's reply states] that the identity information contained in the plaintiff's birth and other certificates are as recorded in the public register and hence true information but that the certificates themselves are forged documents; if we accept this at face value, we cannot deny that it casts grave doubt on the plaintiff's identity. […] Nevertheless, there are some doubts about whether this reply should be accepted at face value as follows. Even before this rejection decision was made, […] there was already a case that took a similar course of events in that an extension application was rejected on the strength of the home government's reply to an inquiry, a doubt about the accuracy of the reply arose after the rejection was executed, and the disposition was eventually withdrawn. Given this precedent, it is questionable if a reply to an inquiry made to a home country should always be trusted as correct information. On this point, witness N who was in charge of the examination relating to disposition in the present case stated in his deposition that he was unaware of the existence of such a precedent. If this information had not been shared among the officers in charge of the examination, that in itself has to mean a flaw in the examination system and therefore this point cannot serve as a reason for exemption from responsibility.

With regard to the plaintiff's birth certificates, the plaintiff's team made an inquiry to the registrar at the first civil registry office of the Riberalta municipal authority and received a document attesting the authenticity of the certificates signed by two officials (although some parts of this document can be interpreted as asserted by the defendants, the document concludes that "This is to certify that the birth certificates numbered 0020957 and 020958 and the marriage certificate numbered 046349 signed by the then registrar Marcial Cuellar Cuellar マルシアル・クエヤル・クエヤル and issued on January 19, 1999, are true and correct copies of the originals recorded in the register", and this confirmation must be considered as strong evidence for the authenticity of the plaintiff's documents), and therefore it is difficult to deny the possibility that the earlier reply was incorrect.

The earlier reply to the effect that the plaintiff's certificates are factually correct but the certificates themselves are forged documents does not explain why they determined the documents to be false despite the correctness of the information therein. Further, a real descendant of the plaintiff's grandfather was involved [...] in the case of a fake Nikkei claiming to be the plaintiff's grandfather's descendant according to intelligence gathered by the Tokyo Regional Immigration Bureau and it would have been easy for these descendants to obtain true copies of identification certificates. It is somewhat puzzling why they would use forged certificates in order to prove their real identities. [...] This line of thinking leads to the view that questions whether the information contained in the government's reply from the home country should have been treated as completely correct in this case even though it is generally reasonable to treat such information as trustworthy.

About the fact that the rejection decision was easily overturned by the additional submission of the military service book, the court concluded as follows:

On the point of the revocation of the rejection decision and the subsequent granting of permission, the defendants argue that "The documents submitted by the plaintiff after the rejection disposition, especially his military service book, served as strong proof of the plaintiff's identity". Accordingly, it is undeniable that the co-defendant officer might have reached a different decision had he asked for additional documents prior to making the rejection decision.

Further, the court concluded:

In consideration of the above factors, it is possible to say that the credibility of the content of the reply, which the co-defendant officer appears to have used as the most important reason for making the rejection decision, was questionable, and in this regard, it is undeniable that a more desirable course of action for the co-defendant officer was to conduct further and more careful investigation, such as trying to find out from the plaintiff how he had obtained the documents and if he had other identification documents, instead of making a decision solely based on a blind trust in the foreign government's reply. It is understandable that the plaintiff claims that the actions of the co-defendants are unlawful.

On this point, the defendants […] made an assertion to the effect that "the required evidence for an extension of residence period is for the plaintiff to supply and the defendants simply have to examine whether the plaintiff's documents are true or false, and therefore the plaintiff's claim on the premise that the co-defendant officers had an active obligation for supplementary investigation is unreasonable". However, […] while it is the plaintiff's responsibility to supply documentary evidence as asserted by the defendants, it is the defendants' responsibility to determine the credibility of the supplied documents accurately and it is reasonable to expect that a certain level of investigation may be needed in some cases. In fact, the defendants made an inquiry to the home government in the present case, so it was possible that further investigation might become necessary if there was any doubt about the reply to the inquiry instead of accepting it without questioning. This means that even though the responsibility to supply evidence to meet the requirements of an extension of residence period rests with the plaintiff, this has no bearing on the defendant's responsibility.

In an unusual move, a witness was called to the stand in this trial. The chief inspector of the Tokyo Regional Immigration Bureau in charge of field operations in this case was examined as a witness. This was because the case raised the question of whether the officers had fulfilled the obligations they were supposed to fulfill in the course of normal operations. The court concurred with A's claim in strong language by stating, for example, 'If the information about the prior case of incorrect reply from the home country was not shared, that in itself has to mean a flaw in the examination system' and 'It is understandable that the plaintiff claims that the actions of the co-defendants are unlawful'. Consequently, it was confirmed that the certificates submitted by A should have been treated as authentic documents.

Although the court accepted the plaintiff's arguments to this extent, it did not go far enough to award government compensation. This was because A's arguments were made in hindsight and sounded reasonable judging from what happened after the submission of his military service book, but this state redress claim trial was concerned with the issue of whether or not decisions made before the submission of the military service book were flawed. From this viewpoint, the only questions to be asked relate to (1) 'the existence of a precedent in which a disposition to reject an extension of residence period made as a result of an inquiry to the home government was revoked' and (2) 'the reliability of the home government's reply in the present case that the plaintiff's certificates were forged even though identity information recorded therein was true and correct'. While the plaintiff's team presented the case referred to in (1) as an example of the rejection decision based on information from the home government, this was 'not sufficient evidence to accept that [incorrect] reply is a common occurrence'. As for (2), the reply in the present case might have had a questionable aspect but 'it was not serious enough to definitively erode the credibility of the home government's reply'.

Above all, 'it is undeniable that there were various doubts' about A's relatives surrounding the question of false identity. In the presence of this condition, whether the submission of A's military service book at this stage 'would have been enough to cause the officers to decide to approve the plaintiff's extension application is open to question, even after taking into account all other concerns'. In rejecting the state redress claim, the court held:

> While the plaintiff's assertions are understandable in part as mentioned earlier, this court cannot accept them in their entirety because declaring the defense officers' actions unlawful would be relying too much on hindsight. […] In the light of the above, for the matter of detention order issuance, this court cannot accept that the issuance of the detention order was unlawful under the State Redress Act.

## Conclusion—Unanswered questions

In this lawsuit, the plaintiff filed a compensation claim through state redress on the basis of the analogous application of Article 29-3 of the Constitution by arguing that loss of employment opportunities amounted to a violation of his property right. However, the court summarily dismissed this point by stating:

> The compensation system based on Article 29-3 of the Constitution is closely linked with the system of appropriation of private property for public use whereas this case's situation in which a person was detained as part of the deportation procedures is clearly different from the situation involving the taking of property for public use and outside the scope of the compensation system, and therefore the argument in relation to the analogous application of the said article must be considered irrelevant.

Nevertheless, winning compensation was not the aim of this state redress claim case. Its aim was to find out (1) why A's application for an extension of residence period was rejected, and (2) why the director of the Tokyo Regional Immigration Bureau subsequently granted him special permission to stay.

Incidentally, it was argued in the Immigration Bureau's pre-trial brief and the court judgment that the military service book was recognized as an important identification document in Bolivia and its submission was crucial in verifying A's identity. However, the recognized importance of the military service book as an ID in Bolivia was not the only reason for the Immigration Bureau to take it seriously. It contained A's fingerprints. His fingerprints were also included on the ID card, which he had been using until just before his arrival in Japan and which was included in his applications for a certificate of eligibility for residence status and an extension of residence period. By comparing the fingerprints in the 1976 military service book and the ID card with those of the person in custody, the Immigration Bureau was able to establish that the applicant was not an imposter.

This case resulted in the overturning of the Immigration Bureau's earlier decision because A happened to be able to find a lawyer for himself. According to Itsuo Sonobe,

# Chapter 1

> The purpose of an action for the judicial review of administrative dispositions is elimination of a state of unlawfulness caused by the enforcement of an administrative agency's primary decision, and the individual's rights and interests are remedied as a consequence. Even when infringement of the individual's rights and interests was caused by unlawful administration, redress may be achieved by way of means other than administrative case litigation such as civil litigation for compensatory damages and injunctions against individual acts or facts in some cases while litigation to recover losses on the basis of the legal burden of public utilities may suit other cases. (Sonobe 1983: 15–16)

In terms of the present case, the lawsuit for revocation of the disposition concerning the rejection of a residence extension application was an action for the judicial review of an administrative disposition and therefore the withdrawal of the rejection and the subsequent issuance of special permission to stay and the granting of a 'long-term residence' visa for one year amounted to an effective remedy of A's rights.

In fact, since granting A special permission to stay and issuing a visa, the Immigration Bureau has stopped listening to A's complaint relying on Tokuji Izumi's view:

> A person having the standing to sue in an action for the revocation of an administrative disposition can be considered as a person whose right or whose interest specifically and concretely protected by the legal basis of the administrative disposition is violated or at risk of being violated as a legal consequence of the administrative disposition, and *for the administrative disposition to be revoked by a court judgment (that is, the benefit of suit in a narrow sense is awarded), that person's right and interest must be in a restorable condition.* It is understood that Article 9 of the Administrative Case Litigation Act defines this relationship and describes the standing to seek restoration of the said right and interest through the elimination of the legal consequence by the revocation of the disposition and the said right and interest restored by the revocation of the disposition as "legal interest". (Izumi 1983: 57; emphasis added)

As stated in the judgment, one of the reasons for the court's denial of the need to award state redress against the Immigration Bureau was that the execution of a disposition based on incorrect information received from the home country, as in A's case, was not a common occurrence although some individual cases might have been detected. According to the plaintiff's pre-trial brief and evidential documents, however, there had been around ten similar cases in the two years immediately before the present case among the cases represented by A's attorney alone. This is no small number for just one attorney. Yet, only the opposing party (the Ministry of Justice / Immigration Bureau) knows how many cases required inquiries to home countries and how many replies were found to be incorrect in the past. The opposing party in a lawsuit would not disclose data that were disadvantageous to themselves.

A similar structural problem can be found in lawsuits against nuclear power plants, but the burden of proof on the part of administrative agencies has been mentioned in these cases. The Supreme Court acknowledged in its ruling on the Ikata Nuclear Power Plant case as follows:

> Although it is normally understood that the burden of claim and proof concerning the unreasonableness of a decision made by the defending administrative agency should be on the plaintiff, in view of the fact that all materials related to safety inspections at this nuclear reactor facility are held by the defendants, the agency needs to argue and prove first on the basis of substantial evidence and material that the agency's decisions were reasonable in terms of the actual inspection criteria and the processes for investigation, deliberation and decision-making; the agency's failure to deliver its full argument and proof will in effect lead to the presumption that the agency's decisions had some unreasonable aspects. (Judgment of the Supreme Court of Japan, 1st Petty Bench on October 29, 1992, in *Saikō saibansho minji hanreishū*, vol. 46, no. 7: 1183)[8]

In comparison, the overwhelming advantage of the administrative agency in immigration administration has never been called into question. The agency approached the case with the view that 'foreign nationals have no standing to sue for state redress' from the onset. There have been situations that

# Chapter 1

raise suspicions that the agency first rejects all doubtful applications for an extension of residence period and only examines cases that are brought to court. We can raise this concern but cannot prove it because all information is monopolized by the administrative agency.

It became apparent during the court proceedings that the Immigration Bureau handled its decision-making on whether or not A was 'fake Nikkei' solely as a matter of documentation. There were just two points of contention in this case: whether the documents submitted by A were forged documents, and if so, which part of them was forged. The Immigration Bureau completely ignored A's offer of taking a DNA test. This is where the essence of the government's definition of 'Japanese descent' comes to the surface.

This total reliance on documentation gives rise to matters that do not match the reality. The Immigration Bureau attached importance to (1) discrepancies between two genealogy charts submitted by relatives at the time of the application for a certificate of eligibility for residence status, and (2) errors in the entries about children in the grandfather's death certificate, among A's submission. The genealogy charts showed the grandfather's six children and their children, i.e., his grandchildren, in Bolivia. We cannot expect the grandchildren to prepare an accurate chart, and the chart has to change depending on the source of information in view of the reality of Japanese immigrants in South America who formed their families as they continually moved from one place to another. Charts are inevitably revised as new information comes to light. The grandfather's death certificate actually contained a note to that effect. The death certificate was filed by another Japanese immigrant who was a friend of the grandfather rather than a family member. The grandfather passed away in his house leaving his young children behind on their own. Because it was his friend in the neighborhood who reported his death and filled out information about his family, errors in the dates of birth of his children were unavoidable (it is normal for a person to know the number of a friend's children but not to know their birth dates). Yet, the Immigration Bureau did not trust this death certificate because of the incorrect birth dates of the grandfather's children.

Foreign workers in Japan do not necessarily come from developed countries. Although their home countries may be undergoing rapid economic development, it is not uncommon for people in some regions to fail to promptly report births and deaths to authorities. As the Immigration Bureau is familiar with this situation, its officials use not only formalized documents but also other reference material on which to base their assessment and the authority of directors of regional immigration bureaus to conduct investigations has been written into law.

There is nothing wrong with case-by-case decision-making. The problem with cases such as the present one is the government's attitude of withdrawing a deportation order and issuing special permission to stay as soon as defeat looms in the trial as well as its unwillingness to disclose reasons for reversing its decision unless a state redress claim is filed with the court. In Japan's depopulating and aging society, sustainable economic growth is becoming increasingly difficult without a considerable injection of foreign labor. To encourage more foreign nationals to come to work in Japan, a rational explanation of visa issuance and extension rules needs to be provided and reasons for the rejection of visa applications must be systematically disclosed. At the minimum, the current attitude of total denial of foreigners' rights has to change if the government wishes to continue accepting foreign workers into the country.

## Notes

1  See Kazumasa Iwata and Nihon Keizai Kenkyū Sentā (eds.) (2016) for these discussions.
2  A prospective foreign worker can apply to the Minister of Justice for the issuance of a certificate of eligibility for residence status in order to facilitate immigration checks on arrival. An organization accepting the worker makes an advance application as a proxy by specifying the purpose of stay, acquires a certificate of eligibility and sends it to the worker overseas. Visa issuance and immigration checks are simplified when the worker produces the certificate upon entry (Hōmu-shō Nyūkoku kanri-kyoku Nyūkoku zairyū-ka 1992).
3  This Guillermo Nema is Genshin Nema, who is a well-recognized bridge-builder between Japan and Bolivia.

4   Under the Family Register Law, records of Japanese citizens on family registers continue to exist even after their death. Once Japanese nationality is confirmed after the person's death, and when the deceased becomes Japanese, they are newly registered in the family register. If it is proved that the grandparents are registered in the family register, their children will be granted the status of residence as the spouse and child of a Japanese national, and their grandchildren will be granted the status of residence as a long-term resident.

5   In this case, supporting documents, including a letter verifying the suspect's identity, were submitted by the then chairperson of the Bolivian-Japanese Association. In particular, the reality of Bolivia's identity registration system can be gleaned from a passage in the letter: 'In Bolivia, the law for compulsory civil registration was proclaimed at the end of 1940 or early 1941. Our municipal registry office opened in 1943. Therefore, there might be some ambiguity in information from before that time and also there might be some errors in the documents of [a personal name] who did not understand Spanish very well and could not write his own signature'.

6   Once A's Japanese ancestry was verified by the military service book, the deportation order against him and the rejection disposition of his application for an extension of residence period were rescinded.

7   Trinidad is the departmental capital where residents in other municipalities can register identification and obtain certificates.

8   See Yasui (2013) for detailed discussions on the significance of the Ikata Nuclear Power Plant case. *Saikō saibansho minji hanreishū* contain judgments on civil and administrative cases, *Saikō saibansho keiji hanreishū* contain those on criminal and public security cases, both of them decided by the Supreme Court. The collection of Japanese Supreme Court precedents is a book that is not commercially available and is not generally distributed. Similarly, *Gyōsei jiken saiban hanreishū, Shōmu geppō* are not commercially available. It is also written in such a way that the author does not know who it is. Privately published precedents collections such as "*Hanrei jihō*" and "*Hanrei taimuzu*", which are commercially available but are also written in such a way that the author cannot be identified. For this reason, I cite these cases explicitly, but not in the bibliography.

# The Sociology of Foreign Juvenile Delinquency

## Introduction

This chapter addresses the issue of the enforcement of a deportation order in the case of foreign juvenile delinquency. It was anticipated that the number of foreign children accompanying their parents coming to Japan for work would naturally increase following the 1990 revision of the Immigration Act. The Ministry of Justice Public Notice No. 132 issued on May 24, 1990 (the so-called Long-Term Residence Notice) lists an unmarried, minor and dependent child of a child of a child of a Japanese national (fourth generation) as a person who is typically granted a visa (Long-Term Residence Notice No. 6). Did Japan prepare itself to receive these children in response to the prediction?

While parents have primary responsibility for taking care of their children, there are situations in which parents alone are unable to fulfill their responsibility and society has to shoulder part of it. Society must be prepared for such situations. The case discussed in this chapter demonstrates Japanese society's lack of preparedness. Our society is structured to lay the onus of child-rearing solely on the parties involved and this perpetuates the absence of a proper system for the acceptance of foreign nationals. However, the Immigration Act recognizes foreigners' rights only within the scope of the act and hence foreign nationals have no freedom of entering or staying in Japan and no capacity to make such demands. From this viewpoint, a system for accepting foreign nationals may be something that is not supposed to exist.

Even if the state is only willing to recognize limited rights for foreigners, it will inevitably be compelled to give special consideration in some situations as long as they are residents of this country. The following case presents cross-purposes between various contradictions arising from the absence of an institutionalized mechanism.

## Juvenile delinquency and nationality: Boy B's life in teenage years

The present case is characterized by the question of why a boy, 'B', could not break free of his delinquent peer group or delinquency cycles. Although his list of misdemeanors does not seem different from that of a typical Japanese juvenile delinquent, the nationality barrier is observable here. Let us confirm the existence of the barrier as we review how he spent his teenage years.

B was ten years old when he was sent for from Peru in 1992 by his mother who was working in Japan.[1] After living in Nara prefecture for a while,[2] they moved to Y city in Kanagawa prefecture when he was in the sixth grade. At this point, B turned to juvenile delinquency, skipping class or leaving school without permission. When he met a classmate who also found it difficult to adapt to the school environment, they began to spend a lot of time in game arcades. B engaged in smoking and shoplifting. He expected his mother to be concerned but she did not seem to care about him. He gradually spent more time at his grandmother's home in the same neighborhood as his own home. When he advanced to junior high school, he fell behind in the classroom because he only understood elementary kanji and could not read the blackboard properly.

The family moved back to Nara at the end of B's first year at junior high school. B found his place in a delinquent group that included one of his former elementary school friends. He learned to ride a moped and to commit theft. The group drove through streets recklessly and got into fights with other groups. Although B spent a lot of time with the delinquent group, he did attend school, which was his only stable environment, every day. Many of the students were from a single-parent family or had been abused by a parent. B was able to identify with those who had experienced some form of family trauma.

B enrolled at an evening high school on the advice of his junior high school teacher. He began to skip class as he found it difficult to keep up. Only two months into the school year, he became involved in a violent incident and left school. Immediately afterwards, B started working as a construction assistant. One day, when he and a workmate were hanging out, they ran out of money and decided to try bag-snatching. When the friend, who was a frequent bag-snatcher, said that he was going to go and snatch a purse, B agreed to go with him without really thinking. The two rode a moped in tandem and snatched a purse from a woman on a bicycle. They were arrested by police when they were sniffing solvent bought with the stolen money. Because the victim had fallen and was injured, the boys were indicted on charges of theft and assault as well as substance abuse.

The court sent B to a juvenile correction institution. He was incarcerated in Kurihama Reform School in Yokosuka, Kanagawa, for one year. Although he was disheartened, he was able to develop his Japanese writing and reading proficiency there. Kurihama Reform School had a special Japanese language education program for foreign youths that involved learning kanji each day for one to two hours. They used workbooks to prepare for regular tests to check their learning progress. In addition, the Japanese teacher was able to speak Portuguese and Spanish and taught the youths with a caring attitude.

B's understanding of Japanese improved rapidly when the meanings of difficult characters and words were explained in his mother tongue. In addition to Japanese characters, he also learned to think and write in sentences for the first time. He became convinced that he needed to be able to read and write kanji if he was to stay in Japan. B began to study voluntarily and often spent a minimum of five hours studying per day even on weekends. He felt happy when he was finally able to read newspapers. As he received Japanese lessons and engaged in his tasks earnestly at the reform school, he was able to sense a gradual change in himself and began to think about his feelings toward his family and his interaction with and consideration for others. He began to confront his own problems from then on.

While B was living on his own in Osaka after being released from the reform school, a former inmate moved into his apartment. Seeing that B was too poor to buy a washing machine, the lodger decided to steal one for him. The friend called for B to help transport the stolen washing machine. The two were arrested for stealing and B was sentenced on January 28, 2004, to eighteen months in prison suspended for five years (under the supervision of a probation officer).

After receiving the suspended sentence, B went to see his probation officer regularly for a while. However, his grandmother, who had been his only supporter when he was feeling unloved by his own mother, passed away in March 2005. Her death filled him with a sense of emptiness and made him temporarily mentally unstable. Around that time, B unwittingly became complicit in the theft of a car. When his cousin was looking for car wheels, B encountered a Brazilian youth dealing in secondhand cars at a club and mentioned this to him. The Brazilian later told B that 'Good stuff has come in' and B went to collect the wheels.[3] The Brazilian told him, 'Help me transport the car because the wheels are still attached; I'll give you 50,000 yen'. While they were in the Brazilian's car discussing how to transport the car in question, B inhaled a stimulant drug offered to him. While B was transporting the car, he was chased by a police vehicle. When the Brazilian confessed to him that it was a stolen car, B realized that he was implicated in car theft. B was arrested. The police also discovered a vapor inhaling apparatus in the car and charged him with violating the Stimulant Drugs Control Act.

B was given an unsuspended sentence for violations of the Stimulant Drugs Control Act and the Road Traffic Act. The suspension of execution of the sentence in the washing machine theft case was revoked and he was ordered to serve his three-year prison sentence in Himeji Juvenile Prison.[4] His visa was due to expire during his prison term and his mother applied for an extension of his residence period as a proxy. However, his application was rejected on the grounds of his conviction for stimulant abuse. As soon as B became an overstayer, the deportation procedures were commenced.

## Family breakups should be prevented

The defense's arguments presented in this section have been put together from the applicant's written statement made in a hearing, a written objection and a statement of reasons for objection as part of the deportation procedures.

The issuance of a deportation order was bound to have a profound impact on B's family. First, B himself would have faced a crisis as he had grown up in Japan and was not fluent in Spanish. Many of his mother's brothers were in Japan and B had had little contact with other relatives in Peru. B's father had gone missing well before B came to Japan. The mother had to obtain consent from the missing birth father's father (B's paternal grandfather, who had passed away by the time of the deportation proceedings) in order to summon B to Japan.

The mother's lack of concern for B had much to do with the fact that she had been betrayed and abandoned by B's father and that she herself had suffered domestic violence. After she began working through these issues, she was able to better relate to B. She apologized to him for past neglect and violence and was endeavoring to improve her relationship with her son. B's Japanese-born younger sister was living with them. B was a father figure to her. His presence became indispensable for her growth as he helped her with her study and played with her.

It became clear from a diagnosis given at a Japanese hospital that the mother's behavior toward B had been influenced by her depression. She continued to work while being treated for depression but working long hours was difficult mentally and physically. Earnings from B's work were absolutely necessary for the family. The mother and the sister were permanent residents and planned to continue living in Japan. In particular, it would have been difficult for the mother to receive treatment for her mental health condition in her home country and she had no choice but to remain in Japan in order to raise B's younger sister. B's deportation would have not only threatened his own existence but also broken up the family and ruined all chance for B, his mother and his sister to live together. The deportation order would have dealt critical damage to the family's existence.

Second, B did not actively seek to use the stimulant. During the stolen car incident, the Brazilian accomplice and his girlfriend began inhaling the drug in the car and pressured B to do the same.[5] This was the only time he had ever inhaled a stimulant drug. Although he was convicted for violating the Stimulant Drugs Control Act, he was not a habitual user. Deporting him for this single-time use would be excessively harsh in comparison with precedents.

The mother was not able to leave Japan due to her illness and her Japanese-born-and-raised daughter's schooling would have been jeopardized if she had returned to the home country. The ill mother's limited income meant that she would not have been able to travel often to see her deported son. As the current Immigration Act bars those who have been deported for violating the Stimulant Drugs Control Act from re-entering Japan, the execution of B's deportation order would highly likely have resulted in the permanent breakup of his family unit. B's deportation would not only burden B with a considerable disadvantage but also cause undue hardship on his mother and sister left behind in Japan.

The 'right to family life' and the 'right to respect for private life' are protected under Article 13 of the Constitution of Japan. The International Covenant on Civil and Political Rights stipulates in Article 17 that 'No one shall be subjected to arbitrary or unlawful interference with his privacy, family, home or correspondence, nor to unlawful attacks on his honour and reputation' and that 'The family is the natural and fundamental group unit of society and is entitled to protection by society and the State' in Article 23.

Despite the postulate that a state is not obligated to accept foreign nationals under international customary law, there is a whole range of international human rights laws and conventions. Arguing for open-ended immigration control policy from the standpoint of 'the freedom of the state' is totally unjustifiable in the contemporary world. In the light of this situation, it is not good enough for the Minister of Justice and directors of regional immigration bureaus to make this string of dispositions from deportation order to special permission to stay solely according to the Immigration Act. Instead, they need to scrutinize them carefully if they are to concord with the spirit of the International Covenant on Civil and Political Rights and other human rights laws.

In one case involving a foreign man who registered marriage to a Japanese woman after his arrest, the court in fact acknowledged the overstepping or abuse of the Minister of Justice's discretionary authority by arguing as follows:

> When our citizen marries a foreign national, except where there are reasonable grounds for not allowing this foreign national to stay in the light of the person's residence conditions as well as domestic and international circumstances, the state should offer some certainty on residency matters so that the two people can fulfill their mutual obligations to cohabit, cooperate and support and build a harmonious

relationship; Article 23 of the International Convention on Civil and Political Rights provides that "The family is the natural and fundamental group unit of society and is entitled to protection by society and the State" and "The right of men and women of marriageable age to marry and to found a family shall be recognized" to express that intent. [...] [C]ondoning the logic of practically refusing to give protection to a genuine marriage that is deserving of consideration and its undesirable consequence in view of the intent of Article 23 of the said convention must be regarded as significantly lacking validity in the light of socially accepted ideas. (Tokyo District Court Judgment November 12, 1999, in *Hanrei jihō* 1727: 103–104)[6]

Decision-makers are bound by international law in some cases.

## Execution of a deportation order equals cumulative penalties

B's defense asserted the following points in their objection to the deportation disposition and subsequent advocacy. First, B is a genuine third-generation Japanese descendant, and this fact alone deserves special consideration. Second, he has resided in Japan for a long period and has not returned to his birth country since coming to Japan at a young age. Third, facts in his violations of the law are not serious enough to necessitate his deportation. Fourth, B's deportation is equivalent to cumulative penalties in effect. Fifth, responsibility for his delinquency and crimes should not be laid on him alone. Sixth, B no longer has any support for daily living in his home country due to his long-term residence in Japan and his deportation will threaten his dignified existence. Seventh, his deportation will break up his family. Eighth, B's deportation will aggravate his mother's mental and physical illness and jeopardize the welfare of his mother and younger sister in Japan. Finally, he is unlikely to reoffend.

Having addressed the above factors, B's defense attorney stressed 'balance between crime and punishment' most strongly. By referring to precedents in US immigration law, which Japan's Immigration Act is modeled on, the attorney argued as follows:

Deportation is a harsh remedy that may result in loss of "all that makes life worth living" (Ng Fung Ho vs White, 259 U.S.276. at 284 [1922])[7] and a drastic measure that can be regarded as a heavy punishment (Costello vs Immigration Naturalization Service, 376 U.S.120 [1964]).[8] Many countries have considered in their legislative process the idea of moderating the enforcement of the state's power of deportation for the sake of respect for the life of the individual and the family as well as where deportation directly removes a person's rights and freedom provided for by the Constitution; for example, Japan's Immigration Act limits the applicability of a deportation order to certain categories of offenders under punitive laws and orders because it is inappropriate in some cases to execute a deportation order against everyone who has received a prison sentence regardless of the severity of punishment (Sakanaka and Saitō 2007: 492), and Article 42 of the Ordinance for Enforcement of the Immigration Act lists "the deportation being significantly unreasonable" as one of the grounds for filing an objection. The deportation of the applicant from Japan will take him away from his family, deprive him of all that he has built up since his childhood, and deny him even the right to a minimum standard of living. This is as harsh a punishment as a death sentence for the applicant.

Moreover, because 'deportation procedures entail detention and forced relocation of a person and relate to physical restraint that has serious implications for the person's interests just as criminal proceedings do', they give rise to the requirement to apply mutatis mutandis or the analogous application of Article 31 onwards of the Constitution according to their nature even though they are administrative procedures. This is a widely accepted doctrine (Takahashi 2006: 396). As for cumulative imposition of criminal and administrative punishments, while Article 39 of the Constitution only refers to criminal penalties, it is necessary to determine whether a punishment is an administrative sanction based on its substance. In one precedent where an offender who evaded corporate tax by fraud and other illegal means was imposed with a fine for tax evasion as well as a substantial additional tax, the fine is a sanction against antisocial conduct whereas the additional tax is an administrative measure to discourage a breach of tax obligations and to improve tax revenues and hence different from criminal punishments in nature. Accordingly, concurrent imposition of the two punishments does not violate Article 39 of the Constitution (*Saikō saibansho minji hanreishū*, vol. 12, no. 6: 938). However, cumulative punishments in this precedent are a fine and an additional tax and the substance of the issue is infringement of the property right. It is not comparable to the enormous losses a foreign national suffers as a result of the execution of a deportation order.

What needs to be considered is the fact that after the person has been subjected to severe punishments in the form of physical restraint and forced relocation, the person is further punished with deportation on the grounds of the same social facts. In this case, the requirement of Article 39 of the Constitution cannot be ignored. Theoretically, where an administrative penalty is administrative in form but a criminal punishment in effect or where it imposes the same level of burden as in criminal proceedings, then it is considered as a criminal penalty in substance and gives rise to the issue of cumulative punishments (Takahashi 2013: 280). B's defense attorney argues that particularly for foreign nationals who came to Japan at a young age and built their life-bases in Japan as they grew up, the deportation procedures uprooting their entire life must be regarded as cumulative punishments in substance unlike in the case of short-term residents and foreign nationals who came to Japan when they were adults.

Is it reasonable to lay all the blame for delinquency on an individual? The direct cause of B's juvenile delinquency is found in his brutal family circumstances. He was beaten and neglected by his mother from infancy to age five and by his stepfather up to age thirteen. He witnessed his mother being raped by his stepfather in Peru and Japan. These experiences led B to believe that he was not loved by anyone, and he lapsed into a distrust of people and experienced low self-esteem. Consequently, he mistrusted his own troubled family and instead turned his relationships with fellow delinquents into his pseudo-family, which he valued. Only the pseudo-family relationships with other delinquents were able to relieve his loneliness and pain.

Had his family been able to safeguard him better at an early stage, things might have turned out differently. However, B never received appropriate protection. Even when he was sliding further into delinquency, his mother left him to his own devices and did not intervene. In any case, her past abuse of B made him distrust her and stopped him from listening to her. There is no doubt that these family circumstances had a major impact on his delinquency. The most crucial factor, however, was the fact that B had little Japanese-language education except for a few months when he was enrolled in elementary school shortly after arriving in Japan and a few months at the end of his third year in middle school. He had to study Japanese and all other subjects on his own. B acquired conversational fluency in Japanese by the sixth grade but his Japanese reading and writing abilities, especially kanji, were very poor. His inability to keep up with his study cannot be attributed to a lack of effort alone. If anything, B is the victim who missed out on an opportunity to receive Japanese-language and other education within an institutional framework.

## Balancing public order and the family

B's objection was sustained and special permission to stay was issued as a result. It was followed by the granting of 'long-term' residence status for one year. In the present case, B's attorney placed a special emphasis on comparing and balancing the maintenance of public order and the interests of the family in a concrete manner and tried to highlight similarities and differences between precedents and B's case from this angle. Let us examine this point more closely.

The defense attorney used the following precedents for comparison.

1 A foreign national married to a Japanese national was granted special permission to stay after being convicted for violating the Opium Law (1999).

2 A foreign national married to a Japanese national was granted special permission to stay after being convicted for importing opioid tablets containing dihydrocodeine (2002).

3 A foreign national married to a Japanese national was granted special permission to stay after being convicted for importing cannabis (2004).

4   A third-generation Japanese descendant married to a second-generation Japanese descendant was granted special permission to stay after being convicted for using a stimulant (1999).

5   A second-generation Japanese descendant was granted special permission to stay after being convicted for using narcotic drugs (2005).

6   A third-generation Japanese descendant was granted special permission to stay after marrying a second-generation Japanese descendant while serving a suspended sentence for using a stimulant in violation of the Simulant Drugs Control Act (2007).

7   A third-generation Japanese descendant was granted special permission to stay after being convicted for violating the narcotics and psychotropics control law and the cannabis control law (2007).[9]

These precedents demonstrate that special permission to stay was granted despite a guilty sentence for the use of stimulant drugs in multiple cases.

Then the attorney presented cases in which special permission to stay was granted to a foreign national who was convicted for crimes other than violations of the Stimulant Drugs Control Act.

8   A foreign national was granted special permission to stay after being sentenced to two years and eight months of imprisonment suspended for three years for violating the Immigration Act and theft on the grounds that the person was the custodial parent of a child acknowledged by a Japanese national and that the person was remorseful for committing the crime (2005).

9   A foreign national was granted special permission to stay after being released from jail at the end of a twenty-two-month sentence. Despite two further convictions, the person was granted special permission to stay on the grounds, among others, that the person grew up in Japan to age sixty-four, had brothers and a child residing

in Japan, and had no relative to depend on in the home country (2005).

The above two cases were disclosed by the Ministry of Justice as examples in which special permission to stay was granted.

10 A Columbian national, who entered Japan on a 'short-term' visa in 1997 and overstayed, was sentenced by the Yokohama District Court to three years of imprisonment suspended for five years for theft (shoplifting) and violating the Immigration Act. The person was immediately taken into custody in the Yokohama branch of the Tokyo Regional Immigration Bureau and deportation procedures were commenced. However, special permission to stay was issued in December 2006 on the grounds that the person was the custodial parent of a Japanese child, which was followed by the granting of 'long-term' residence status for one year.

11 A Peruvian national, who entered Japan on a 'short-term' visa in 1992 and overstayed without extending the visa or changing status, was arrested for suspicion of indecent assault in December 2000. The person was subsequently charged with a violation of the Immigration Act alone and sentenced by the Tokyo District Court to two years and six months of imprisonment suspended for four years on March 23, 2001. The person was detained by the Tokyo Regional Immigration Bureau as part of deportation procedures but special permission to stay was granted in October 2002 on the grounds of the person's marriage to another Peruvian national after the arrest followed by 'long-term' residence status for one year.

12 A Chinese national married a Japanese businessperson in China and came to live in Japan in 2002 on a 'spouse of a Japanese' visa in 2002. The person was convicted for violating the Anti-Prostitution Act and sentenced by the Yokohama District Court to eighteen months in prison suspended for four years and a fine of 300,000 yen in July 2003. The person was immediately detained at the Yokohama branch

of the Tokyo Regional Immigration Bureau as part of deportation procedures. In August 2003, however, special permission to stay was issued and 'spouse of a Japanese' residence status for one year was granted.

13 A Chinese national, who was married to a Japanese national and living in Japan on a 'spouse of a Japanese' visa, was convicted for violating the Anti-Prostitution Act and sentenced by the Tokyo District Court to one year of imprisonment suspended for three years and a fine of 200,000 yen in May 2003. The person was immediately detained as part of deportation procedures by the Tokyo Regional Immigration Bureau but received special permission to stay and 'spouse of a Japanese' residence status for one year in July 2003.

These two Chinese nationals were involved in the operation of brothels.

14 A Peruvian national of second-generation Japanese descent entered Japan on a 'short-term' residence visa in 1992 and became an overstayer when an application for change of residence status was rejected even though the person was a second-generation Japanese. In December 2005, the Yokohama District Court sentenced the person to two years of imprisonment suspended for three years for violating the Immigration Act and inflicting bodily injury. After the person's deportation procedures were commenced on the grounds of overstaying, special permission to stay was issued in February 2006 followed by the granting of 'spouse of a Japanese' residence status for one year.

15 A Brazilian national of third-generation Japanese descent, who arrived in 1991 with 'long-term' residence status, was sentenced to two years of imprisonment suspended for three years for inflicting bodily injury and causing bodily injury resulting in death in November 1999. The person received an unsuspended sentence of eight-months in prison for attempted extortion in November 2002. The person's application for an extension of residence period was

rejected and a deportation order was issued but the person was subsequently granted special permission to stay on the grounds of marriage to a third-generation Japanese descendant.

In cases where a foreign national with a criminal record was granted special permission to stay, the existence of a family was one of the key factors. These cases illustrate that suspension of the deportation process at least once is no exception where the foreign national exists as part of a family unit, regardless of whether the family includes Japanese nationals. In view of this, halting the deportation process and granting special permission to stay in B's case would be in accordance with precedents.

In the case under discussion here, consideration should have been given to the lives of B's mother and sister if he were to be deported. The mother was sincerely dealing with her history of abusive treatment of B while B had come to understand the pain he had inflicted on her. This situation deserves full attention in considering their family circumstances. For the welfare of the family, including the younger sister, giving B a chance to rehabilitate accords better with the social equity principle than deporting him out of Japan. The attorney's assertion was that a stay of execution of B's deportation order would better serve the public welfare from the standpoint of the family comprising B, his mother and his sister.

## From the final hearing to special permission to stay

The last hearing was conducted inside the Himeji Juvenile Prison on August 21, 2008. B nervously conveyed his feelings to a special inquiry officer. The officer listened in a respectful manner and skillfully put together a report. After the issuance of special permission to stay, B sent a thank-you letter to this special inquiry officer.

> I am truly glad to receive this special visa and feeling relieved after spending many days worrying so much. Thanks to you, I was able to obtain this wonderful outcome, which allows me to stay with my mother and sister. I am eternally grateful to you. Now that I'm permitted to stay in Japan, I am determined to lead a decent life and never to commit

a crime again. I will work hard, keep good company and be a good son. To make up for the suffering I caused to my mother, I will endure hardships in society and behave responsibly. I want to abandon my self-centered thinking and have concern for my family and others in order not to repeat the same mistake. That is my promise. My mother, sister and I have decided to move to Saitama in order to make a fresh start. I am still living with my mother in Osaka but we will go to Saitama before the end of this month. I want to find casual work to help my mother until then. I will remember to live the rest of my life as best as I can because I will not get a second chance. Once again, I thank you from the bottom of my heart for trying to help this sinful man and giving me the visa.

B's mother found a law firm run by Spanish-speaking attorneys and administrative procedures specialists in a Japanese Spanish-language magazine and contacted them in mid-July 2007. Special permission to stay was issued approximately one year after the appointment of an attorney. A large number of evidential documents were submitted by the applicant's attorney during this period.[10] The submission included statements from B and his mother and petitions from the mother, her brothers in Japan, B's cousins in Japan, B's former probation officer and the mother's attending doctor in a hospital. A number of letters exchanged between these people and B were also submitted as evidence. All of the letters, except the mother's, were hand-written in Japanese (thanks in part to the Japanese language learning program at Kurihama Reform School).

In addition to precedents in which special permission to stay was issued despite an applicant's criminal record, detailed reports of individual circumstances in the cases personally handled by the attorney were also submitted as evidence. This was the attorney's attempt to demonstrate the grounds for the applicant's argument based on these precedents. However, what staggered me as a researcher in this case was a set of documents concerning the family's life history documenting in concrete terms the history of B's time in Japan, the course of his mother's illness, how their family life was formed in Japan from the sister's birth to schooling, and the relationships B, his mother and his sister built in Japanese society. For example, photographs of the sister's preschool excursions and sports days and her elementary school reports, essays and paintings were submitted to illustrate her growth process and the extent to which the family was integrated in Japanese society. The sister's letters to her brother demonstrated family bonds. This evidence made it very easy to imagine the situation into which the mother and the sister would be thrust by B's deportation. In my mind, this overwhelming amount of the family's life history materials had the effect of moving the Immigration Bureau to issue special permission to stay more than any logical reasoning.

## Conclusion: Acceptance of foreign nationals

B's delinquency was largely attributable to the hardships that troubled him and his family. Nevertheless, we must not set it aside as a special case.

B turned to juvenile delinquency. He was never given a chance to mend his ways. While he experienced many school transfers in elementary and secondary education, only one elementary school and one junior high school supported his learning by way of a special class or supplemental study. B was finally able to learn functional Japanese reading and writing thanks to the Japanese language learning program at Kurihama Reform School. *B would not have developed his Japanese writing and reading skills had he not committed a crime and been sent to a reform school.* It is ironic that he was only offered an opportunity to learn after he became a criminal, but this is the reality.

Since the introduction of the public notice on long-term residence, it is no longer possible to claim that the admittance of foreign nationals is determined on a case-by-case basis. Now that anyone can enter the country, it is inevitable that some of them will be troubled people. However, B's treatment suggests that there has been no consideration for these people. In the case of children who had no choice but to accompany their parents to Japan, the entire responsibility for adaptation to life in Japan is placed on themselves and their parents. Those who come to Japan as business executives or university professors may have the financial and cultural resources to pay sufficient attention to their children's education. On the other hand, foreign nationals who come to take on demanding, dirty and dangerous jobs unwanted by Japanese are unlikely to have such resources. Most of them would not come to work in Japan if they had such resources. They came because they were 'have-nots'.

Those without resources will quickly fall into a crisis if they lose their jobs. Many of the foreign nationals of Japanese descent have been employed as non-regular workers because it is too costly to hire them as regular employees. Japan has been using these people as flexible labor to deal with fluctuations in production. This is why the Japanese government had to set up the repatriation support program for unemployed foreign workers of Japanese descent when various problems arose after the Lehman Shock economic slump. It is inevitable that some of the people accepted into the country fall outside of the scope of the assumption. However, it is unacceptable for a modern law-governed state to eject some people just because it did not anticipate their arrival. The case discussed in this chapter has revealed the consequences of the state's failure to define the foreigner's 'status as a person' in advance so that any person arriving in Japan can be dealt with appropriately.

## Notes

1   His mother arrived in Japan in 1991.
2   He was initially enrolled in the first grade at a Nara elementary school. He mastered conversational Japanese within several months and was transferred to the fourth grade, which was a year behind the grade for his age.
3   B sought assurances from the Brazilian when he mentioned needing wheels in the first instance and when he went to collect them, he again asked for confirmation that they were 'definitely not stolen goods'. As the Brazilian assured him that they were not, B went to collect them.
4   As B watched his mother break down crying in the court, he was disappointed with himself for lying and failing to keep promises He blamed himself for making his mother unhappy. He used to attribute his struggles to ill treatment by his mother, but he came to realize that he also contributed to her hardships in life.

5   When the two placed a substance in a glass apparatus and inhaled vapors, the car was filled with smoke. B asked them to open windows or turn on the air conditioning. B realized that they were using a stimulant only when he asked what they were inhaling and they said it was '*curica*' (probably crack cocaine).

6   In this case, a Bangladeshi man overstayed his visa and was arrested for violating the Immigration Act while he was in a de facto relationship with a Japanese woman. They married after his arrest. As the woman was the eldest daughter caring for her ill mother, the couple chose to support her mother in Japan rather than moving to Bangladesh.

7   The case report can be accessed here: https://supreme.justia.com/cases/federal/us/259/276/case.html

8   The case report can be accessed here: https://supreme.justia.com/cases/federal/us/376/120/case.html

9   Cases 2, 3, 5, 6 and 7 occurred after the 2001 revision that added a suspended sentence to the list of grounds for deportation. Cases 6 and 7 occurred after the good conduct requirement was added to the criteria for third-generation applicants in the revision of the public notice on long-term residence.

10  I used ten notebooks to study these documents. This task took me almost three years, from May 2014 to October 2016. The attorney who represented B was the leading attorney in the case on which the Supreme Court ruled on June 4, 2008, that certain conditions in the Nationality Law were unconstitutional. I used twelve notebooks on that case. Even though B's case did not go to court, the amount of documentary evidence gathered was not far behind that in the Supreme Court case.

# LGBT Foreign Nationals and the Sociology of Deportation Orders in Japan: Protecting the Rights of a Minority within a Minority

## Introduction

In this chapter, I argue that in Japan's legal system the deportation order issued for a trans foreign national, C, was highly extraordinary and discuss its problematic aspects, which were compounded by the fact that she is transgender.[1] In my opinion, the mandate given to directors of regional immigration bureaus to decide on special permission to stay (*zairyū tokubetusu kyoka*) has been widened by administrative notices, a type of internal document that, since its legislation in Article 69(2) of the Immigration Control and Refugee Recognition Act (hereafter 'the Immigration Act'), figures in the chronology of events to date. These decisions made by the directors of regional immigration bureaus on special permission to stay, whose scope was gradually widened during the 1990s, depend on pre-determined enabling requirements and in nature differ significantly from decisions of the Minister of Justice. As a result, the directors of the branches of the Tokyo Regional Immigration Bureau as the adjudicating administrative agencies have zero degree of freedom in their decisions. With regard to the execution of the deportation order in this case by the supervising immigration inspector of the Yokohama branch of the Tokyo Regional Immigration Bureau as the executing administrative agency, controls under the principle of the proportionality of law enforcement and the principle of equality based on current domestic and international civic environments are necessary. From this standpoint, I consider the rights of foreign-national sexual minorities in Japan who constitute a minority group within a minority.

The reason the deportation order was issued for C was a previous criminal conviction for a violation of the Stimulant Drugs Control Act. However, multiple precedents exist where the immigration authority has issued a special permission to stay and permitted residence visa status after the issuance of a deportation order upon conviction in cases of violation of the Stimulant Drugs Control Act. Compared with these equivalent precedents, the treatment of C is problematic because her status as a transgender person has structurally expelled her from the framework of precedents.

## Summary of the facts

The defendant, C, of Japanese descent in the third generation (so called 'Sansei') arrived at New Tokyo International Airport Authority in 1997 with the objective of finding work as a foreign laborer. Between that time and April 2011, her foreign resident registration had been amended seventeen times. During this period, she never returned to her home country, Brazil. In September 2012 she was arrested by the Metropolitan Police Office (Keishichō), Ōi Police Station, for violating the Stimulant Drugs Control Act. On November 14 in a ruling of the Tokyo District Court she received an eighteen-month prison sentence with three years' stay of execution. The ruling became final on November 29.

On February 4 and 14, 2013, officers of the Tokyo Regional Immigration Bureau, Yokohama Branch, investigated her in connection with a violation of the Immigration Act. On May 27, a detention order was issued on grounds of violating the Immigration Act. The order was executed on May 29, and she was placed into detention. On the same day, she was tried for violation of the Immigration Act. She was found in breach of the act and was informed of the finding. She requested an oral hearing and was provisionally released on the same day.

In the interval, she opened a restaurant. On September 6, the oral hearing was held, which did not change the deportation decision. On the same day, she filed an objection with the Minister of Justice. On September 12, the adjudicating administrative agency (the director of the Tokyo Regional Immigration Bureau) found the filing of objection groundless and notified the executing administrative agency (the supervising immigration inspector of the Tokyo Regional Immigration Bureau, Yokohama Branch). On October 24, the executing administrative agency enforced the deportation order and placed her in detention. On October 28, she filed a complaint with the Tokyo District Court. She was again provisionally released on November 28.

To date, she has spent eighteen years in Japan, never returning to her home country, changing her foreign resident registration without delay with every change of address. With a 'long term resident' visa status, she has renewed her visa eight times while in Japan. Her conviction for the violation of the Stimulant Drugs Control Act stemmed from the use of stimulant drugs upon encouragement from her male partner at the time. Moreover, during her residence in Japan, she underwent a gender transition from male to female that altered her appearance.

## Assertions of the parties and first ruling

The complaint filed for the plaintiff with the Tokyo District Court made the following assertions. The plaintiff, C, is a Brazilian citizen of Japanese descent in the third generation. (i) This point must be taken into account because the residence qualification of non-Japanese nationals of Japanese descent is granted with consideration of the strong linkages with Japan. (ii) She has lived in Japan for eighteen consecutive years. Her long-term residence deserves consideration. (iii) She is a transgender person whose male gender appearance has become almost indiscernible. Upon return to Brazil, her access to the labor market would be extremely difficult. It is uncertain if her family and relatives would accept her. (iv) The violation of the Stimulant Drugs Control Act committed by C was due to personal use of stimulant drugs. Multiple precedents exist for like cases where special permission to stay was granted. The case of C corresponds to such precedents.

The immigration authority rebutted these assertions. Specifically, the immigration authority held that 'The country is neither obligated by international convention or law to admit foreign nationals nor does the

Constitution guarantee foreign nationals freedom to enter Japan, the right to take residence in Japan, or to demand continuation of residence in Japan'. 'Holders of a permanent resident qualification are no exception and are not exempt from the deportation proceedings provided under the law'. The Nagoya District Court also stated in its ruling on January 29, 2009, that although 'having permission for permanent residence' is one of the grounds on which the authority 'may grant the suspect special permission to stay' (Article 50(1)(i) of the Immigration Act), it is 'merely one factor that may be considered in rejecting special permission to stay'. Because 'whether or not special permission to stay should be granted is decided with consideration of the individual circumstances of the affected foreign national's entire conduct and various other matters such as the maintenance of domestic public peace and public order and morals as well as the preservation of health and hygiene and the stability of the labor market' by the Minister of Justice and the immigration authority under them, Japanese ancestry or permanent residency is just one of the factors they may or may not take into consideration.

With regard to C's status as a transgender person and the possibility of her return to Brazil, the immigration authority held (i) that the matter of C being a transgender person was not at issue at the stage of the investigation and the oral examination[2] and (ii) that 'the Brazilian government has established information and support centers for Brazilian workers for laborers returning from abroad to rejoin the Brazilian labor market (NIATRE) and centers operating as employment agents for repatriating workers, in the light of which an inability of C to find work after repatriation is baseless conjecture'.[3]

For the purposes of its ruling, the Tokyo District Court split the dispute into two points at issue. The first concerned the lawfulness of the decision as to whether or not special permission to stay was to be granted. The second issue concerned the lawfulness of the deportation order, i.e., whether or not she was to be expelled from Japan. I begin the discussion with the perception of the Tokyo District Court concerning the lawfulness of the decision on special permission to stay.

> Under the Immigration Act, Article 69(2), and the Immigration Act Enforcement Rules, Article 61(2), the Minister of Justice can delegate

the authority to decide on special permission to stay to the directors of the regional immigration bureaus. Since the case at hand was decided by the pertinently authorized director of the Tokyo Regional Immigration Bureau, it applies that this decision on special permission to stay was passed by authority of the Minister of Justice. The Constitution stipulates nothing about foreign nationals entering and residing in Japan and imposes no duty on the immigration authority to let foreign nationals enter or reside in Japan. Absent a special treaty, a nation is under no obligation to admit foreign nationals into the country. Hence, whether or not foreign nationals are admitted into the country and, if admitted, on what conditions, is to be determined at the discretion of the subject nation. These questions and the question of whether to grant special permission to stay are conceptually the same. Consequently, for a decision on special permission to stay passed by the Minister of Justice to be unlawful, it would either have to fully fail to grasp the facts and circumstances at issue, or it would in significant measure have to fall short of general accepted ideas prevalent in society. Only these cases would amount to a departure from the scope of discretionary authority, or its abuse, vested in the Minister of Justice.

As to the second point, the lawfulness of the deportation order, C started using stimulant drugs around 2007 or 2008 encouraged by her then-boyfriend. Stimulant drugs can not only affect users themselves but can also give rise to crime, become widespread in society, corrupt civic spirit and threaten a nation's existence. The defendant thus acted against the preservation of domestic public peace and public order and morals. On the other hand, the fact that homophobic incidents have occurred in Brazil does not provide sufficient grounds to conclude that C will encounter such incidents shortly after her repatriation. This consideration therefore failed to qualify as a specific concern for the physical safety of C.

Hence, 'even taking into account the best possible considerations in favor of the plaintiff, there is no basis for holding that the decision to deny special permission to stay fully fails to grasp the facts and circumstances at issue or in significant measure falls short of general accepted ideas of society. Since the court found that with regard to the decision on the special permission to stay or the lawfulness of the disposition of a deportation order no departure from or abuse of the scope of discretionary power granted to the Minister of Justice had occurred and that the decision was therefore lawful', the court ruled against C's complaint.

## Assertions of the parties in the appeal proceedings and decision of the appellate court

On April 25, 2015, C filed an appeal with the Tokyo High Court on grounds that the decision in the first instance was passed in error. In the appeal proceedings the plaintiff side took issue with the guidelines published by the Ministry of Justice concerning decisions on special permission to stay. The guidelines are subdivided into four points that are to be taken into account in passing decisions. These are factors for particular consideration in favor, other factors for consideration in favor, factors for particular consideration against, and other factors against, along with criteria for their clarification. If based on individual consideration of the various factors the circumstances for consideration in favor clearly outweigh the factors against, deliberations are to be conducted with a view to granting special permission to stay. However, even when a factor in favor exists, it will not necessarily prompt a review with a view to granting special permission to stay. Likewise, a factor against does not mean the review will be conducted with a view to denying special permission to stay.

According to the assertion of the immigration authority and the ruling in the first instance, these factors are but one angle in considering a foreign national's special permission to stay for long-term residence, and need not be considered by necessity. However, the guidelines issued by the immigration authority note, as one of the 'other factors for admission to be given consideration', the question of whether 'the foreign national's residence in Japan has been long-term and whether the foreign national has assimilated in Japan'. This means the question of assimilation in Japan must be given full review. In the case of C, the only 'factor against' is her conviction in connection with a violation of the Stimulant Drugs Control Act. This is also clear from the ruling in the first instance, where the conviction in a criminal case 'is to be rated as an important factor against'. However, according to the guidelines, not all drug-related offences constitute 'other factors against to be given particular consideration'. Cases that fall into the latter category are 'cases of convictions for the illegal import and trafficking in harmful goods such as illegal drugs and firearms, etc'. Consequently, a violation of the Stimulant Drugs Control Act due to the possession of drugs for personal use corresponds only to the category of 'other factors against'. C has never experienced hallucination or an altered mental state nor caused harm to society or the people around her.

Indeed, in the case of C, circumstances in favor to be given particular consideration do exist. These concern the protection of the rights afforded to homosexual persons and transgender persons. The rights afforded to these minorities are anchored in the United Nations resolution of June 2011 (A/HRC/17/L.9/Rev.1) adopted at the United Nations Human Rights Commission. The resolution expresses 'grave concern' over the violence and discrimination against individuals on grounds of sexual orientation and gender identity and posits that the rights of sexual minorities must be approached from international frameworks. Thus, according to the Office of the United Nations High Commissioner for Human Rights, the right of sexual minorities to protection from homophobia is acknowledged in the Universal Declaration of Human Rights, Article 3, the International Covenant on Civil and Political Rights, articles 6 and 9, and the Convention Relating to the Status of Refugees, Article 33(1).[4] The right of homosexual persons to be protected from torture and inhumane treatment and violation of human dignity is acknowledged in the Universal Declaration of Human Rights, Article 5, the International Covenant on Civil and Political Rights, Article 7, and the Convention against Torture, Article 1(1) and Article 2(1).[5] Discrimination on grounds of homosexuality is banned in the Universal Declaration of Human Rights, articles 2, 7, 9 and 12; and in the International Covenant on Civil and Political Rights, articles 2(1), 6(2), 9, 17 and 26.[6] Discrimination on grounds of sexual orientation and gender identity is banned in the Universal Declaration of Human Rights, articles 2 and 7; and in the International Covenant on Civil and Political Rights, articles 2(1) and 26; in the International Covenant on Economic, Social and Cultural Rights, Article 2; and in the Convention on the Rights of the Child, Article 2.[7] Moreover, the Universal Declaration of Human Rights, articles 19 and 20(1), and the International Covenant on Civil and Political Rights, articles 19(2), 21 and 22, stipulate the freedom of expression and the freedom of association of LGBT persons.[8] The human rights of sexual minorities are guaranteed in established international human rights law and have been the subject of a range of efforts by the United Nations. The ruling of the district court considered only domestic law and neglected the responsibility as a member of the international community based on the principle of internationalism which finds expression also in international law and the Constitution of Japan.

The immigration authority frontally rebutted this statement of reasons for the appeal. Specifically, it was argued that essentially the guidelines 'indicate no univocal, fixed standard for special permission to stay. Instead, they indicate only general, abstract examples of matters or consideration in deciding on such a permission'. A grant of special permission to stay:

> [...] constitutes a beneficial measure that needs to be determined individually based on the comprehensive consideration of the circumstances at large, predicated on the wide-ranging discretionary rights of the Minister of Justice, with no extant administrative precedent that would preclude a decision of denial or permittance and without extant univocal, fixed standards. With respect to the special permission to stay, the law contains no specific provision concerning requirements under which permission should be granted but leaves discretion to the Minister of Justice to adjudicate its denial, which is apparent from the intent of affording this discretionary right its wide scope.

The immigration authority thus argued that the decision on special permission to stay was entirely at its discretion, as though asserting it was not bound even by its self-issued guidelines.

Despite this, according to the immigration authority, the guidelines were kept and even augmented because, in the proceedings concerning the 'Act on the Partial Revision of the Special Measures Act Concerning the Immigration Act (Law No. 79 of 2009)' passed into law at the 171st Ordinary Diet Session, Article 60(2) of the supplementary provisions of this law was revised by adding a stipulation to the effect that 'Deliberations shall be held on measures to further enhance the transparency of the operations of permissions under Article 50(1) and other measures for the promotion of applications, and the implementation of measures for reducing the number of illegal residents'. In fact, as the plaintiff asserts, the guidelines indicate a concept for the adjudication of denial of special permission to stay based on the categories of 'factors for admissions to be given particular consideration', 'other factors for admission to be given consideration', 'other factors against to be given particular consideration', and 'other factors against'. However, in its attempt at transparency, this revision does no more than offer various examples of considerations 'in favor of special permission to stay' and 'against special permission to stay', and for each individual case comprehensively considers the applicant's (i) reason for desiring special permission; (ii) family situation; and (iii) conduct; as well as (iv) circumstances in Japan and abroad; (v) the need for humanitarian consideration; and (vi) general circumstances including effects on illegal residents in Japan. This means that the guidelines indicate only example considerations but no criteria. Moreover, with respect to the rights of sexual minorities argued by the plaintiff, the immigration authority holds that Brazil supports the resolutions adopted by the United Nations Human Rights Commission, and since the Brazilian government has been making efforts to protect the rights of homosexual persons, no problems exist in connection with the repatriation of C.

The Tokyo High Court made minor corrections to the wording of the first decision and added the following language:

> The conviction of the appellant in this criminal case concerns the personal use of illegal drugs. This is no circumstance corresponding to "factors against to be given particular consideration" under the guidelines but signifies only other criminal law violations or corresponds to improper conduct mentioned as "other factors against". The appellant therefore asserts that in the decision of these criminal proceedings the assessment of the use of stimulant drugs as serious occurred in error. However, in light of the intent associated with conferring upon the Minister of Justice the authority over the special permission to stay, as stated in the above opinion (a), there is nothing unreasonable in assessing the fact that the appellant has regularly used stimulant drugs

while resident in Japan and has been given a criminal conviction as a serious "factor against" in the decision of denial of special permission to stay passed against the appellant.

In its decision, the Tokyo High Court thus almost fully followed the assertions of the immigration authority.

## Review of the authority to decide on special permission to stay

Based on the foregoing, the discussion will now turn to points of concern regarding the assertions of the immigration authority and the decision of the court.

In its decision, the Tokyo District Court held as follows:

> The directors of regional immigration bureaus can be mandated to execute the authority of the Minister of Justice under the Immigration Act, Article 69(2). Since the director of the Tokyo Regional Immigration Bureau is for the purposes of this case mandated with such authority, it applies to the director of the Tokyo Regional Immigration Bureau to make pronouncements concerning special permission to stay under the authority of the Minister of Justice.

As to the reason, the Tokyo District Court found as follows:

> It is held, and this interpretation concurs with the view, that no provision exists that imposes a duty on the nation to admit foreign nationals into the country or to permit residence, the reason being that under international convention or law no nation is obligated to take in foreign nationals and absent a special treaty a nation can decide at its discretion whether and based on what conditions it admits foreign nationals into the country.

The entire argument originates from this point.

The immigration authority asserts that once the legal procedures are in place for delegating to the directors of the regional immigration bureaus the authority conferred upon the Minister of Justice, decisions passed respectively by the Minister of Justice and the directors of the regional immigration bureaus are entirely the same. However, as foreign nationals have no right to enter Japan from the outset, they have no right to ask to continue residing in Japan. Indeed, foreign nationals are unable to invoke a right to enter Japan. However, neither does the Immigration Act allow the immigration authority to deny entry of foreign nationals who carry a valid visa.[9] Although the Immigration Act does not refer to any right of foreign nationals, the immigration authority is not entirely free in its actions with regard to the entry and residence of foreign nationals as suggested by this provision to prevent it from denying entry of foreign nationals with a valid visa.

In practice, effects equaling rights in substance have been put into place through procedural stipulations. Likewise, deportation procedures allow for the filing of objections and litigation in court. Incidentally, special permission to stay originally served, in light of a person's special circumstances and based on specific 'merits', to enable legal residence of persons who otherwise were on legal grounds unable to take residence in Japan. It is for this reason that a person who is not granted special permission to stay must be deported. Consequently, in a sense, any decision granting special permission to stay bends the law and naturally the decision-maker must be equipped with significant discretionary authority. However, this strong discretionary authority or a wide scope of discretion does not bestow free rein on the decision-maker.

How is the right to decide on special permission to stay delegated from the Minister of Justice to the directors of the regional immigration bureaus and what is the nature of the decisions by the directors of the regional immigration bureaus in this regard? In practice the range of discretion on special permission to stay has been changed by way of official notice. The Ministry of Justice Immigration Bureau Director's notices dated April 8, 1992, and August 1, 1996 ('Spouse Notice') stated as follows:

> Special permission to stay is to be granted if all of the following conditions are met: (i) with respect to cases of unlawful entry, unlawful landing or unlawful residence in Japan, at least three years of residence in Japan have passed after landing (whether unlawful or lawful); (ii) marriage to a Japanese citizen or permanent resident, with the credibility and stability of the marriage holding up to inspection; (iii) the subject foreign national has applied for special permission to stay. (iv) In cases that correspond to the above criteria, the directors of the regional immigration bureaus shall decide at discretion on special permission to stay (determination by the Minister of Justice).

Subsequently, the Spouse Notice underwent enlargement and on July 30, 1996, became the 'Notice concerning the treatment of foreign nationals who support their own Japanese child' ('Long-Term Resident Mother and Child Notice'). As a result, foreign parents having and supporting their own Japanese child became eligible to obtain residence qualification. Next, in the notice issued on April 6, 1999, the Spouse Notice was revised (hereafter referred to as the 'Marriage Notice'), rescinding the residence period requirement for spouses of Japanese citizens, irrespective of whether they have children.

What kind of circumstances surrounded this delegation of the authority to decide on special permission to stay to the directors of the regional immigration bureaus? The answer can be gleaned from the Ministry of Justice Immigration Bureau Director's Notice dated April 16, 1999 ('Notice of 1999'). This notice issued the following instruction: 'For the sake of administrative simplification, except for important cases, such as cases that may have political or diplomatic implications or affect public peace, etc., in instances where a marriage exists with a Japanese citizen and the marriage is judged credible and stable, the directors of regional immigration bureaus can decide at their discretion'.

What then is the common denominator of the Spouse Notice, the Long-Term Resident Mother and Child Notice, the Marriage Notice, and the Notice of 1999? The Spouse Notice empowers the directors of the regional immigration bureaus to decide at their discretion in cases that meet four requirements. The Long-Term Resident Mother and Child Notice expands the scope to foreign nationals who are the parent of a child holding Japanese citizenship. The Marriage Notice authorizes the directors of the regional immigration bureaus to decide at their discretion while a marriage to a Japanese citizen continues, irrespective of children and irrespective of a foreign spouse's period of residence in Japan. The Notice of 1999, for the sake of administrative simplification, enables the directors of the regional immigration bureaus to decide at their discretion on special permission to stay, provided political and diplomatic interests and public peace are not under threat, and provided an extant genuine marriage with a Japanese citizen. In order to statutorily buttress the delegation of the authority over special permission to stay to the directors of the regional immigration bureaus advanced through the internal documents of an administrative agency, their content was integrated into the text of the current Immigration Act, Article 69(2), and the Immigration Act Enforcement Rules, Article 61(2). Considering that the act for partial revision containing the provision to delegate the minister's authority to the directors of the regional immigration bureaus was promulgated as Act No. 136 of 2001 following its passage in the 153rd extraordinary Diet session, my interpretation that the aforementioned two articles are an extension of the prior notices is logical.

These notices demonstrate that unlike assertions by the immigration authority and the courts, decisions on special permission to stay passed by the directors of the regional immigration bureaus are not entirely identical to decisions passed by the Minister of Justice. *The decision-making authority delegated to the directors of the regional immigration bureaus is predicated on cases that meet certain conditions.* These conditions are prescribed in the notices. What the decisions of the Minister of Justice and of the directors of the regional immigration bureaus have in common is only the effect of enabling a grant of residence qualification for persons who have lost that qualification. The decision-making criteria for the minister and the directors are not the same.

Incidentally, not all immigration administration notices are made public. The 'Long-Term Resident Mother and Child Notice' was widely and generally publicized, which makes it an exception. Consequently, as special permission to stay became immigration offices' routine work as cases increased in number, an array of doubts were raised concerning the scope of discretion involved. As a result, the immigration authority, finding it impossible to ignore these voices, started in 2003 to publish on the website of the Ministry of Justice Immigration Bureau the very small number of cases where special permission to stay was granted. Moreover, in order to further increase the transparency of the administration of special permission to stay, guidelines for special permission to stay (the point at issue in the appeal proceedings considered here) were published.

In the assertions of the immigration authority and the court rulings, the decision in the case at hand is discussed as if it were completely identical in nature to the McLean case precedent (discussed below). However, the Immigration Act, Article 69(2), also in the text body, excludes from the authority delegated to the directors of the regional immigration bureaus decisions concerning (i) permanent residence permits, (ii) permanent resident permits for refugees, and (iii) revocations of refugee status. As mentioned above, up to this point, the authority to decide on special permission to stay that had come to be delegated to the directors of the regional immigration bureaus had its scope of discretion established through notices, and for the sake of administrative simplification, directors of regional immigration bureaus were enabled to decide on cases that met certain requirements. This is entirely different from decisions passed by the Minister of Justice based on assessments made at a high political level.

## Conditions in practice

How does the question of discretion in deciding on special permission to stay relate to the actual practice? In the McLean case, which figures also in the assertions of the immigration authority and the ruling of the Tokyo District Court, the point at issue was the scope of discretion of the Minister of Justice regarding applications for renewal of the period of stay. The case is routinely cited in precedent collections and legal papers in connection with the scope of foreign nationals' human rights.

> With respect to the decision to approve or deny the renewal of a residence period, the vantage point of the Minister of Justice with respect to foreign nationals is the protection of national interests, such as the preservation

of domestic public peace as public order and morals, preservation of health and hygiene, and the stability of the labor market. The Minister of Justice considers not only the appropriateness of an applicant's application but also general circumstances, such as the applicant's entire conduct during the period of residence, domestic political, economic and social conditions, international affairs, diplomatic relations and the comity of nations, and must in a timely manner pass relevant appropriate decisions. Decisions of this kind cannot be expected to yield appropriate results unless left to the discretion of the Minister of Justice, who is responsible for the administration of immigration control.

This language has been repeatedly cited in rulings in cases of dispute over special permission to stay.

As discussed in the previous section, however, in the case at hand the authority to pass a decision rests with the director of a regional immigration bureau and not the Minister of Justice. Decisions are made by just one of the directors of the eight regional immigration bureaus subordinated to the central Immigration Bureau, which forms a section of the Ministry of Justice. As a cabinet member, the Minister of Justice also makes political decisions at a high level, and it is understandable that cases associated with this kind of high-level political decision-making require wide-ranging discretionary authority.[10]

However, special permission to stay now differs in significant ways from the time of the McLean case. Before the issuance of Ministry of Justice Notice No. 132 of 1990 (the so-called 'Long-Term Residence Notice'), which enabled non-Japanese nationals of Japanese descent to take up work, around 400–500 special permissions to stay were issued each year. Calculated according to public agencies' business days, this means about two cases were decided each day. After the revision of the Immigration Control and Refugee Recognition Act of 1990, the number of grants of special permissions to stay increased by orders of magnitude. Over the last ten years, the number topped 10,000 in the busiest year. Although 2014 was the quietest of those ten years, the count still came to 2,289 cases (see Figure 3.1).

After the authority to decide on special permission to stay had to be delegated to the directors of the regional immigration bureaus, unconditional

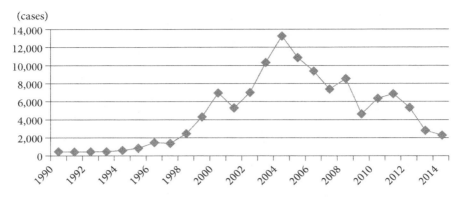

**Figure 3.1** The number of special permissions to stay issued
Source: Prepared by the author based on the 1990–2014 editions of *Shutsunyūkoku kanri tōkei* (Statistics on legal migrants) (Hōmushō Daijin Kanbō [eds.]).

discretion to decide on special permission could not be tolerated. The approximately 3,000 cases of special permission to stay in years with low counts means around 250 cases per month and a little over sixty cases per week (the number of decisions increases if rejected cases are included). At one or two decisions per day, decisions may have been passed entirely according to discretion, but today special permission forms an administrative act that is entirely driven by routine. Precisely because this situation had become permanent, the authority to decide on special permission to stay was delegated to the directors of the regional immigration bureaus. Considering the nature of this action, even if wide-ranging discretion is permitted by law, there is a need for strong controls through general administrative principles such as the principle of administration by law, the principle of equality and the principle of proportionality.

In the case under discussion here, denial of special permission to stay resulted in the execution of C's deportation order. After the abduction and murder of a young girl by a Peruvian citizen of Japanese descent that occurred in November 2005 in Hiroshima, the immigration authority instituted criminal record inquiries when foreign nationals of Japanese descent apply for the issuance of a residence visa and the renewal of residence periods.[11] Although persons with a deportation record are already barred from entry into Japan, C with her deportation order on grounds of a Stimulant Drugs Control Act violation can never return to Japan. For her the execution of the deportation order approaches the implications of a death sentence. Biologically she is alive but her relationships with those around her will be permanently lost and her life in Japan will disappear forever. This can only be termed a 'social death'. *The Immigration Act is a law designed to preserve internal order and public peace. If the execution of a deportation order means for the affected foreign national a 'death' in this country, this state of affairs must call for controls by the principle of proportionality and the principle of equality.* Even the examples of cases of special permission to stay published on the Immigration Bureau's website include an arrest and conviction for the use of stimulant drugs, testifying to the existence of numerous cases where the possibility of 'social death' must be taken into account.

The Guidelines on Special Permission to Stay published by the Ministry of Justice Immigration Control Bureau in October 2006 (the so-called 'old guidelines') stated as an example of (iv) special circumstances requiring humanitarian consideration that the foreign national has 'assimilated in Japan and would find it extremely difficult to live in the country of nationality because her/his connection to it has become tenuous'. The old guidelines questioned not only whether the foreign national could be deported but also whether they were expected to face difficulty living there after deportation. In the so-called new guidelines revised in July 2009, this part was changed to '(v) whether the foreign national's residence in Japan has been long-term and whether the foreign national has assimilated in Japan' as one of the 'other factors for admission to be given consideration'. The new guidelines kept the question of assimilation in Japan and removed the question of difficulty living in the country of nationality after deportation from consideration.

In the case of C, the foreign national at issue has through operating a restaurant created a diversity of social interconnections within Japan and this, it has been acknowledged, has given shape to her assimilation in Japan, which would have been difficult to acknowledge during her time as a foreign laborer. She has used stimulant drugs, but never for the purpose of transferring or selling drugs. It deserves repeating with renewed emphasis that the case examples published by the Ministry of Justice where special permission to stay was granted include several cases of violations of the Stimulant Drugs Control Act involving only personal use.

Chapter 3

Japan adopts the warrant principle under which the issuing of arrest warrants and detention warrants to physically restrain/detain its nationals must be checked and approved by the court at each stage, except when they are caught in the act. Further, the quasi-appeal system is in place to facilitate a prompt release of the arrested/detained persons from physical restraint by granting bail or rescinding the detention order. On the other hand, the issuing of deportation orders in immigration violation cases is enforced by the supervising immigration inspector and does not involve prior approval by the court. If the foreign national cannot be deported immediately, the law allows detention for the indeterminate period of 'until such time as deportation becomes possible'. There is no judicial supervision of long-term detention / physical restraint, and the suspect is not given an opportunity to raise an objection to physical restraint. Even a provisional release from detention is determined by the head of the detention facility or the supervising immigration inspector without judiciary involvement. Thus, due process of law is hardly guaranteed in the Immigration Act. Judicial involvement in terms of human rights protection is minimized in the Immigration Act. Under this statutory construction, public welfare is better served by active utilization of discretionary authority. Furthermore, C's deportation needs to be considered very carefully because it will cause irreparable harm to herself and those around her.

Accordingly, the difficulty of living she would experience after deportation is clearly foreseeable in reference to the old guidelines as well. Granting C special permission to stay would not imply stepping over any lines that have been drawn thus far (as per one case example of a violation of the Stimulant Drugs Control Act for personal use). Moreover, since the use of stimulant drugs, as the immigration authority pointed out, has a strongly addictive element, the person concerned will inevitably re-offend, at which time it would be still early enough for the execution of the deportation order. Considering that successful assimilation in Japan has been acknowledged, causing social death equivalent to a death sentence appears vastly disproportionate to the gravity of the violation. *Administering a disposition equivalent to a death sentence for a first offence eligible for a stay of execution deviates significantly from the principle of equality and the principle of proportionality.* The fact that there are other cases where amid identical circumstance special permission has been granted raises strong misgivings that the denial may have been based on C's identity as a transgender person. Enforcement of deportation orders that may invite such misgivings demands a more scrupulous approach.

## Does Japan ignore the rights of persons who are not subsumed in a family?

In my opinion, the fact that in the case at hand the deportation order against C was executed and special permission to stay denied has its ultimate cause in C's being unable to have a family resident in Japan. Within the scope of independent research I conducted, (i) special permission to stay was granted in the case where a foreign national married to a Japanese citizen had a conviction for violation of the Opium Act; (ii) special permission to stay was granted in the case where a foreign national married to a Japanese citizen had a conviction for the attempted import of tablets containing the narcotic dihydrocodeine; (iii) special permission to stay was granted in the case where a foreign national married to a Japanese citizen had a conviction for the attempted import of narcotics; (iv) special permission to stay was granted in a case where a foreign national of Japanese descent in the third generation married to a foreign national of Japanese descent in the second generation had a conviction for personal use of stimulant drugs; (v) special permission to stay was granted in a case where a foreign national of Japanese descent in the second generation had a conviction for personal use of narcotics; (vi) special permission to stay was granted in a case where a foreign national of Japanese descent in the third generation had a conviction for violation of the Stimulant Drugs Control Act due to personal use of drugs and during the stay of execution period married a foreign national of Japanese descent in the second generation, whereupon special permission to stay was granted; and (vii) special permission to stay was granted in a case where a foreign national of Japanese descent in the third generation had a conviction for a violation of the Narcotics and Psychotropic Drug Control Act and the Cannabis Control Act (these cases were discussed in Chapter Two). There is no explaining why the immigration authority has frequently mentioned that its decision considered the wrongfulness of the violation of the Stimulant

Drugs Control Act committed by C when special permission to stay was granted in multiple cases where the person concerned had a history of arrest for violation of the same act in connection with personal use.

Incidentally, as discussed above, the requirements for cases that the director of the regional immigration bureaus can decide at their discretion have been increasingly widened through a range of notices, i.e., the Spouse Notice, the Long-Term Resident Mother and Child Notice and the Marriage Notice. This can be seen as a move to accommodate changes over time in marriages between Japanese citizens and foreign nationals. Thus the Spouse Notice instructed the affordance of residence when a genuine marriage exists between a Japanese parent and a foreign parent to a child born to them. The Long-Term Resident Mother and Child Notice introduces change to the extent that if such a marriage ends in divorce, the foreign parent who ceases to be the spouse of a Japanese citizen will still be granted residence if the foreign parent is the caregiver to the Japanese child. Subsequently, the Marriage Notice granted residence for foreign spouses irrespective of whether or not children exist provided the marriage is genuine. From this succession of notices, it becomes apparent that the familial relationship with a Japanese citizen is used as an indicator of assimilation, and that this indicator has been progressively loosened from 'marriage and child', to 'caregiver to a Japanese child', then to 'marriage with or without child'. In other words, the immigration authority accommodated the changes by changing the definition of the family and gave significance to being part of the newly defined family.

Reference to family formation with Japanese citizens can also be found in the guidelines and it is clear that this serves as an important indicator of assimilation in Japan. However, at issue in the case at hand is a foreign national who identifies as transgender. For C, a change of gender in Japan is next to impossible due to her nationality. Nor does Japan allow same-sex marriage. Hence, for C, family formation with a Japanese partner in Japan is not possible. To the extent that family formation serves as an indicator of assimilation in Japan, persons belonging to a sexual/gender minority who would be granted residence if they were heterosexual cannot on structural grounds obtain permission of residence.

Certainly, family formation was never an absolute in either of the guidelines, new or old, and was only one factor indicating assimilation into Japan. Even so, compared with the cases published to date in which special permission to stay was granted despite a violation of the Stimulant Drugs Control Act, one can readily conjecture that what C lacks is 'family formation in Japan'. *What the immigration authority demands is civil marriage with a Japanese citizen or a foreign national resident.* Unlike many Western societies, Japan has not introduced a civil partnership system and neither has the municipality in which C resides. This compels the exclusion of homosexual persons.

According to the Committee on the Elimination of Discrimination against Women, even if discrimination against older women is not simply discrimination against women but is due to the stronger effects of composite factors that combine age with other attributes, such discrimination must be corrected as discrimination against women (United Nations Convention on the Elimination of All Forms of Discrimination against Women, 2010). This issue is also cited in the report on 'International Human Rights Laws of Sexual Orientation and Gender Identity' which discusses 'prohibiting discrimination based on sexual orientation and gender identity'. *The United Nations Resolution on Gender Identity and Sexual Identity, which Japan supported, prohibits discrimination against sexual minorities that results from composite factors* (United Nations Human Rights Office of the High Commissioner 2012: 43–44).

The Immigration Act excluded suspended sentences from the list of reasons for deportation by stating in Article 24-4(i) that, 'In addition to persons listed in sub-items (d) to (h), a person who was sentenced on or after November 1, 1951, to imprisonment with or without work for life or for a period exceeding one year will be deported. However, this shall not apply to those who were found guilty with suspension of execution of sentences'. However, suspended sentences were included as a reason for deportation in the 153rd Extraordinary Diet Session at the same time as the delegation of authority for granting special permission to stay to the directors of regional immigration bureaus was added to the act.

## Chapter 3

At the Committee on Judicial Affairs of the 153rd Extraordinary Diet Session where this revision was deliberated, the director of the Ministry of Justice Immigration Bureau, Takumi Nakao, pleaded:

> Back then, the majority of foreign nationals residing in Japan were South or North Korean residents in Japan *who fundamentally were strongly assimilated into Japan in what we call long-term patterns of residence. Since they took the top rank among long-term resident foreign nationals, with this class of foreign nationals in mind, it is my understanding that they are excluded from deportation on grounds of a conviction with a stay of execution.* Consequently, in my understanding the intent is that with regard to this class of foreign nationals, given their strong assimilation, they will not be immediately deported but allowed to rehabilitate themselves in Japan. (The 153rd Meeting minutes of the Committee on Judicial Affairs No. 12 [November 21, 2001]; emphasis added)

Because the Immigration Act was formulated to account for strongly assimilated people in 'long-term patterns of residence' at the time, a stay of execution was not included as a reason for deportation and foreign residents with suspended sentences only were allowed to rehabilitate in Japan.

According to the explanation offered by Nakao, there are two reasons why a stay of execution was added to the reasons for deportation. Firstly, 'Due to the steep rise in newcomers, the number of registered foreign residents climbed to about 1.62 million. Out of these, over one million were newcomers, changing the percentages from earlier periods'. Secondly, 'Crime committed by foreign nationals increased strongly. If stay of execution is granted for robbery and burglary, perpetrators belonging to criminal organizations who are granted a stay of execution and permission to stay for the remainder of the residence period would return to their organizations and commit new crimes. This kind of interconnection strengthened'. According to this explanation, convictions with stays of execution were added as a reason for deportation primarily targeting organized crime committed by newly arriving foreign nationals. However, according to the explanation, the Immigration Control and Refugee Recognition Act was from the start devised to leave room for accommodating people with a strong preparedness to assimilate and has been operated in that manner.

The Immigration Act requires 'assimilation into Japanese society', which must be substantiated. The Immigration Act does not preclude alternative indicators in cases where familial inclusion is impracticable. A situation where a business has been established and continues operating should be acknowledged as a reasonably sufficient indicator of 'substantiated assimilation in Japan'. This assumption is based on the fact that running a business requires winning the trust of a diversity of persons and organizations, such as by renting business premises, conducting trading activities necessary for day-to-day operations and transactions with financial institutions, contracting between employer and employees, and forming relationships with customers. The status of an ongoing business can be used as an indicator of the trust that Japan's society places in C on a more objective basis, in a sense, than the trust invested by people only in the narrow relationship of a family.

The immigration authority asserts that since decision-makers have discretion, their decisions are neither wrongful nor do individual decision standards exists. If this is the case, the standard of assimilation into Japanese society must be used from various angles. If decisions generally emphasize only family relationships, individual decisions will be reduced to a mere shell. Even if special permission to stay is subject to individual decisions with wide-ranging discretion, their supposed purpose is to judge whether assimilation is in substance present. As C's assimilation into Japan was considered from a one-dimensional and irrelevant viewpoint, both the administrative agency and the court deserve criticism for making decisions without considering what they were supposed to consider. Enforcement of the deportation order in particular is open to serious question. For C as a transgender person, her assimilation in Japan must be judged in a manner more adapted to reality and the deportation disposition must not generate concern that her sexual/gender minority status has somehow been implicated in the decision.

## Conclusion

The starting point for the enactment of the Constitution of Japan after the end of WWII was the emphasis on respect for the individual and gender equality. The concept of gender equality derived its meaning from its denial in the Japanese family system (*ie*) until the prewar years. Nowadays, since Japan has adopted the United Nations resolution on sexual orientation and gender identity (A/HRC/17/L.9/Rev.1), there can be no doubt that the gender equality anchored in the Constitution has transformed into 'equality of all genders'. If this is the case, it is unacceptable that persons who would be eligible to stay if they were heterosexual are denied eligibility when they are not. It is unacceptable that persons with a past conviction for personal use of stimulant drugs are permitted to stay only if they are part of a civil law family. The logic of judging their assimilation on a case-by-case basis requires updating, such as introducing indicators other than family inclusion.

Japan's modernization since the Meiji period resulted in the proactive adoption of Western European systems of law and value preferences. The article 'The Civil Code is created, but it destroys the loyalty and filial piety of the Japanese' was discussed by the legal scholar Hozumi Yatsuka, and the Civil Code controversy arose. The old Civil Code passed through the Imperial Diet but was not promulgated. On the other hand, Westernization and the retention of indigenous values sometimes violently clashed, but both have always coexisted in Japanese society. With the fundamental reforms accomplished with the transition from the Meiji Constitution to the Japanese Constitution after the end of WWII, in a groundbreaking change the value emphasis that centered on the family was supplanted by a value preference for respecting the individual. However, considering that a marriage to a Japanese or permanent resident has been used as a determining factor in deciding whether to give protection to a foreign national, the Japanese family value seems to live on in a different form and continue to affect the individual as we have seen in this chapter.

The assertions of the immigration authority and the rulings of the courts take the stance that rulings occur only within the scope of Japanese law and are barely affected by international laws unless special treaties exist. However, there can be no doubt that the legal terms 'nation' (*kokumin*) and 'citizen' (*shimin*), not to mention 'human rights' (*jinken*) and also the concept of 'family' (*ie*), have been formed during the Meiji period through Japan's chance encounter with Western Europe. Incidentally, the social security of resident foreign nationals and their children's right to education has come to be acknowledged through the relaxation of national regulations by ratification of the Convention Relating to the Status of Refugees and the Convention on the Rights of the Child. Likewise, the fact that the social rights of foreign nationals in Japan are effectively safeguarded is a variation of the encounter with Western Europe. Even then, the state continues to assert that these rules/measures are merely applied 'mutatis mutandis' and foreigners have no right to demand to receive health insurance, the national pension or compulsory education. Nevertheless, leaving aside the question of rights, the first question is whether they can actually receive these benefits.

In a ruling dated June 4, 2008, concerning Article 3 of the Nationality Act, the Grand Bench of the Supreme Court found the matter unconstitutional, holding:

> When only one parent is a Japanese citizen, with regard to the circumstances of familial life, such as whether cohabitation is present or not, an assessment of the status of civil marriage and the parent-child relationships in its foreground *are more complex and multi-faceted than when both parents are Japanese citizens*, and the degree of strength of the relation that the child has to Japan cannot be immediately determined based on whether or not a civic marriage exists between the parents. (*Saikō saibansho minji hanreishū*, vol. 62, no. 6: 1374; emphasis added)

Exactly the same could be said in relation to sexual minorities. Unlike in situations where no problem arises when both sides of a couple are Japanese citizens, the relation with Japan becomes complex and multi-faceted the moment one side is a foreign national.

This Supreme Court ruling references international law ratified by Japan, noting 'The International Covenant on Civil and Political Rights and the Convention on the Rights of the Child are ratified by Japan', and continuing as follows: 'seen in the light of the changes in the domestic, international and societal environments of Japan, it is difficult to discover a reasonable connection between the purpose of the legislation mentioned above, which requires legitimation by submission of an acknowledgement of paternity after birth as a necessary requirement for obtaining Japanese nationality' (*Saikō saibansho minji hanreishū*, vol. 62, no. 6: 1374). In this way, in June

2008 the Supreme Court ruled that what was still constitutional at the time of the revision of the Nationality Act in 1984 is now unconstitutional. It is obvious that the domestic, international and social environments have changed even more since the Supreme Court handed down the McLean ruling in October 1978. Do the immigration authority and the court believe that only the environment surrounding decision-making on special permission to stay and deportation has escaped these changes?

Yasuhiro Okuda offers the following exposition in an opinion that he wrote to the Supreme Court in the above case where the Nationality Act was found unconstitutional.

> Concerning the ruling of unconstitutionality of the stipulations for severe punishment of parricide, while there are no grounds for a right to demand a light punishment, compared with the stipulations for ordinary homicide the punishment appears nonetheless excessively heavy. For the case that, based on an unreasonable discrimination, the difference is due to the notion of empathy for the victim, the requirement operates that this should be treated in the same way as a common homicide. Likewise, currently there exists a stipulation that allows a legitimate child by notice to obtain Japanese citizenship. If compared with this, only because the father may not be married, the way to citizenship is blocked and as a result the right of residence under the citizenship of the father is denied, the requirement operates that the treatment shall be the same as that for a legitimate child. (Okuda 2010: 21)

The issue of C is entirely the same, inasmuch as the path to residence in Japan is closed in circumstances that would allow for residence if civil marriage were possible. Moreover, the special gender characteristic of C, who belongs to a sexual/gender minority, introduces a difference based on an attribute beyond her control.

Since the McLean case, Japan has ratified and endorsed a variety of international treaties and United Nations resolutions. It stands to reason that the conduct must be consistent with those resolutions. It is not sufficient if the Immigration Act is operated only in accordance with precedent. In order to achieve consistency with domestic administrative precedent and international treaties, even if residence is granted only as a favor, in case new constituencies, such as sexual/gender minorities, arise within the scope of administration, the assessment on 'substantiated assimilation in Japan' must be different from what is has been to date. Moreover, the deportation of foreign nationals belonging to a sexual/gender minority must be positioned in the overall legal order of Japan. When on grounds of a minor offence 'social death' is imposed on persons with special attributes by permanently denying residence in Japan, it is without doubt discrimination against them (or their exclusion).

## Notes

1   This paper is a revised opinion paper I submitted to the Supreme Court.
2   The immigration authority perceived that the plaintiff's sexual/gender minority status is a makeshift argument she started using mid-course. However, the immigration authority initiated the actual investigation based on suspected violations and its special inquiry officer conducted a hearing in the form of questions and answers to verify the inquiry findings. This process is very different from court proceedings that allow the foreign national to prepare and present her arguments in a structured manner. Further, the records of the violation investigation and examination are not disclosed to the suspect prior to an oral hearing. The suspect is given only a short time to read when she finally gets to see them at the start of the oral hearing. Accordingly, it is unreasonable to imply or assume that the suspect has been given enough opportunities and time to lay out her case thoroughly.
3   The immigration authority makes this assertion in Brief No. 1 dated October 14, 2014. However, this assertion was rebutted by the plaintiff in Brief No. 4, noting that NIATRE was dissolved on December 25, 2014. Given the fact that the decision to dissolve NIATRE occurred early, it is difficult to see why an organization scheduled to be dissolved was mentioned in support of the possibility of the repatriation of C. By the time I conducted research in Brazil in August 2015, NIATRE was already defunct and the first basement floor of Sao Paulo Bunkyo Building previously occupied by the organization was being refurbished, leaving no traces of its former existence (other occupants of the building include the History Museum of Japanese Immigration in Brazil and the Centro de Informacao e Apoio ao Trabalhador no Exterior [CIATE: the Ministry of Health, Labor and Welfare's local agency]).

4   United Nations Human Rights Office of the High Commissioner (2012: 14).
5   United Nations Human Rights Office of the High Commissioner (2012: 22).
6   United Nations Human Rights Office of the High Commissioner (2012: 29).
7   United Nations Human Rights Office of the High Commissioner (2012: 39).
8   United Nations Human Rights Office of the High Commissioner (2012: 55).
9   The Immigration Act, Article 9(1) prescribes 'If a foreigner meets a condition for a landing permit (Immigration Act, Article 7(1)) a landing permit must be issued'.
10  However, also with regard to the refugee status determination over which the Minister of Justice has discretion, the question as to what extent proof is required has been thrown back at the administrative authority as follows: 'The extent of proof required is unclear. With regard to the denial of refugee status in the case at hand, the plaintiff was interviewed and on the basis thereof proof was submitted. If in spite of this a disposition is made to the effect of denial of refugee status because of missing concrete proof, the grounds for the administrative disposition are entirely lacking in the absence of an indication of the reasons for the finding that evidence is insufficient based on the proof provided, the assessment of proof and the extent of proof required. With the reasons given in this case, the decision process is entirely unclear and careful judgement is not possible. Even an appropriate response such as a filing of opposition is rendered impracticable because no object of opposition has been stated' (*Hanrei taimuzu*, No. 1210, 107–108). This means that the existing objection procedures are inadequate for meeting the intent of the objection system.
11  Issued as 'Ministerial Notification No. 172 of the Ministry of Justice'. The requirement of 'good conduct' was added in order for someone to qualify as a long-term resident.

# The Sociology of LGBT Foreign Nationals and Post-Deportation Concerns

## Introduction

In this chapter, I attempt to demonstrate that the issues confronting C, as discussed in Chapter 3, are applicable to foreign nationals subjected to deportation in general and not limited to the special circumstance of her being transgender. Specifically, I will address the following three points: (1) C would be subjected to severe discrimination and prejudice in Brazil; (2) Brazil's social environment could pose a threat to her physical safety; and (3) the deportation order against C shows a significant lack of the balance between crime and punishment and is strongly suspected of contravening articles 31 and 39 of the Constitution of Japan.

C's argument is about whether there is a reasonable level of equality between her and those who were granted special permission to stay after being convicted under the Stimulant Drugs Control Act for personal use. The pathway to maintain residency in Japan on the grounds of family bonds that has been used in precedents is closed to C as a transgender person.

The defense brief and the rulings of the district court and the high court describe the plaintiff's argument on risks she would be exposed to upon returning to her home country as 'general and abstract criticisms'. However, is it adequate to assert that C would not face any problems in Brazil solely on the grounds that same-sex marriage has been legalized there and prisons have separate areas for LGBT prisoners without assessing actual conditions in Latin American societies? When we look at how things are in Latin American societies, it is the view of the immigration authority and the courts that seems too 'general and abstract' about risks to C's physical safety as their opinion is simply based on the existence of proper systems.

Moreover, the issues addressed in chapters 1 and 2 are entirely applicable to a stay of execution of a deportation order against C, and in particular, the relevance of the issue of proportionality here is not surprising at all. I will argue this point in conjunction with a number of constitutional questions that arise when deporting LGBT people by simply acting on precedents.

## The gap between the legal system and society in Brazil

According to the immigration authority's brief in the LGBT case: (1) Brazil's Supreme Federal Court ruled in 2011 that the civil law provision limiting marriage to heterosexual unions was unconstitutional, prompting its states to accept marriage registration by same-sex couples; (2) while there were some states that did not accept same-sex marriage registration, the National Justice Council decided in 2013 that marriage registration by same-sex couples should not be rejected; and (3) some prisons provide a separate building for homosexual inmates. Therefore, 'Homosexual people in Brazil are no more unjustly discriminated or adversely treated in their marriage system than in Japan, and in a similar vein, it is understood that reasonable consideration is made to them in prisons as well'. The immigration authority asserts that homophobia and transphobia in Brazil are not worth considering.

In reality, however, there is a significant gap between the legal system and the actual social landscape in Brazil and other Latin American countries. Laws of the Latin American countries in general have been known for their spirit of equality and orientation toward actively safeguarding the disadvantaged. It has been a legally progressive part of the world where decisions have been made in some jurisdictions to usher in women's freedom to choose their own nationality, such as the resolution made at the 1922 Buenos Aires Conference of the International Law Association to accept the principle of married women's freedom to choose their nationality as much as possible and the passing of the 1933 Convention on the Nationality of Married Women in Montevideo (Ninomiya 1983: 15–16).

It was only recently that Japan reviewed a legal provision discriminating against extra-marital children after the court ruled it unconstitutional. On the other hand, Colombia developed a progressive legal system rejecting discrimination against extra-marital children much earlier than Japan. Article 1 of Colombia's Law 45 of 1936 (Ley 45 em 1936: a series of laws on extra-marital children in Colombia's Civil Code) defines the extra-marital child as a child who was born of parents not married to one another at the time of conception and recognized or declared as such according to the rule of law. The fact of being born of a single woman or a widow is sufficient for a child to acquire this status. Article 18 provides that legitimate children, adopted children and extra-marital children shall receive inheritance in equal shares to the exclusion of all other heirs. However, they shall not prejudice the spouse's share.[1]

Brazil's labor laws, which are said to have been modeled on Mussolini-era Italy, are known for powerful protection of workers' rights. Regular employees are given strong rights and benefits. For example, employers are obliged to cover half the cost of their regular employees' lunch and to pay a year-end bonus equivalent to one month's salary (often called the 13th-month salary [*13º salário*]) in addition to forty days of paid annual leave, regardless of the size of the company. Workers continuously employed for over two years must be made regular employees. For this reason, employers prefer to keep employees' period of employment to less than two years in order to avoid their obligation to place them on the regular payroll.

Brazil is a signatory to the International Covenant on Economic, Social and Cultural Rights and provides free education according to Article 13 of the covenant. Admission and tuition fees are free at all federal and state universities and student dormitories are also free (not only for Brazilian students but also for Japanese and other overseas students). This is designed to provide people of all social classes with opportunities to receive higher education. Although there are private universities in Brazil, a succession of Brazilian presidents have been alumni of free public universities. The University of São Paulo has produced the largest number of presidents, followed by the Federal University of Rio de Janeiro and the State University of Campinas. In reality, however, it is almost impossible to gain entry to these elite universities from free public high schools. Tuition fees at private high schools are very high, ranging from 2,000 to 3,000 reais per month (approximately 80,000–120,000 yen at the June 2015 exchange rate), often costing over one million yen per year at the high schools leading to admissions to the University of São Paulo. While Brazil's social system offers everyone access to higher education, it is only accessible to wealthy people in reality.

This situation is not viewed favorably, and federal universities are supposed to allocate places to black (*preto*) people. However, around 75 percent of the total population reportedly fall in this category based on self-declaration in national censuses. Brazilian society has undergone a high level of racial mixing and the category accounts for various degrees of blackness. For this reason, state universities such as the University of São Paulo are trying to secure higher education opportunities for low-income people by allocating places to public high school graduates rather than based on race.

In his many writings, Florestan Fernandes, Brazil's leading sociologist in the post-WWII era, described conflict between 'white' (*branco*) and 'black' as Brazilian society's trait and argued that there was an uncrossable boundary between them despite the national policy of democracy without racial barriers and the fact that this boundary was redrawn as society seemingly moved closer to a non-racial democracy in the process of the increasing social mobility of non-white people (Fernandes 1968). The division has become more intense and violent in today's society. While Rio de Janeiro's shantytowns are world-famous, there are over 800 slums (favelas) in the City of São Paulo alone. Residents of these favelas relocate when they are evicted by government agencies or land-owners. It is widely known that many gated communities surrounded by high walls have appeared in and around the city in order to keep favelas from creeping into their neighborhoods (Caldeira 2001). The extreme geographical and hierarchical division in the face of potential exposure to physical violence stemming from wealth inequality is the real social situation in an increasingly affluent Brazil.

As above, the existence of a progressive social system has not necessarily led to the development of a society in alignment with the objectives of the system in Brazil and other Latin American countries. In fact, a legal system always embodies an ideal society while in reality, society lags behind. The large-scale demolition of favelas by the Brazilian government in preparation for the hosting of the 2014 Soccer World Cup and the 2016 Rio de Janeiro Olympics drove Comando Vermelho and other drug syndicates from their bases in favelas to other areas. As this phenomenon has increasingly sparked the transformation of wealthy neighborhoods into gated communities, society as a whole has been transfigured into one with vastly different crime rates, and, most of all, perceived security between communities. For this reason, it is impossible to gain an accurate understanding of the risks involved in living in Brazil based on national-level statistics.

## Social background to the formation of militias

The history of Latin America as a recorded history is usually limited to the past 500 to 600 years. As evident in Machu Picchu and Nazca in Peru and scattered archaeological sites in Bolivia and Peru's Lake Titicaca, ancient writing systems used by many of its indigenous peoples are currently undecipherable or being studied and have little connection to the history of people living in the present world. In this sense, Latin American history is the history of conquistadors.

The Portuguese word *bandeirantes* is translated as explorers or settlers in the history of the conquest of Latin America. It also means roving raiders. These explorers wielding guns and axes ventured deep into 'undiscovered jungles' for exploitation in Brazil, Peru, Argentina, Bolivia, Venezuela and other lands. However, the jungles were undiscovered only from the conquerors' perspective and their guns were more often pointed at indigenous inhabitants (*indigenas*) than large animals such as jaguars and anacondas.

The conquest aspect of Latin American history is not confined to the period prior to the nation-building phase in the eighteenth century. Similar stories have been told by some of the postwar immigrants from twentieth-century Japan. My interview surveys of Japanese immigrants in Paraguay found multiple incidents of attack on Japanese immigrants by the indigenous Guarani people in settlements provided by Japan Emigration Services (one of the predecessors of the Japan International Cooperation Agency) near the city of Encarnacion (where some settlers shot dead some Guarani attackers in self-defense). Although the settlements were established through formal purchases of land titles recognized by the host government from the immigrants' viewpoint, the indigenous Guarani people saw the settlers as invaders exploiting their forest without their permission.[2]

## Chapter 4

Latin American societies were built on a history similar to that of the Wild West. Brazil is no exception and its regions have retained their uniquely local social structures controlled by local political bosses despite the presence of a powerful federal government. Although power was transferred from the military regime to the democratic government in 1985, the old political structures controlled by bosses did not change. For this reason, some people view democratization after the transition as 'democracy without equity' and note that change in the distribution of wealth has always been made by government intervention, which has been dictated by political connections that have characterized inequality within Brazil in the past (Montero 2006: chapter 5). This view cannot be ignored in light of the recent ousting of the leftist government of the Partido dos Trabalhadores (Workers Party) due to corruption scandals.

In this historical and social context, each locality has local political connections with its state and federal representatives and these connections extend into public officials in the police and the municipal offices and create local vigilante group-like organizations. They are called militias or paramilitary groups as they are armed with guns.[3] Militias are closely involved in local politics and have a powerful influence on people's everyday lives. In Brazil, it is public knowledge that many members of these militias are public service employees.[4] The international human rights organization Amnesty International is concerned that militias in Brazil pose a serious threat to the human rights of the general public and reports that the involvement of public security and law enforcement officers, including off-duty soldiers, police officers, prison officers and firefighters, in their activities is highly noticeable.[5]

As mentioned earlier, the Japanese immigration authority claimed in its brief for the appeal court proceedings that homophobia and transphobia in Brazil are not worth considering for the following three reasons: (1) Brazil's Supreme Federal Court ruled in 2011 that the civil law provision limiting marriage to heterosexual unions was unconstitutional, prompting its states to accept marriage registration by same-sex couples; (2) while some states did not accept same-sex marriage registration, the National Justice Council decided in 2013 that marriage registration by same-sex couples should not be rejected; and (3) some prisons provide a separate building for homosexual inmates. Therefore, 'Homosexual people in Brazil are no more unjustly discriminated or adversely treated in their marriage system than in Japan, and in a similar vein, it is understood that reasonable consideration is made to them in prisons as well'. This argument completely overlooks the reality in which prison officers often support the oppression of human rights in spite of the country's progressive legal system.

Japan's administrative agencies and courts assume that various types of discrimination will gradually disappear as the legal and social systems develop. However, the realities of Latin American societies necessitate some reservations about that assumption. The question of C's safety after her deportation needs to be assessed in light of a more realistic understanding of Brazil's social conditions because that country's social progress is lagging behind its institutional development in some aspects.

## Deep-rooted homophobia and transphobia

São Paulo hosts Latin America's largest gay pride parade in June each year. The parade has become a major tourist event attracting three million participants and spectators in recent years.

As a largely Catholic society, Brazilian society has deeply patriarchal roots. However, the recent economic growth has ignited changes in various aspects of society and those who have been marginalized by this process (or those who want more rapid changes) have joined evangelical Protestant organizations in phenomenal numbers. They have introduced a new style of worship by holding mass televised services in huge gymnasium-like churches (similar to the style of US televangelists). These new churches urge new followers to donate large sums from their worldly possessions, causing social problems. Moreover, the evangelicals are also gaining political power.

When the gay pride parade was held in São Paulo on the first weekend of June 2015, a transgender actress appeared dressed as Jesus. In response, the leader of the Partido da Social Democracia Brasileira who was lobbied by evangelicals proposed a bill to impose harsher penalties on acts insulting or hindering religion in the Federal Chamber of Deputies on the following day (June 8, 2015). According to *The São Paulo Shimbun*, the activity of evangelical deputies supporting the proposal created an uproar in the plenary session. The actress reportedly received numerous threats and abuse (*The São Paulo Shimbun*, June 12, 2015: 2).[6]

Since Japanese-Brazilians began to travel to Japan for work, returnees have often been subjected to robbery at airports, while traveling home and as they go about their daily life.[7] It is essential for the returnees to have the support of their family and relatives when they go home. However, it would be very difficult for C to secure the necessary support from her family network in the remote countryside now that she looks physically different. If she has to live in isolation from her family in Brazil, it is highly likely that she will be alone in a society prejudiced against LGBTs. As she is not expected to find a high-income job (and therefore not able to live in a gated community), her risk of being exposed to physical harm is also very high.

## The severity of the deportation disposition against C

As presented in chapters 1 and 2, there have been many cases in which special permission to stay was issued to a foreign national who had received a suspended prison sentence for violating the Stimulant Drugs Control Act similar to that of C. Let us consider the severity of the deportation disposition against C in comparison with cases in which special permission to stay was issued to a person convicted of crimes other than drug use.

1. A foreign national was granted special permission to stay after being sentenced to two years and eight months of imprisonment suspended for three years for violating the Immigration Act and theft on the grounds that the person was the custodial parent of a child acknowledged by a Japanese national and that the person was remorseful for committing the crime (2005).

2. A foreign national was granted special permission to stay after being released from jail at the end of a twenty-two-month sentence for fraud. Despite two further convictions, the person was granted special permission to stay on the grounds, among others, that the person grew up in Japan to age sixty-four, had brothers and a child residing in Japan, and had no relatives to depend on in the home country (2005).

Both cases have been published on the web page of the Ministry of Justice. The following cases were found through my own independent research.

3   A Colombian national, who entered Japan on a 'short-term' visa in 1997 and overstayed, was sentenced by the Yokohama District Court to three years of imprisonment suspended for five years for theft (shoplifting) and violating the Immigration Act. The person was immediately taken into custody in the Yokohama branch of the Tokyo Regional Immigration Bureau and deportation procedures were commenced. However, special permission to stay was issued in December 2006 on the grounds that the person was the custodial parent of a Japanese child, which was followed by the granting of 'long-term' residence status for one year.

4   A Peruvian national, who entered Japan on a 'short-term' visa in 1992 and overstayed without extending their visa or changing status, was arrested for suspicion of indecent assault in December 2000. The person was subsequently charged with a violation of the Immigration Act alone and sentenced by the Tokyo District Court to two years and six months of imprisonment suspended for four years on March 23, 2001. The person was detained by the Tokyo Regional Immigration Bureau as part of deportation procedures but special permission to stay was issued in October 2002 on the grounds of the person's marriage to another Peruvian national after the arrest followed by the granting of 'long-term' residence status for one year.

5   A Chinese national married a Japanese businessperson in China and came to live in Japan in 2002 on a 'spouse of a Japanese' visa in 2002. The person was convicted for violating the Anti-Prostitution Act and sentenced by the Yokohama District Court in July 2003 to eighteen months in prison suspended for four years and given a fine of 300,000 yen. The person was immediately detained at the Yokohama branch of the Tokyo Regional Immigration Bureau as part of deportation procedures. In August 2003, however, special

permission to stay was issued and 'spouse of a Japanese' residence status for one year was granted.

6   A Chinese national, who was married to a Japanese national and living in Japan on a 'spouse of a Japanese' visa, was convicted for violating the Anti-Prostitution Act and sentenced in May 2003 by the Tokyo District Court to one-year imprisonment suspended for three years and a fine of 200,000 yen. The person was immediately detained as part of deportation procedures by the Tokyo Regional Immigration Bureau but received special permission to stay and 'spouse of a Japanese' residence status for one year in July 2003.

These two Chinese nationals were involved in the operation of brothels.

7   A Peruvian national of second-generation Japanese descent entered Japan on a 'short-term' residence visa in 1992 and became an overstayer when an application for change of residence status was rejected even though the person was a second-generation Japanese. In December 2005, the Yokohama District Court sentenced the person to two years of imprisonment suspended for three years for violating the Immigration Act and inflicting bodily injury. After the person's deportation procedures were commenced on the grounds of overstaying, special permission to stay was issued in February 2006 followed by the granting of 'spouse of a Japanese' residence status for one year.

8   A Brazilian national of third-generation Japanese descent, who arrived in 1991 with 'long-term' residence status, was sentenced to two years of imprisonment suspended for three years for inflicting bodily injury and causing bodily injury resulting in death in November 1999. The person received an unsuspended sentence of eight months of imprisonment for attempted extortion in November 2002. The person's application for an extension of residence period was rejected and a deportation order was issued but the person was

subsequently granted special permission to stay on the grounds of marriage to a third-generation Japanese descendant.

Special permission to stay was issued even though cases 1 and 3 involved convictions for theft, case 2 for fraud, case 4 for indecent assault, cases 5 and 6 for violations of the Anti-Prostitution Act (operating brothels) and cases 7 and 8 for inflicting bodily injury. Unlike the potential threat to society allegedly posed by C's stimulant use, these cases clearly caused harm to specific individuals or, in the case of prostitution, public morals and health. Special permission to stay was issued to even these people.

In all of the above cases, 'family' formation in Japan was the key consideration in granting permission to stay. Perhaps C has to be excluded from such consideration because she lives alone and cannot position herself in relation to those who are recognized as family members under Japanese law. However, it is obvious from a comparison between her crime and the crimes committed by others that her punishment is grossly disproportionate to her crime especially given that the authority is unwilling to consider any mitigating circumstances.

## Conclusion

This chapter focused on the issues that confronted C by consolidating the problematic viewpoints in the previously discussed cases. I have presented C's case in this way in order to look at her issues from an etic perspective. In particular, I would like to emphasize that my points of argument in both the 'fake Nikkei' case and the 'foreign juvenile delinquency' case are very much relevant to her case. However, the very concerning questions in the two cases were circumvented when special permission to stay was issued.

On the other hand, these questions are unavoidable in C's case. Although the Immigration Bureau claims to conduct an emic case-by-case assessment, it does not seem to find meaning in the facts of individual cases at the emic level. I cannot help but think that the immigration authority used an etic approach in denying C a special permission to stay in the sense that the agency's preoccupation with 'family' led to its decision that it was not necessary to grant her special permission to stay.

Moreover, while the Ministry of Justice states that it uses an emic approach in considering the issuance of special permission to stay, it appears that only the cases in which it was issued were assessed from an emic perspective, whereas those in which it was denied were not assessed in this way. The statement that the ministry conducts case-by-case assessment does not necessarily mean that it does so for all cases. Looking at the facts, I suspect that the Immigration Bureau actually conducts etic assessment of a majority of cases and only takes an emic case-by-case approach to some cases in making decisions on special permission to stay.

## Notes

1. This part is from the revision made by Law 29 of 1982 (Ley 29 em 1982).
2. Based on the author's surveys in the city of Posadas, Misiones Province, Argentina in August 2006 and in the city of Encarnacion, Itapua Department, Paraguay in August 2009.
3. It is widely known that the militia issue has bearings on the fundamental character of society in Brazil. The crime film *Tropa de Elite* portraying a paramilitary troop in Rio de Janeiro won the Golden Bear at the 2008 Berlin Film Festival. The story was later turned into a TV series. Based on a true story, the film featuring the relationship between the paramilitary force, drugs and local politics in Rio de Janeiro reached a broad audience in and outside Brazil.
4. See a typical report in *The Nikkey Shimbun* at http://www.nikkeyshimbun.jp/2014/140809-22brasil.html (in Japanese).
5. Amnesty International is one of the few organizations reporting on Brazil's militia problem. See http://www.amnesty.or.jp/news/2009/0311_998.html (in Japanese).
6. The following article reports on the social issue of rising violence against LGBT people while the gay pride parade's popularity grows, under the heading of 'Brazil Is A Gay Traveler's Paradise, But Violence Against LGBTs is on The Rise' (http://www.queerty.com/brazil-is-a-gay-travelers-paradise-but-violence-against-lgbts-is-on-the-rise-20120409).
7. One such incident was reported in *The Nikkey Shimbun* (http://www.nikkeyshimbun.jp/2009/090723-73colonia.html).

# The Sociology of the Hate-Speech Rally Ban: The Case of Kawasaki

## Introduction

On July 17, 2016, *The Kanagawa Shimbun* published a Kyodo News story online about a hate rally in Osaka.

> A street rally calling for the exclusion of Zainichi Koreans and severing diplomatic relations with South Korea was held near the Consulate General of South Korea in Chūō ward, Osaka city, on July 17. The rally was publicized on the internet by a person who is believed to be connected to Zainichi Tokken wo Yurusanai Shimin no Kai [the Association of Citizens against the Special Privileges of the Zainichi; "Zaitokukai" for short] and elicited accusations of "hate speech" from Zainichi Koreans. About ten protesters carrying loudspeakers and old Japanese military flags gathered at 3pm and chanted slogans such as "Koreans go home". Counter-protesters also began to gather, calling "Stop racial discrimination". The two sides continued to shout at one another for about an hour and a half with dozens of police officers standing guard in the middle on a five-meter-wide sidewalk across from the consulate building.

On June 5, just over a month prior to the above incident, a hate rally was blocked after marching for only ten meters and was forced to break up near Nakaharaheiwa Park not far from Musashikosugi train station in Nakahara ward, Kawasaki city. The news was widely reported by national TV networks that day and in morning newspapers the following morning. As the Act on the Promotion of Efforts to Eliminate Unfair Discriminatory Speech

Chapter 5

**Photo 5.1** A hate rally in front of Nakaharaheiwa Park on June 5, 2016
Source: Photo by Kazuki Tanno.

and Behavior against Persons with Countries of Origin other than Japan (hereafter referred to as the 'Anti-Hate Speech Act') came into force on June 3, the incident was described as the first example of an effort to regulate hate speech. Some commentators even called it the 'Kawasaki model'.

However, a close examination of this case has revealed various issues that go beyond a mere idealistic theory in considering foreigners' rights. This chapter discusses these issues with 'foreigners' dignity' as the key.

## Hate speech and the Sakuramoto community

After exiting JR Kawasaki train station and walking eastward for three kilometers along Prefectural Highway No. 101, you reach the Yotsukado intersection. Turn left here, and you will find yourself in the neighborhood of Sakuramoto, Kawasaki's Korean town. It is an ordinary-looking residential district with no tall buildings and has a shopping street running through its center. There is no suburban shopping mall as train stations are not close enough and there is no land for large car parks. For this reason, the shopping street functions well with good foot and bicycle traffic through it. It is clear from the presence of many barbecue restaurants and several Korean grocery stores that this is the Korean town, but it feels very different from Ōkubo in Tokyo or Tsuruhashi in Osaka. This town is compact and there is nothing spectacular about it.

On September 5, 2015, an anti-war march in Sakuramoto drew a large number of participants, including *halmeonis* ('grandmothers' in Korean).[1] Sakuramoto people's reaction to ethnic hatred began to change around this time. The most symbolic statement was made by Tomohito Miura, chairperson of Seikyū-sha and former director of Kawasaki municipal Fureaikan hall: 'I am going to stop shielding children and *halmeonis* from hatred. I have been holding back from telling children about some ugly things because I don't want them to go out into the world with a negative bias. I have been keeping from *halmeonis* anything that brings back painful memories. From now on, I am willing to communicate to them that "These things still exist in society"'.

This resulted in the *halmeonis* organizing their own peace march in Sakuramoto rather than letting haters march in Sakuramoto unchecked. Hate speech and Japan's tilt to the right are linked and the presence of Zainichi Koreans itself is intertwined with prewar Japan's expansionist stance. Partly spurred by the security legislation revision issue that became a hot topic in national politics at the time, Sakuramoto people organized an anti-war march on September 5, 2015. For a majority of older demonstrators, including those in their eighties and nineties, this march was the first social movement in which they had ever participated (Zainichi Kōreisha Kōryū kurabu Torajinokai 2015; Kawasaki no Zainichi Kōreisha to musubu 2000-people Network [eds.] 2017).

It was found that a group of Korean-haters had applied to hold a counter-rally on November 8, 2015, marching from Fujimi Park along a bus route (Prefectural Highway No. 101) to Sakuramoto and heading for Kawasaki Daishi Temple. It was a rainy day, and the rally drew only eleven demonstrators chanting hateful slogans. The sight of eleven people marching while being surrounded by a 100-strong anti-riot police squad was rather peculiar. The march proceeded on the perimeter of Sakuramoto to Daishimachi (and broke up in front of Kawasaki Daishi train station).

Sakuramoto residents gathered and lined both sides of the road in order to prevent the demonstrators from entering their town.

It was not the first time that a hate rally had come to Kawasaki (the first one was held on May 12, 2013). However, previous rallies were staged in locations outside of the Zainichi neighborhood such as in front of Kawasaki station. From this time onward, though, rally organizers began to target the local community where people had been living in peace and quiet. Sakuramoto was the target of the November 8, 2015, rally and one held on January 31 in the following year. Both rallies planned to march from Fujimi Park near Kawasaki station to Sakuramoto. The latter rally was one of the largest in Kawasaki, drawing over fifty demonstrators (seventy according to the police), more than five times the November rally. However, the waiting 700 counter-protesters easily outnumbered the demonstrators by ten to one. As usual, the hate group continued to march, guarded by the riot police, and reached the Yotsukado intersection just before Sakuramoto. Seniors and young people staged a sit-in protest near the intersection to stop the demonstrators and police vehicles. The police intervened at this point and the demonstrators gave up on their plan to enter Sakuramoto and returned to Kawasaki station. In the end, they marched to Keikyū Kawasaki station and disbanded.

On January 23, 2016, the Kawasaki Network of Citizens Against Hate Speech was formed by citizens and NPOs operating in Kawasaki city and Kanagawa prefecture as well as city councilors in order to make a concerted city-wide effort to combat hate speech.[2] Against this backdrop, it looked as if the citizens' movement and the local community acted in unison in mounting the counter-protest against the hate rally on January 31 and 'stopped the hate group's march though Sakuramoto'. In truth, the demonstrators could not enter Sakuramoto because the police made them deviate from the approved course for public safety reasons even though they were still expecting to march through Sakuramoto.

## The filing of complaints

With the ingress of hate speech into Sakuramoto, three local residents filed individual complaints for human rights violations with the Yokohama

District Legal Affairs Bureau. The complainants included D, who was a first-generation Zainichi Korean, E, a third-generation Zainichi Korean and F, who was married to E. They submitted their complaints, together with a large amount of supporting evidence, that their right to live in peace and quiet in their place of residence was significantly violated by (1) the staging of twelve hate speech rallies since May 2013; (2) the fact that the twelfth rally had headed for Sakuramoto, which is their home base; and (3) the incitement of racial and ethnic discrimination over a loudspeaker at the meeting of demonstrators in the Fujimi Park gathering point. Each person's complaint is summarized below.

D complained of being treated in a cruel fashion at the ripe old age of seventy-eight by people who wanted to exclude her from society. The experience was affecting her health as she felt depressed and slept poorly when she thought of hate speech that denies her pride in her contributions to the local community and Japanese society and everything else about her life. She was worried that her daughters and grandchildren would continue to be subjected to this discriminatory treatment and the thought of being exposed to another hate speech rally aroused a strong feeling of fear in her.

E went to the hate rally's departure point in Fujimi Park on January 31, 2016 and became directly exposed to hostile hate speech. Not going there was not an option for her because her middle-schooler son had made his own decision to protest against hate speech. She not only found herself at the receiving end of hate speech but also had to watch her child, who had been developing his identity as a Korean Double (someone with Korean-Japanese dual nationality), shedding bitter tears as he told her that he was 'feeling as if his body was cut in half and his heart was torn apart'. She began to live in anxiety and fear that another hate speech rally might descend on them to trample on her and her son's lives.[3] She claimed that these were the harmful effects inflicted on her.

F, who is E's spouse, had been working hard to rid the local community of ethnic discrimination. Despite his efforts, he could only watch as his spouse and child were put into a position where they were subjected to hate speech and compelled to protest. This caused him great pain and unbearable sadness. He claimed that the family could not restore the peaceful life they had had prior to the hate speech rallies because the family's loss of dignity would continue until hate speech was stopped.[4]

The complaints outlined above explain that the harms these individuals have suffered are not baseless. First, there have been twelve hate speech rallies. Second, the hate speech rallies have become increasingly intent on intimidating the community where Zainichi people live and those involved have put that intent into action. Third, a hate crime has already been perpetrated in Kawasaki in which a hate speech demonstrator attacked an unrelated citizen with an imitation sword and caused an injury requiring treatment that spanned one week.[5] As I discuss in more detail in the next section, these hate speech activities not only damage the dignity of Zainichi Koreans but also bring threatening behaviors into the local community, causing anxiety and pain in the everyday living environment.

## A true picture of hate speech in Kawasaki

Evidential documents accompanying the aforementioned complaints about human rights violations devoted many pages to what was actually said at the rallies in order to paint a true picture of hate speech. Amongst them was a transcript of the audio recording made at the rally held on January 31, 2016 from beginning to end. Let us look at the hate speeches made by the demonstrators at the rally as cited in the June 2, 2016 ruling of the Yokohama District Court Kawasaki Branch as the reason for granting a provisional injunction forbidding hate speech rallies from entering Sakuramoto.

The following are some of the remarks that were shouted out at the gathering point and throughout the march.

> Those long-term travelers[6] over there are liable to military service, too. South Koreans call their own country Hell Joseon. You should go home. We'll kick all of you out of Japan. You say "Don't come to Sakuramoto". This is Japan, we will never let you have your own way, never!.
>
> I'll tell you one more thing. You said to us, "Don't come to Sakuramoto". Are you kidding? I'll tell you many times, Sakuramoto is Japan. We Japanese can stage a demonstration here, by right, no problem. You were finished when you said it. We'll finish you!

We'll never forgive you. We'll pressure you until you go mad. We'll choke you very slowly and steadily. Until the last Korean has left Japan, you understand.

We'll not dirty our hands by killing you with our hands. We'll legally and calmly do things that drive you mad and back to the place you call Hell Joseon.

Go home, go home, Koreans, go home, go home, Koreans, go home, go home, Koreans, go home, go home, Koreans.

The following remarks made by a participant distills the essence of the hate speech rally even better than the organizers' statements.

They've just told us to stop discrimination but is there discrimination in this country? I bet you have never heard or seen discrimination. The Republic of Korea, South Korea, and North Korea are our enemy nations. The whole nation of South Korea spreads baseless views and says nasty things about Japan around the world trying to damage Japan's reputation. It has usurped part of Japanese territory by illegally occupying Takeshima Island. If this isn't an enemy nation, what is? Listen, it is normal to call for killing enemy aliens. I tell you, calling for killing enemy aliens is normal in war. I'll show you evidence. This thing from wartime America says "Kills Jap". It's a "Let's Kill Japs Game". It's a picture-story show titled "Kills Jap". The USA and Japan were fighting against each other during WWII and that's the type of language they used against their enemy. Admiral William Halsey's dictum is the most famous. He popularized the phrase "Kills Jap" [sic; Halsey's phrase was actually "Kill Japs"]. He was the man who evacuated aircraft carriers from Pearl Harbor before the Japanese air raid. The word "kill" is commonly used against enemy aliens. Because they are the enemy. Where do you find a fool who tells you to respect your enemy or protect your enemy's human rights? Nowhere in the world. America tells you to batter your enemies to death. *This is no discrimination. Anywhere in the world, anyone in a state of war says "kill"*. Japanese don't use words like "die" and "kill" only because they are emotionally unaccustomed to them, but they all use these words during wartime. The USA did, and so did Germany and the UK. They called for killing Japanese during wars. Koreans are Japan's enemy aliens. It is not discrimination to tell them to go home or die or whatever. Don't be fooled by the term "hate speech". Let's speak out proudly, everyone. Koreans, go home. Koreans, go home. Cockroaches. Cockroach Koreans, go home. It's OK to say anything. Now in Kawasaki, and Osaka the other day. Hate speech ordinances? What are they talking about? There is no such thing as hate speech in this country. People, don't be hoodwinked by this term. It's right to say, kill the enemy. Nowhere in the world will you find fools who respect enemies and protect their human rights. Kill your enemy is the right thing to say. There is no hate speech in this country. (emphasis added)

The hate speeches quoted above are totally consistent with Jeremy Waldron's argument. According to Waldron, the typical hate speech pattern sends the following message to minorities.

> Don't be fooled into thinking you are welcome here. The society around you may seem hospitable and nondiscriminatory, but the truth is that you are not wanted, and you and your families will be shunned, excluded, beaten, and driven out, whenever we can get away with it. We may have to keep a low profile right now. But don't get too comfortable. Remember what has happened to you and your kind in the past. Be afraid. (Waldron 2012a: 2–3)

At the same time, it conveys the following message to the rest of the community.

> We know some of you agree that these people are not wanted here. We know that some of you feel that they are dirty (or dangerous or criminal or terrorist). Know now that you are not alone. Whatever the government says, there are enough of us around to make sure these people are not welcome. There are enough of us around to draw attention to what these people are really like. Talk to your neighbors, talk to your customers. And above all, don't let any more of them in. (Waldron 2012a: 2–3)

The hate speeches delivered in Kawasaki followed this pattern.

## Opposition to hate speech and the anti-war/peace rally

The titles of hate speech rallies set forth by the organizers have changed over time since the first rally in Kawasaki on May 12, 2013. Starting with 'Protect Kawasaki from anti-Japan leftwingers and anti-Japanese foreigners', they gradually changed to 'Stop anti-Japan'. The later rallies that attempted to enter Sakuramoto had 'Cleanse Japan' as the theme. It is no surprise that this became the theme of the hate speech rallies organized by Zaitokukai without any change in the contents of the discourse of the speeches targeting Sakuramoto quoted in the previous section.[7] Nevertheless, a review of the actual remarks from the rallies informs us why people on the receiving end had to style their counter-protest as an 'anti-war/peace rally'. This was because the haters called Zainichi Koreans 'enemy/enemy aliens' and used the logic that it is fair to call for their 'death/killing' 'in a state of war'.

Around the time the local residents began to organize the counter-rally, Sakuramoto started offering 'education' on how to conduct a demonstration. Former director of Kawasaki municipal Fureaikan hall Tomohito Miura thought that people needed to demonstrate 'the community's will' but also recognized that the demonstration needed to be conducted lawfully with permission from the police. The education program was designed to prevent a situation where inexperienced demonstrators would be arrested due to not being aware of the rules. The program set its sights on the eventual arrival of a hate speech rally in Sakuramoto.

On January 31, 2016, their knowledge was put into practice when the community group kept the hate speech demonstrators out of Sakuramoto. However, the direct cause of this outcome was the police advising the demonstrators to change their route in order to avoid unnecessary trouble when they faced the well-mobilized counter-protesters. In comparison, the significance of the rejection of a hate speech rally planned for June 5, 2016 is completely different. This rally initially had a strong element of revenge for the blocking of the January rally's passage through Sakuramoto. For this reason, the group applied to march along the same route as the January rally.

However, the city mayor of Kawasaki refused the use of Fujimi Park by the hate speech rally in turning down the application.

National newspapers reported this matter solely in connection with the passing of the Anti-Hate Speech Act in the Diet. If we look further, however, the hate speech rally was subsequently given permission to march in Nakahara ward, Kawasaki city, by an alternative route starting from Nakaharaheiwa Park, even though the initially planned route through Sakuramoto was rejected. We cannot attribute the thwarting of the plan for the June 5 hate speech rally in Sakuramoto entirely to the effect of the newly passed Anti-Hate Speech Act. The real reason for the decision not to allow the hate speech rally into Sakuramoto was the fact that the Yokohama District Court Kawasaki Branch issued a provisional injunction against holding hate speech rallies within 500 meters of Seikyū-sha, a local social welfare organization for Zainichi Koreans, on June 2 (Yokohama District Court Kawasaki Branch Judgment June 2, 2016). The applicants were the same individuals who filed the aforementioned complaints about human rights violations. It is likely that the city mayor was able to refuse the use of Fujimi Park based on this court injunction as the planned rally route encroached on the banned area.

Let us briefly examine the court judgment in this provisional injunction case. It makes an argument for the validity of the disposition to ban hate speech rallies on the grounds of the International Convention on the Elimination of All Forms of Racial Discrimination (Treaty No. 26 of 1995), the Anti-Hate Speech Act due to come in force on the following day, and the Social Welfare Act (Act No. 45 of 1951). It recognizes Sakuramoto as a community with a high concentration of Zainichi Korean residents and acknowledges the facts, among others, that they have lived there in peace and quiet, that Seikyū-sha has been providing a range of community support services from child care and after-school care to aged care, and that there have been significant violations of personal rights denying the residents' existence and dignity through hate speech at twelve demonstrations in Kawasaki including phrases such as 'Die/kill', 'Go back to the peninsula', 'We'll kick all of you out', 'We'll choke you slowly' and 'Cockroach Koreans, go home'. The judgement then prohibits hate speech rallies from entering within a 500-meter radius of Seikyū-sha's headquarters.

The Anti-Hate Speech Act neither defines what constitutes hate speech nor contains any provision to ban it. The intent of the legislators of this law is stated in a book called *Heito supīchi kaishō hō—Seiritsu no keii to kihontekina kangaekata* (The hate speech elimination act: Its enactment process and basic thinking) as follows.

> This act takes the form of a philosophical law and not a ban. Our greatest concern was, in essence, to maintain the constitutionally guaranteed right to freedom of expression, that is a principal value we must protect. As a result of that consideration, we declare in the Preamble that unfair discriminatory speech and behavior towards non-Japanese residents will not be tolerated in order to strengthen our efforts to eliminate unfair discriminatory speech and behavior by spreading awareness among the general public and promoting their understanding and cooperation through further human rights education and awareness-raising activities. (Uozumi et al. 2016: 8)

They also state the following about how to control hate speech and behavior with the help of this philosophical law.

> We must not allow such speech and behavior, including at various levels of government. There are many existing laws and regulations that can be used for that purpose. We believe that this legislation will provide guidance in interpreting various laws such as the noise prevention ordinances and the defamation law. The governments can use their inhibitive power, including this combination technique. (Uozumi et al. 2016: 39)

In other words, the Anti-Hate Speech Act places responsibility on the national and local governments for taking appropriate measures to protect victims of hate speech by invoking powers bestowed upon them under existing legislation instead of laying down prohibitive rules to control those who make hate speeches. In fact, this is the logic used for the injunction order against hate speech rallies in Kawasaki. From the opposite perspective, this means that hate speech rallies could be allowed, in terms of the Social

Welfare Act, (1) if the community of Zainichi Koreans did not exist; (2) even if it existed, if there were no organization similar to Seikyūsha; or (3) if the actual speech and behavior at hate speech rallies had not been verified. It is expected that each case would be closely examined against these conditions. It becomes obvious that the Kawasaki Model cannot become a universal model if we consider why a hate speech rally that cannot be held in Kawasaki ward is allowed to proceed in Nakahara ward. The Anti-hate Speech Act is not a panacea in that attempting to regulate hate speech on a case-by-case basis using a combination of laws can produce inconsistent outcomes. Japan's experiment to turn the Kawasaki Model into something more adaptable to other communities has only just begun.

## Linking nationality and family may open a new horizon

The ruling made by the Yokohama District Court Kawasaki Branch explains the permanent residents' right to live in their community in peace and quiet on the basis of personal rights protected by Article 13 of the Constitution. It is unusual to invoke Article 13 of the Constitution in a legal dispute brought by foreigners, be it an administrative lawsuit or a civil action. This is because the Japanese courts have rarely recognized 'foreigners' right to the pursuit of happiness'. As Junji Annen questions in his *'Gaikokujin no jinken' saikō* (Rethinking 'foreigners' human rights'), 'foreigners' human rights' and 'the Japanese people's human rights' look alike but are different in substance even though foreigners' human rights are recognized according to constitutional interpretation—the courts have found no problem when freedoms to choose and change occupation and residence, which are usually considered to form part of basic human rights, are defined by the type of residency status under the immigration law, and foreigners' freedom is restricted accordingly (Annen 1993).

A permanent resident in Ōita Prefecture applied for public assistance when she fell into poverty due to abuse by her brother-in-law. Her application was rejected and she resorted to a court action in which the question of the right to life was raised. The Supreme Court categorically refused to recognize foreigners' right to life (*Shōmu geppō*, vol. 61, no. 2:

356–391). Although administrative agencies have been providing foreigners with public assistance out of considerations at an operational level, articles 1 and 2 of the Public Assistance Act specifically state that the law is applicable to Japanese citizens. Because the letter of the law has never been changed, only Japanese citizens are entitled to request public assistance as their right. The plaintiff was a foreigner with permanent resident status who was not entitled to receive public assistance and hence had no right to apply for it. While the permanent resident had Chinese nationality, she was born and raised in Japan and married in Japan. She had never been to the country of her nationality. Japan does not recognize the right to life even of a person like this (Nagano 2015). The creation of the Anti-Hate Speech Act does not change the lack of foreigners' access to human rights in Japan.

This issue is not limited to the Public Assistance Act. The same problem occurs in relation to all legislation with the citizenship rule. For instance, Article 1 of the Act on Access to Information Held by Administrative Organs (Act No. 42 of 1999) states: 'The purpose of this Act is, in accordance with the principle of sovereignty of the people, and by providing for the right to request the disclosure of administrative documents, etc., […] thereby ensuring to achieve accountability of the Government to the citizens for its various activities, and to contribute to the promotion of a fair and democratic administration that is subject to the citizens' appropriate understanding and criticism'. This means that foreigners are barred from requesting the disclosure of administrative documents concerning dispositions against themselves under this act. The Administrative Complaint Review Act (Act No. 68 of 2014) does not have the citizenship rule, but Article 7-1(x) provides that 'dispositions concerning departure and immigration or naturalization of foreign nationals' are the types of dispositions and inactions to which 'The provisions of articles 2 and 3 do not apply'. On the other hand, foreigners can go to the court in the immigration law violation cases under the Administrative Case Litigation Act simply because it does not have the citizenship rule. Article 9-1 states as follows:

> An action for the revocation of an original administrative disposition and an action for the revocation of an administrative determination may be filed only by a person who has legal interest to seek the revocation of the original administrative disposition or of the administrative determination (including a person who has legal interest to be recovered by revoking the original administrative disposition or administrative determination even after it has lost its effect due to the expiration of a certain period or for other reasons).

The act says nothing to the effect that foreigners are afforded such a right.

Despite this situation, the Yokohama District Court Kawasaki Branch recognized 'permanent residents' personal rights' in its decision. Why was it able to make that decision? The Anti-Hate Speech Act had a major impact in this respect. While the issue of foreigners' human rights may be raised in a dispute pertaining to the Immigration Act, foreigners' dignity has never been an issue. Because foreigners' freedoms to choose and change their occupation or residence is restricted and their freedom to bring their family with them is predetermined according to their visa category, it is impossible to talk about foreign residents in general as having a 'dignified existence'. However, the Anti-Hate Speech Act accepts that foreign persons have personal dignity by definition. Its legislators argue as follows:

> Hate speech, which is speech or behavior intended to exclude persons of a specific ethnicity or nationality from the local community or Japanese society on the grounds of their ethnicity or nationality—an attribute that is impossible or difficult to change by themselves—significantly damages personal dignity and leads to a divided community and of course must not be tolerated.
>
> [It] deeply harms the dignity of the targeted minority people and inflicts serious damage on their mind, body and life. It spreads hatred and discriminatory sentiments throughout our society and therefore it is absolutely unacceptable. (Uozumi et al. 2016: iii, vii)

Incidentally, hate speech is by definition not directed at a particular individual. The hate demonstrators did not name any individuals when they chanted 'kill' or 'go home' as shown in evidential documents accompanying the complaints regarding human rights violations. If defamatory or violent speech is directed at particular individuals, the offenders can be penalized and the victims can receive relief or reparative measures. These penalties and relief measures are only available when speech is directed at a specific person. Utterances such as 'We'll not dirty our hands by killing you with our hands. We'll legally and calmly do things that drive you mad and back to the place you call Hell Joseon' have been treated as one form of free expression under Japanese law.

Sang-gyun Kim addresses this structural issue based on the intermingling of a 'vertical relationship' with a 'horizontal relationship'. The vertical relationship exists where, after an individual's standing is lowered in an attack from the perpetrator, forces are exerted to lower the perpetrator's standing by imposing penalties, or to return the victim to the original standing as much as possible by instituting relief or reparative measures to the individual victim. When the 'individual' is replaced with the 'group' of Zainichi Koreans, which includes men and women, children and seniors, first-generation Koreans and younger-generation residents with South/North Korean nationality or Japanese nationality, their attributes become too diverse to be understood in terms of the vertical relationship. When the group with diverse attributes is categorized as the horizontal relationship, it no longer fits into the framework of the victim required under Japanese law.[8]

On the other hand, the 'vertical relationship' and the 'horizontal relationship' are examined in the opposite direction in the decision made by the Yokohama District Court Kawasaki Branch. The applicants asking for relief from human rights violations included (1) a first-generation Zainichi woman, (2) a third-generation Zainichi woman, and (3) the Japanese spouse of (2). Also, there was a child with dual nationality born of (2) and (3) who was necessarily given consideration in the court's deliberation process even though he was not among the complainants.

The commonality of their arguments rested in their Zainichi Korean identity. The question of their individual identity is also the question of their family identity, including for those who have Japanese nationality. In reality, Zainichi families without Japanese members (Japanese citizenship holders) are in the minority these days due to the generational change among the

Zainichi population. The court recognized permanent residents' personal rights under Article 13 of the Constitution by taking this 'horizontal relationship' into consideration.

We must acknowledge, however, that acceptance of the personal rights of permanent residents in the 'horizontal relationship' cannot be equated with acceptance of 'permanent residents' personal rights' in general. As in the Supreme Court Second Petty Bench's decision in the aforementioned Ōita case on July 18, 2014, a foreign national as an individual is judged on the basis of their foreign nationality alone and cannot assert any constitutional rights regardless of their personal circumstances. Assuming that this view of the Supreme Court still stands, permanent residents' personal rights under Article 13 of the Constitution accepted by the Yokohama District Court Kawasaki Branch would not be recognized in the case of a foreign individual. The latter court held that where individual permanent residents exist as part of a family including Japanese citizens who together form a certain community (i.e., being in the 'horizontal relationship'), these people's personal rights are guaranteed under the Constitution.[9]

Did the recognition of foreigners' personal rights from the 'horizontal relationship' angle suddenly arise out of the hate speech issue? I do not think so. I believe there is a connection between this question and a higher probability of the issuance of special permission to stay to applicants who are married to a Japanese citizen or a permanent resident or who have children with a Japanese or permanent resident partner. The authority cannot find a 'benefit' to grant when it sees a case as involving only an individual. When it can see the case as a problem for a family, including that individual, it shifts their viewpoint to the horizontal relationship, and if it considers the case on this plane, it can find a path to confer a 'benefit' upon that individual. While we cannot discuss the 'benefit' of special permission to stay on the same footing as 'dignity' under the Anti-Hate Speech Act, we cannot overlook the analogy between them either. It is the existence of the individual's personal rights that are realizable in communal life such as the local community and the family.

## Conclusion: Permanent residents' right to peaceful existence and the Japanese Constitution

From the start, the main point of contention over the anti-hate speech legislation was how to reconcile it with freedom of expression. The ruling of the Yokohama District Court Kawasaki Branch explains this point as follows:

> Where the violator, who is aware or able to discern easily that the right holder is living in peace and quiet in their place of residence, engages in discriminatory speech or behavior in serious violation of the right holder's personal right to peaceful existence at their residence, including demonstrating or parading around while using a loudspeaker or sound truck or shouting loudly in the neighborhood, it is reasonable to find that the right holder has the right to seek an injunction against the discriminatory speech or behavior as part of the right to petition for the removal of obstruction on the basis of the personal right to live peacefully at one's residence. […] Hence the violated personal right is a robust right guaranteed and protected by the Constitution and law; on the other hand, the illegality of the violation is significant and clearly falls outside of the bounds of the freedoms of assembly and expression guaranteed by the Constitution and also constitutes abuse of rights in private law on the grounds that discriminatory speech or behavior constitutes a violation of this personal right intentionally or by gross negligence as stated above, that it involves publicly announcing an intention to harm the life, body, freedom, honor or property of people of non-Japanese origin or slandering or severely denigrating their reputation for the sole purpose of promoting or inciting discriminatory sentiments against them, and that it adopts the aforementioned modes of conduct such as the use of a loudspeaker and sound truck.

The court held that this rationale is applicable to Seikyū-sha as a social welfare juridical person as much as the individual applicants. This means that, on balance, personal rights protected by Article 13 of the Constitution deserve protection more than freedom of expression and therefore the latter has to be subjected to certain restrictions in some cases.

The purport of this decision has so far been accepted by the Ministry of Justice. On August 1, 2016, the Human Rights Bureau of the Ministry of Justice issued an advice to the organizers of the hate speech rally in Kawasaki. According to a newspaper report,

> [The bureau] acknowledged that these speeches and behavior were "illegal activities violating the personal rights of Zainichi Koreans in that they interfered with their enjoyment of basic human rights on an equal footing with Japanese people and other foreign nationals by inciting hatred and hostility towards them in an attempt to exclude them from Japan", and advised them in writing to repent their conduct "consisting of unfair discriminatory speech and behavior to violate human dignity which cannot be overlooked from the viewpoint of human rights protection" and not to engage in similar activities in future. (*The Kanagawa Shimbun* August 2, 2016: 1).

The advice restates the logic found in the judgment of the Yokohama District Court Kawasaki Branch.

There still is uncertainty over the question of how hate speech and hate rallies can be stopped. Nevertheless, the court ruling clearly states that permanent residents' personal right for peaceful existence at their residence is guaranteed by Article 13 of the Constitution and the Ministry of Justice Human Rights Bureau advised the rally organizers on the basis of the court's interpretation. This view must be usable in supporting legal arguments in cases unrelated to hate speech as well. In the past, the scope of foreigners' human rights has been considered only in relation to the Immigration Act. The Anti-Hate Speech Act has cleared a path to approach foreigners' rights outside of the logic of the Immigration Act. It was a major step in this respect.

## Notes

1 The march was documented in Zainichi Kōreisha Kōryū kurabu Torajinokai (2015) and footage can be viewed at https://www.youtube.com/watch?v=0PGTNR_TJTI.

2 The path to the formation of the city-wide network was reported in detail in Kanagawa Shimbun 'Jidai no shōtai' Shuzai Han (ed.) (2016).

3 This is explained more specifically in her statement of facts. 'When we desperately called to stop discrimination, the hate rally participants ranted over the loudspeaker, "They are Koreans", "Koreans are the enemy of Japan", "It's fair to say, kill the enemy". The sight of a grown man goading people to "kill" over the microphone with a straight face filled me with great fear for my life. We feel as if our hearts were killed at that time'. This makes it clear that the hate rallies instilled a deep fear in the victims.

4 He says in his statement that the experience had an enormous impact on his daily life: 'This is not a guess or my imagination but I seriously think I am a prime candidate for a mental illness or PTSD'.

5 It happened inside JR Kawasaki train station on February 2, 2014. After a passing train user threw an anti-hate speech pamphlet into a trash box, one of the hate rally participants mistook the person as a counter-protester and attacked, shouting 'What kind of Japanese are you?' (as reported in *The Kanagawa Shimbun* on March 4, 2014).

6 The term refers to Zainichi Koreans with special permanent resident status.

7 They are no different from those reported in Yasuda (2012), Nakamura (2014), Noma (2015) and others.

8 This point is discussed from different perspectives in Kim (2014) and Mori (2014).

9 In addition, there is no doubt that the Kawasaki court decision was prompted by a desire to reflect the legislative intent of the recently enacted Anti- Hate Speech Act.

# Japanese Management through the Lens of Foreign Labor: The Significance of Foreign Workers to Enterprises and the Community

## Introduction

I once received a request to review a book entitled *Toyota to Toyota—Sangyō gurōbaruka senshin chiiki no genzai* (Toyota City and Toyota Motor: The current state of an advanced area of industrial globalization; Nibe, Okamura and Yamaguchi [eds.] 2014) based on my experience in research on the foreign labor issue. The book contained studies on wide-ranging topics written by various authors. This was necessary as it aimed to present a comprehensive discussion of the civic life of Toyota city residents. On the other hand, it seemed to me that the diverse mix of the authors' methodologies, standpoints and areas of expertise in studying the same geographic location resulted in some inconsistent evaluations of the subject across chapters. I would like to raise some questions by re-examining the significance of foreign labor research to the theory of Japanese-style management represented by the Toyota Production System.

## Japanese-style management and Toyotism

Yoshio Sugimoto divides the history of the analysis of Japan into several phases in *An Introduction to Japanese Society* (4th edition; 2014). The first phase (to the 1950s) involved comparison with Western society using an approach derived from the cultural anthropological framework.[1] The second phase (from the 1950s to the 1960s) featured Japan's modernization and postwar recovery as research themes with the use of empirical and universal data sets. Discussions during these phases were largely guided by studies conducted by overseas scholars. The third phase (from the late 1960s to the 1970s) saw the rise of Japanese thinkers such as Chie Nakane (*Tate shakai no ningen kankei* [Japanese society]; 1967) and Takeo Doi (*'Amae' no kōzō* [The anatomy of dependence]; 1971). Discussions centered on specific aspects of the Japanese people and the organizations they create and the main academic interest shifted to a broader perspective, including the family and enterprises. The fourth phase was spearheaded by *Japan as Number One: Lessons for America* by Ezra Vogel (1979). Discussions on the central subject of Japanese-style management went beyond corporate structures into analysis of the Japanese people (Japanese society) (Sugimoto 2014: 16–21).

The Toyota Production System is one of the topics that has garnered much attention in this context. Literature on the topic ranges from that written from a business perspective, including *Toyota seisan hōshiki—Datsukibo no keiei wo mezashite* (Toyota Production System: Beyond large-scale production) by Taiichi Ōno, former vice president of Toyota Motor Company who is considered to be the father of the system (Ōno 1978),[2] and *Toyota shisutemu—Toyota shiki seisan kanri shisutemu* (Toyota system: Toyota-style production control system) by Yasuhiro Monden (1989), to studies from a more academic perspective such as *The Machine That Changed the World: The Story of Lean Production—How Japan's Secret Weapon in the Global Auto Wars will Revolutionize Western Industry* (Womack, Jones and Roos 1990).

Japanese-style management typified by the Toyota Production System drew attention not merely because of Japan's postwar economic recovery and the strong economic performance of individual enterprises or the evolution of Japanese studies as outlined by Sugimoto. Studies of Japanese-style management provided excellent material to the emerging academic fields of 'information economics' and 'law and economics' and promoted the formation of a social theory with a certain level of universality beyond Japanese studies. Leading figures include Masahiko Aoki and Banri Asanuma. Aoki transposed the themes of Kazuo Koike's empirical research into organizational analyses from the standpoint of information economics and conducted economic analyses of the mechanisms that were supposed to be uniquely

Japanese, including the seniority-based salary system, lifelong employment and enterprise unionism. He discovered the existence of a universal principle of good organizational management in a comparison between the J-firm (Japanese companies) and the A-firm (American companies) (Aoki 1988). Asanuma studied 'long-term contracts' in intra-group transactions between Japanese companies and found that the seemingly incomplete contracts acted as a mechanism for inter-organizational adaptability to environmental changes due to allowances they made for advances in skills and technology and fluctuations in the economic environment over a long period (Asanuma 1997).

The studies by Aoki, Asanuma and others successfully incorporated Japan analysis into the framework of comparative institutional analysis by explaining the behaviors of Japanese enterprises and workers, which were often regarded as Japanese peculiarities, in terms of the 'new institutional economics' of Ronald Coarse and Oliver E. Williamson (Aoki and Okuno [eds.] 1986; Aoki and Dore [eds.] 1995; Aoki 2001). The once distinct and particular studies of Japanese enterprises and labor relations have become part of a universal social models analysis. It was the Toyota Production System that convinced the world of Japan's universality. The concept of *kaizen* (continuous improvement) was translated into English and an introductory book became a best-seller (Imai 1986). As the word found its way into the English lexicon, manufacturing facilities all over the world introduced quality control circles / *kaizen* groups to practice this management technique.

## Toyotism and foreign workers

When I met Eishi Fujita, a leading expert in the field of automobile industry research, for the first time in 2003, I told him about a sense of discomfort I had felt after reading a study conducted by his team. It was inconceivable that a large volume of menial repetitive work that any short-term worker could handle (as was the case for most Nikkei contract workers) would be generated in automobile production sites where workforces were strictly controlled and trained to become highly skilled tradespeople under long-term employment and organized via group activities held outside regular work hours. Communities with a high concentration of Nikkei residents were experiencing social problems. Corporate governance was supposed to prevent these problems. I asked Fujita why this situation was happening. He replied, 'I don't know why, either; something must have changed'.

In my view, Japan's industrial society and labor society revealed by Fujita and others were expressed schematically in Hiroji Baba's theory of '*kaishashugi*' (companyism). According to Baba, companyism refers to:

> [T]he employee's strong feeling of belonging to an enterprise on one hand. Common terms such as *kaisha ningen* [company-first person] are used in this sense. On the other hand, companyism is a blanket term for a social system in contemporary Japanese society. Both are mediated by a form of enterprise organization called company. [...] The behavioral pattern of large companies became the goal and the norm for small-to-medium-sized enterprises. *It governs the lives of people who are employed by companies and defines society as a whole, including people who are not employed by them.* (Baba 1991: 62–63; emphasis added).

Companyism served as a circuitry for macro-economic growth based on the following logic.

> Loyal employees are highly motivated and willing to work long hours. As they see company development as a good thing, they accept rationalization and actively participate in improving productivity as long as they remain employed. Enterprise unionism means that the company minimizes losses from labor disputes and the employees withhold wage demands during recessions. These factors support company expansions, including technological innovation, and an aggregation of concurrent expansions of many companies leads to rapid economic growth. (Baba 1991: 68)

Companyism was strengthened even further as the rapid economic growth opened up another circuitry.

> It first absorbed an abundant supply of young workers from the rural area. Their employment brought average wages down and promoted the

system of in-house education to develop a highly adaptive labor force through on-the-job training. Company-specific skills development accompanied frequent job re-assignment fostering cross-trained workers with a wide interest in the company's business. Workers were reluctant to move to another company as company-specific skills were not easily transferrable while employers were disinclined to lose workers given the cost of training them. This long-term employment condition further enhanced in-house skills development and strengthened the seniority-based system. (Baba 1991: 68)

Consequently, companyism acquired the following reputation.

Under companyism, workers were positioned as agents, or rather forced to become agents from the viewpoints of competition and communality, and eventually headed in the direction of voluntary productivity improvement for their company as the capital. *This is why companyism became the best institution for productivity improvement in human history and even reached a stage where it was difficult to imagine a better system.* (Baba 1991: 74; emphasis added)

Companyism turned Japanese employees into cross-trained workers and gave Japanese companies with highly productive cross-trained workers a reputation as 'the best institutions in human history' that 'even reached a stage where it was difficult to imagine a better system'. Just as companyism reached its apogee, great numbers of Latin Americans of Japanese descent were arriving in Japan to work and the largest receptacles for these Nikkei workers were the electric and electronics industry and the automotive industry, which were Japan's biggest foreign currency earners thanks to companyism. How can we interpret this phenomenon? Why did utilization of nonskilled foreign labor for menial tasks expand in the automotive industry, the sector most steeped in Japanese-style management? Neither exponents of Japanese-style management nor its critics have raised this question to date.

Chapter 6

# Toyota and foreign labor

The comprehensive research on the automotive industry by Fujita's team covers a wide range of topics from its production sites and workers' home life to the relationship between enterprises and the community and resulted in the publication of two books, *Kyodai kigyō taisei to rōdōsha—Toyota no jirei* (The giant corporation and its workers: The case of Toyota; 1985) by Yōichi Oyama (ed.) and *Jidōsha sangyō to rōdōsha—Rōdōsha kanri no kōzō to rōdōsha zō* (The automotive industry and its workers: Labor management structure and worker profile; 1988) by Hikari Nohara and Eishi Fujita. Having conducted a survey of business establishments in Toyota city in the late 1990s, I recognized a marked change in 'the relationship between enterprises and workers' and 'the relationship between enterprises and the community' reported in these books. As I was co-authoring *Kao no mienai teijūka: Nikkei Burajiru-jin to kokka, shijō, imin nettowāku* (Invisible residents: Japanese Brazilians vis-à-vis the state, the market and the immigrant network; hereafter *Invisible Residents*; 2005) with Takamichi Kajita and Naoto Higuchi at the time, I expressed this sense of incongruity to Fujita.

As I mentioned in the previous section, Japanese-style management represented by Toyotism builds on lifetime employment and the seniority system and turns individual employees into cross-trained workers through skills development by on-the-job training over a long period based on the theory of learning by doing. Japanese management theory posited that this mechanism enabled Japanese enterprises to achieve high productivity.[3] In the aforementioned book, Nohara and Fujita cast light on the negative aspect of Japanese-style management in which quality control and *kaizen* activities practiced daily on the shop-floor as part of the cross-training of workers compels workers to think continually about 'the company's future' and 'my work at the company' during and after work hours and turns them into company-first people. In reality, this seldom generates *kaizen* suggestions that directly contribute to productivity improvement even though these practices are thought to lead to some productivity benefits. The book portrays the process of developing 'intellectual skills' proposed by Kazuo Koike (1990), which refers to a worker's growing proficiency in the overall workflow over a long period, as a process in which the individual's work achievement (and the company's growth as a collective achievement) deepens their self-alienation.

While Oyama's book is a community-level analysis of the same subject, it came to a theoretical conclusion along the lines of Nohara and Fujita's argument that a social structure was in place through which Toyota as the controlling company could extend its dominion to various parts of the community and keep its critics small, localized and isolated. These views implied that the concomitant formation of workers' in-company identities based on lifelong employment and a community of people aligned with the company's activity in the local community exerts intense peer pressure at work and in the community, keeping nonconformists excluded or in a minority.[4]

The presence of Toyota's rapidly expanding foreign workforces runs directly counter to this understanding of corporate society and the local community. The principal role in *monozukuri* (manufacturing/craftsmanship) that forms the core of the company's production has been passed on to newly arrived foreign workers, who do not receive any special training to develop their individual skills or competency. *Many of the tasks that used to be performed by highly skilled workers and those in the ongoing skills development process have been quantified and converted into programs to run numerically controlled machine tools (NC machine).* While small numbers of workers continue to undertake the role of maintaining skills for the *narai* process, teaching machines to copy the technique of highly skilled workers, production line work itself has come to be regarded as a job anyone can perform. In one subcontract factory, non-permanent foreign workers were assigned even to the testing process, which is said to be the most important part of product quality control (Photo 6.1).

When I asked, 'What would you do if you had no foreign labor?' in my hearing survey of Toyota's primary subcontractors, most firms replied that they would 'deal with it by further automation and mechanization'. When I asked, 'Then, why are you employing foreign labor instead of mechanizing?', they gave me a reply to the effect that, 'Mechanization requires a certain level of capital investment and we need to get at least ten years' worth of use out of the machine. We don't know if we'll still be in business then, and a machine generates a lot of waste unless a certain volume of stable production can be

## Chapter 6

**Photo 6.1** Brazilian workers assigned to product testing
Source: Photo by Akihiro Nomura.

maintained. We can respond to fluctuations in production more readily if we use human labor'.

This means that a group of easily replaceable workers in menial jobs face the constant threat of job loss and are actually hired or fired at the mercy of production fluctuations. The presence of these people has become a social problem and the studies conducted by Fujita's team do not explain why this situation emerged. In other words, the presence of foreign workers embedded in the Toyota-style production management system opens a crack in the conventional arguments of Toyotism and Japanese-style management.

## Foreign labor and institutional sociology

Can we understand what has changed in the Toyota Production System and Japanese-style management theory by analyzing foreign labor? I believe we can grasp a certain aspect of it by approaching foreign labor as an institution (Kamata 1982). Here, I am referring to the situation where various foreign nationals enter Japan under various visa categories, including foreigners of Japanese descent, technical intern trainees and IT and other skilled personnel. While I am aware of their different residency qualifications, I do not differentiate these people according to visa categories. Where foreign labor takes on a certain social function, it is regarded as a single institution based on the difference in economic function or the socioeconomic difference, rather than the difference in residency or legal status. From a strictly methodological viewpoint, my foreign-labor-as-an-institution approach does not conform to the definition of institution. Nevertheless, I adopt a social-functional approach unconstrained by the legal discrepancy for a reason.

I was involved in a residents' attitude survey conducted by the city of Hamamatsu, Shizuoka prefecture, in 2014. Participants were randomly chosen from the city's basic resident register and included 2,000 residents with foreign nationalities and 1,200 Japanese residents. The number of foreign residents of each nationality was determined according to the nationality-based population ratio in the city and resulted in the inclusion of 853 Brazilians, 292 Filipinos, 251 Chinese, 176 other South Americans and 428 other nationalities. The city had been conducting a survey of the living and working conditions of the South American residents, mainly targeting Brazilians, every four years since 1992. The non-South-American nationals were added to the survey in 2014 due to an exodus of South-American Nikkei residents during the global recession. Hamamatsu's Brazilian population halved in five years from 2008 (Hamamatsu-shi Kikakuchōsei-bu Kokusai-ka 2014), the beginning of the global financial crisis (GFC).

A similar situation was found in Toyota city. Based on *Gaikokujin shimin ishiki chōsa* (Foreign residents' attitude survey) conducted by the city of Toyota, Nibe reported:

> More than a quarter of Brazilian, Korean and Filipino respondents identified themselves as "job seeker (unemployed)", giving a glimpse of the significant impact of the global financial crisis of 2008. It is noteworthy that unemployment among Chinese respondents was only 6.2 percent while the ratio of "trainee/technical intern" reached 36.2 percent. [...] [W]ith a stronger tendency for permanent residency on

one hand and an increased fluidity of employment due to deteriorating economic conditions on the other hand, the city's ethnic composition is changing gradually. We must remember that the situation has changed considerably since prior studies were undertaken in the 1990s to the early 2000s. (Nibe, Okamura and Yamaguchi [eds.] 2014: 38)

My question stems from the transition outlined above. The shift in the ethnic composition occurred in Hamamatsu as well. The domination of a largely Brazilian Nikkei population has become a thing of the past and other ethnic groups have joined the ranks of city residents. Has this change caused the employment structure to change? While the city of Hamamatsu was undertaking its attitudinal survey, I was conducting a survey of business establishments in Hamamatsu city, as outlined below.

I have conducted an annual hearing survey of some of the subcontract businesses with which I made contact during my first business establishment survey in Hamamatsu in 1996–97.[5] In the 2014 survey, in addition to subcontract factories, I interviewed business contracting firms supplying foreign workers to them. The survey uncovered a strange phenomenon. Some of the business contracting firms were supplying both Nikkei foreign workers and technical intern trainees. Nikkei workers and technical intern trainees belong to different legal categories and therefore cannot be supplied by the same corporate organization. Each of these business contracting firms was operating by dividing their organization into a production contracting service division (or company) dispatching Nikkei workers to production sites and a not-for-profit business cooperative receiving technical intern trainees and dispatching them to production sites. Although these sub-organizations appeared to be separate entities because of their different names, they were actually operating under the same management and supplying both Nikkei workers and technical intern trainees.

The business contracting firms presented a statement of costs for the supply of Nikkei workers and a statement of costs for the supply of foreign technical intern trainees to their client factories to allow them to choose their preferred labor (tables 6.1 and 6.2). Table 6.1 shows the costs involved in accepting a Nikkei worker from a business contracting firm. The host enterprise pays 1,988 yen per hour per worker (base unit price) to the firm, which in turn pays the worker 1,187.50 yen per hour. There is an allowance of 9,500 yen for perfect attendance as an incentive to improve attendance as well as a transfer allowance based on a Japanese-worker model. The 'costs to be borne by the firm' (for health insurance, employee pension, employment insurance, labor insurance, liability insurance, job advertising, medical examination, accommodation and transport) are paid by the business contracting firm, not the host enterprise (but passed on to the host enterprise). The total cost to the host enterprise is a sum of pay for ordinary hours worked, overtime (working on holidays) pay, late-night (overtime) pay and late-night allowance under the subheading of 'Invoiced to (the host enterprise)'. The amount invoiced to the host enterprise includes the salary portion per worker of 283,277 yen, the overhead costs borne by the business contracting firm of 55,957 yen and the cost of labor management by the business contracting firm. Consequently, the gross margin for the business contracting firm is shown to be 71,387 yen per month.[6]

Table 6.2 may seem unfamiliar even to some researchers working on the foreign labor issue. It shows a breakdown of the cost of dispatching a foreign technical intern trainee. Unlike Nikkei workers, technical intern trainees are permitted to come to Japan only once for a period of up to three years in principle and must return home at the end of the period under a rotation policy. The first item in the cost statement is an advance preparation cost of 307,100 yen and the last item is a repatriation cost of 105,000 yen. The program's underlying principle manifests in the form of the rule that makes the host enterprise responsible for the advance payment of the costs of bringing the intern to and from Japan.

The 'management cost', 'other costs', 'insurance, allowance, wage and costs borne by the host company' and 'accommodation cost' are incurred monthly for the duration of the internship. As far as calculation is concerned, these monthly costs are determined at the same time as the prior preparation cost and the repatriation cost. Part of the management cost is paid to a recruitment agency in the intern's home country. The amount may also include the cost of pre-employment training. For this reason, the pre-employment training cost, the repatriation-related costs and the costs of staying for the duration of the internship are not determined separately as they become assessable only after the total costs have been calculated.

## Chapter 6

**Table 6.1** Statement of costs per Nikkei employee

Statement of costs  Attention to [host company's name]  (1 April 2007)

| | Item | Base (yen/month) | Formula | Notes |
|---|---|---|---|---|
| Paid to employee | 1 Salary | 205,200 | = 1,187.5/hour × 8.0 hours × 22 days | 1. Based on assignment to the head factory. |
| | 2 Overtime (holiday) | 33,666 | = 1,246.88/hour × 125% × 22 hours/month | |
| | 3 Late-night (overtime) | 0 | = 1,246.88/hour × 125% × 0 hour × 0 day | 2. Monthly employment assumes the following: |
| | 4 Late-night allowance | 0 | = 311.72/hour × 25% × 0 hour × 0 month | |
| | 5 Early-morning allowance | 0 | = 0/day × 0 day | (a) 21.6 operating days |
| | 6 Full-attendance allowance | 9,500 | Purpose: to improve attendance rate | (b) 172.8 work hours |
| | 7 Paid leave | 15,738 | = 283,277 Total Items 1–11 × 3 months ÷ 90 days × 10 days ÷ 6 months | (c) 21.6 overtime hours (1.0 hour/day). |
| | 8 Transfer expenses | 5,720 | = 34,320 ÷ 6 months (one-way travel cost between Sapporo and Nagoya) | 3. The base assumes the average monthly sum per employee working regular hours. |
| | 9 Homecoming expenses | 5,720 | = 34,320 ÷ 6 months (one-way travel cost between Sapporo and Nagoya) | |
| | 10 Supplies | 3,333 | = 20,000 (uniform, cap, shoes) ÷ 6 months | |
| | 11 Commuting expenses | 4,400 | = 4,400 (estimated from average annual sum per employee) | |
| | Total I (1–11) | 283,277 | = Average monthly sum paid to employee | |
| Borne by the firm | 12 Health insurance | 12,875 | = Total I × health insurance rate 0.04545 | |
| | 13 Employee pension | 19,234 | = Total I × employee pension rate 0.06790 | |
| | 14 Employment insurance | 2,479 | = Total I × employment insurance rate 0.00875 | |
| | 15 Labor insurance | 5,949 | = Total I × labor insurance rate 0.02100 | |
| | 16 Liability insurance | 920 | = 275,910 ÷ 300 employees | |
| | 17 Job advertisement | 10,000 | = 36,000,000/year ÷ 12 months ÷ 300 employees | |
| | 18 Medical checkup | 333 | = 2,000 (at the time of hiring) ÷ 6 months | |
| | 19 Share of accommodation cost | 4,167 | = 350,000 (management fee) ÷ 84 | |
| | 20 Transport | 0 | = Annual cost ÷ 12 months ÷ 300 employees (vehicle lease, insurance, fuel) | |
| | Total II (12–20) | 55,957 | = Average monthly sum borne by this firm | |
| | Total III (I + II) | 339,233 | | |
| Invoiced to [the host company's name] | 1 Regular hours | 343,526 | = 1,988/hour × 8.0 hours × 22 days | |
| | 2 Overtime (holiday) | 67,095 | = 2,485/hour × 125% × 22 hours/month | |
| | 3 Late-night (overtime) | 0 | = 2,485/hour × 125% × 0 hour × 0 day | |
| | 4 Late-night allowance | 0 | = 497/hour × 25% × 0 hour × 0 day | |
| | Total IV (1–4) | 410,621 | = Average monthly sum paid to employee | |

| Asking price | Base unit price | 1,988/hour |
|---|---|---|
| | Overtime unit price | 2,485/hour |
| | Late-night premium | 497/hour |

**Table 6.2** Running costs per technical intern/trainee for three years

| | Cost Item | Unit Price | Quantity | Total | Notes |
|---|---|---|---|---|---|
| **Prior preparation costs** | Acceptance procedure (visa) | 25,000 | 1 | 25,000 | Immigration application expenses |
| | Pre-employment (home country) | 30,000 | 1 | 30,000 | Pre-departure training cost in the home country |
| | Departure preparation (local interview etc.) | 30,000 | 1 | 30,000 | Job interview expenses in the home country |
| | Travel (home country to Japan) | 100,000 | 1 | 100,000 | One-way airfare from home country to Japan |
| | Trainee insurance | 27,100 | 1 | 27,000 | Compulsory |
| | Post-arrival group training | 40,000 | 1 | 40,000 | Group training cost in Japan |
| | Domestic transfer (airport to accommodation) | 5,000 | 1 | 5,000 | Transfer from the airport to the accommodation |
| | Post-arrival purchase of daily necessities | 50,000 | 1 | 50,000 | Costs of essential goods to live in Japan |
| | Total 1 (fee per person per application) | | | 307,100 | Expenses per trainee to arrival in Japan |
| **Management costs** | Trainee management (year 1) | 35,000 | 12 | 420,000 | Management fee for the cooperative and in the home country |
| | Trainee management (year 2) | 35,000 | 12 | 420,000 | Management fee for the cooperative and in the home country |
| | Trainee management (year 3) | 35,000 | 12 | 420,000 | Management fee for the cooperative and in the home country |
| | Total 2 (management cost per trainee per 3 years) | | | 1,260,000 | Costs to maintain and manage a trainee |
| **Other costs** | Transport/management between accommodation and factory | 40,000 | 36 | 1,440,000 | Bus and driver |
| | Internship examination (year 2) | 20,000 | 1 | 20,000 | Compulsory (if advancing to intern status) |
| | Immigration application (3 times) | 6,000 | 3 | 18,000 | Stamp duty + proxy application |
| | Total 3 (miscellaneous expenses per trainee per 3 years) | | | 1,478,000 | |
| **Insurance, allowance, wages, costs borne by the host company** | Intern insurance (years 2 & 3) | 15,940 | 1 | 15,940 | Optional |
| | Social insurance (year 1) | 14,047 | 12 | 168,564 | Compulsory (trainee's share to be deducted from pay) |
| | Social insurance (year 2) | | | | Compulsory (trainee's share to be deducted from pay) |
| | Total 4 (insurances per trainee per 3 years) | | | 365,032 | |
| | Training allowance (year 1) | 69,000 | 12 | 828,000 | Living expenses in Japan |
| | Minimum wage (year 2) take-home pay 80,000 | 115,770 | 12 | 1,389,240 | (681 × 170 hours) × 12 |
| | Minimum wage (year 3) take-home pay 90,000 | 125,770 | 12 | 1,509,240 | (681 × 170 hours + 10,000) × 12 |
| | Merit bonus | 100,000 | 1 | 100,000 | On completion of training/internship |
| | Total 5 (personnel cost per trainee per 3 years) | | | 3,826,480 | Living expenses the host company pays the trainee |
| **Accommodation costs** | Trainee accommodation (year 1) | 25,000 | 12 | 300,000 | 20,000–30,000 per trainee |
| | Trainee utility charges (year 1) | 5,000 | 12 | 60,000 | The host company's share (up to 5,000 per trainee) |
| | Intern accommodation (years 2 & 3) | 25,000 | 24 | 600,000 | 20,000–30,000 per trainee |
| | Intern utility charges (years 2 & 3) | 5,000 | 12 | 60,000 | The host company's share (up to 5,000 per trainee) |
| | Accommodation cost deduction (years 2 & 3) | (15,000) | 24 | (360,000) | (deduction from intern's pay) |
| | Total 6 (accommodation costs per trainee per 3 years) | | | 720,000 | Utility charges are born by the host company throughout |
| **Repatriation costs** | Domestic transfer (to the airport) | 5,000 | 1 | 5,000 | Optional (transfer from accommodation to the airport) |
| | Travel (Japan to home country) | 100,000 | 1 | 100,000 | One-way airfare |
| | Total 7 (repatriation costs per trainee per travel) | | | 105,000 | |

In any case, the key point in Table 6.2 for a technical intern trainee is the monthly management cost of 35,000 yen. Let us compare this with the table for a Nikkei worker. The business contracting firm dispatches a Nikkei worker at an hourly wage of 1,187.50 yen and gains a gross profit of 71,387 yen per month. When the firm dispatches a technical intern trainee at an hourly wage of 681 yen, it gains a gross profit of 35,000 yen per month. The business contracting firm calls the ratio of the total amount it pays the worker to the total amount it receives from the host enterprise the 'cost percentage'. Although the profits in absolute amounts are different, the cost percentages are almost the same whether the firm supplies a Nikkei worker or a technical intern trainee.[7] As far as the foreign labor dispatching business goes, the Nikkei worker and the technical intern trainee are just different product brands offered by the firm.

However, tables 6.1 and 6.2 are not the actual statements for a cost comparison between a Nikkei worker and a technical intern trainee that I was shown during my survey in Hamamatsu.[8] These were used by a foreign labor dispatch firm in Nishimikawa region surrounding Toyota city from 2007 to 2008, before the GFC. Under the Immigration Act revision of July 6, 2009, trainee status was merged into technical intern trainee status (the first year is called 'technical intern training [i]' and the second and third years are called 'technical intern training [ii]'). The Act on Proper Technical Intern Training and Protection of Technical Intern Trainees (Act No. 89 of 2016; hereafter referred to as the 'Technical Intern Training Act') was proclaimed on November 28, 2016 and came into operation from November 1, 2017. The act instituted 'technical intern training (iii)' for certain skill types, affording intern trainees who have progressed to technical intern training (iii) a maximum of five years of training in total. The title of Table 6.2, 'Running cost per trainee/technical intern for three years', is based on the fact that the document was used prior to the 2009 law revision. As at September 2014, the figures used by a Hamamatsu firm were very close to the earlier figures thanks to Abenomics, which boosted manufacturers' operating rates and lifted Nikkei workers' hourly wages almost back to the pre-GFC level. Therefore, the information gleaned from a comparison of the two tables here is still useful in understanding the shift in the foreign labor market from Nikkei workers to technical intern trainees.[9]

Nikkei workers, who are received as long-term residents, and technical intern trainees, who are confined to designated activities and cannot change employer or place of residence, belong to different legal categories. However, this legal distinction means nothing in Japan's economic reality where the two groups are options in the same category from which a client can choose. They are merely high-wage foreign labor and low-wage foreign labor supplied by the same firm. As for the decline in the population of Brazilian residents and the increase in other foreign nationals, it would be possible to say that the foreign labor market has not changed if the latter were to consist of an increase in the number of technical intern trainees.

## The impact of institutional change on the local community

Among Japan's Nikkei resident population, the Brazilian group recorded the most pronounced decrease. Their population continued to decline from around 326,000 shortly before the GFC to 173,038 in June 2015. Although the number began to recover slowly to reach 184,967 in June 2017, the rate of increase was smaller compared with other nationalities. After the fall of 2008, the Japanese economy remained depressed for a long period partly because it was struck by the Great East Japan Earthquake just when it was showing some signs of recovery. It feels unreal that it was only in July 2008 when the Japan Federation of Economic Organizations and the ruling Liberal Democratic Party's national strategic division project team on the foreign labor issue each announced its own distinct foreign labor policy proposal.

Faced with the GFC and the major natural disaster, manufacturing and production by Japanese enterprises contracted. However, the situation was vastly different overseas. Toyota Brazil's Sorocaba plant doubled its annual production from 130,000 vehicles in 2008 to 260,000 vehicles in 2013. Its Indaiatuba plant also lifted production. Toyota was not the only corporation expanding its production capacity. Nissan Brazil acquired a site and commenced the construction of a new plant in Rio de Janeiro in 2013 as it outgrew the Curitiba plant jointly used by Renault. Honda also began constructing its second plant when the first São Paulo plant became too small. Besides the automotive industry, Panasonic built and commissioned a new home appliances plant on the state border between São Paulo and Minas Gerais after it stopped white goods production in Japan. The jobs that had disappeared from Japan were being created one after another by Japanese companies in the Nikkei Brazilians' home country.

Businesses from other countries were also actively investing in Brazil. Strong job growth pushed up the rising minimum wage. Brazil's minimum wage rose from 300 reais in 2008 to 645 reais in 2013 and again to 724 reais in 2014. It rose further to 788.06 reais in 2015 (and 905 reais in the State of São Paulo where wages were generally higher). There is a big difference between how the minimum wage is set in Japan and Brazil in terms of whether or not it is set to the minimum amount necessary to lead a comfortable life. In Brazil, it is generally thought that a household of parents with two children in compulsory education requires monthly earnings of at least around seven times the minimum wage. If the household wishes to send a child to university, it needs to earn around twelve times the minimum wage. Based on the exchange rate current at the time of writing, the former amounts to approximately 237,000 yen and the latter 406,000 yen per month (based on São Paulo's minimum wage, approximately 272,000 yen and 467,000 yen).

The rise in the required cash earnings is leading to a substantial increase in the general cost of living, especially in terms of real estate prices. In Liberdade, known as a Japanese town, a thirty-year-old three-bedroom family-size apartment sells for around 35,000,000 yen while a newly-built similar property costs more than double that price. These prices are not so different from those in Japanese cities. Under these conditions, Brazilians are no longer able to build wealth with income from overseas work. For Brazilian workers who were considering returning home, the post-2008 economic growth in their home country changed the meaning of working in Japan completely.

Japan's foreign labor system as a 'cross-border employment system' was impacted most by this change. The cross-border employment system operates through the tie-in arrangement between Japanese-affiliated travel agencies recruiting workers overseas (Japanese-managed travel agencies selling air tickets to Japan and information about employment in Japan as a package) and business contracting firms in Japan allocating workers to factories. In the past, a prospective Nikkei worker would convey their wish to find employment in Japan to a travel agency, which would forward their personal information to a business contracting firm in Japan to decide on their application. If the applicant was successful, they would be issued with a plane ticket to Japan. The airfare and the brokerage fee would be deducted from the worker's monthly salary. The workers were able to go to Japan without paying travel expenses upfront as long as they were willing to work (Tanno 2013: Chapter 10). However, this mechanism collapsed during the GFC. Amid the shrinking employment of temporary workers, payments from foreign workers' salaries to travel agencies stopped. As these recruiter-travel agencies had already paid the travel costs on behalf of the workers, they suffered losses in Brazil. The cross-border employment system linking the supply source and demand center for labor had completely collapsed by early 2009.

A totally different travel arrangement was introduced from 2009. An applicant wishing to work in Japan had to pay around one half of the combined cost of the airfare and the brokerage fee to a travel agency before their departure and pay the balance through deduction from pay once they started work in Japan. Since Japan's manufacturing sector made a quick recovery under Abenomics, the remaining Nikkei labor market regained vitality and the wage level returned almost to the pre-GFC level. The demand for labor recruitment activity in Brazil has naturally increased but the mechanism for the payment of travel and recruiting costs has not reverted to the previous one.

When we treat foreign labor as a social institution, we can grasp the dynamics behind the change at the local level. The fall in the population of Brazilian residents in Japan cannot be explained by Japan's economic recession (and resultant job losses) alone. The dynamics involved can be summarized as follows.

1 Brazil's economic growth led to job creation and wage rise domestically.

2 Brazil's economic growth led to inflation especially in real estate prices, making it impossible for Nikkei workers to realize the goal of building wealth with income from working in Japan.

3 The mechanism of labor movement between Japan and Brazil collapsed amid the GFC and has not been reinstated despite a fast economic recovery in recent years (2008–2018).

When Japan's recovery from the GFC and the Great East Japan Earthquake became evident, the Abenomics policy favoring a weaker yen acted as the direct trigger for the tightening of the local labor market. However:

4 More than a quarter of a century after the 1990 revision of the Immigration Act allowing employment of up to the third-generation foreign nationals of Japanese descent, Nikkei workers living in Japan have steadily become older.

5 The factories that laid off Nikkei workers during the recession wish to rehire but they prefer younger workers because they want to strengthen their production activity.

6 Consequently, there is a broad shift from Nikkei labor to technical intern trainees and hence Asian countries have replaced Latin American countries as the major sources of labor.

Despite this apparent shift, it is possible to say that foreign labor as a social institution has not changed. This is because the transition from Nikkei workers to technical intern trainees is merely a change of recruitment areas while the shift in visa categories from long-term/permanent residency to designated activity residency has not changed the overall system of labor force movement itself. The system is fundamentally operating in the same way by drawing workers from overseas labor reservoirs and funneling them to where they are needed in various localities across Japan through the same intermediary organizations.

The change in the composition of foreign residents in the local community represents the combined effect of domestic and overseas factors. The only way to understand this change is to treat it as a process by integrating domestic and overseas factors. The decline in the population of Nikkei Brazilian residents is part of the constantly changing global dynamic. Moreover, the shift from Nikkei workers to technical intern trainees is not a simple transition. It strongly suggests that technical intern trainees cater for the demand for cheap labor in regular production activity[10] whereas Nikkei workers tend to be employed in more unstable sectors or in more variable production activity.

## Conclusion: Rethinking 'invisible residents'

So, what has foreign labor contributed to our perspective on enterprises and local society? It has elucidated the presence of a type of 'mode of incorporation' of people other than regular members of society and become an indicator of change in the community. As far as this mode of incorporation is concerned, Japanese seasonal workers and fixed-term contractors preceded the arrival of foreign workers and in fact the business contracting industry used to be the labor outsourcing industry dispatching Japanese seasonal and short-term workers. As the market shifted the source of labor from Japan to overseas, the business contracting firms adapted their operation to different legal requirements for different worker categories and formatted their business to cater for both Nikkei workers and technical intern trainees, broadening the labor outsourcing market.

Has the presence of foreign workers changed any of the mechanisms operating within the community? It certainly has. The situation has changed greatly since my co-authors and I published *Invisible Residents*. I defined 'invisible residents' as 'people who are attempting to gain a foothold as part of an invisible workforce' in the local community where 'foreign workers exist, but their existence is not recognized by the local community due to their lack of social life' (Kajita, Tanno and Higuchi 2005: 72). I used the issue of out-of-school Nikkei children of compulsory schooling age as an example of this invisibility. In Toyota city, their out-of-school rate fell from 40 percent in 2001 to below 10 percent in 2004. This sharp drop in a short space of time came to light when the city undertook a survey of all households with school-age children (Kajita, Tanno and Higuchi 2005: 241–243). On the other hand, the 2014 Hamamatsu residents' attitude survey initially found that 5.4 percent of the sample responded that the first-born child was out of school although they were of compulsory schooling age. The figure was 9.3 percent for the second-born child. Shortly after, however, we discovered that the figures included some children who were 'not in senior high school' and children who were 'living outside of Japan and not in compulsory schooling'. We noticed this error without having to undertake a survey of all households.

When we first raised the issue of 'invisible residents', foreigners were required to complete alien registration only at the time of moving into a municipality whereas Japanese citizens were required to register residence when they relocated into and out of a municipality. As foreign residents did not report to the first municipality when they moved out or moved to a different municipality, they continued to exist in the administrative system of the first municipality. This procedural flaw was responsible for the overestimation of the out-of-school rate to a significant degree (and hence the rate suddenly fell when the survey of all households was conducted). Now the alien registration law has been abolished and foreign residents are integrated into the system of basic resident registration along with Japanese residents. They are issued a 'residence card' instead of an alien registration card and recorded in the municipal resident register. Today, foreigners' residency information is centrally managed under the residence card database. Because of this availability of information on foreign residents' movements between municipalities as well as to and from Japan, the city of Hamamatsu was able to immediately discover that the residents' attitude survey results did not reflect the actual condition due to erroneous responses. The process of 'making residents visible from above' was progressing rapidly.

Municipal governments' move to make foreign residents visible in this way inevitably leads to an expansion of administrative services to cater for their circumstances. The results of the Hamamatsu residents' attitude survey indicate that foreign residents who send their children to public schools, use the Japanese language to communicate with Japanese residents, and see a doctor for their own or a family member's illness without using a medical interpreter are becoming mainstream. This does not necessarily mean that they are heading directly to stable long-term residence. In light of Japanese residents' responses, there is little contact outside the workplace between foreigners and Japanese people, except those who participate in support activities for foreign residents or live in a community with high proportions of foreign residents. While almost 100 percent of Japanese children advance to senior high school, only 72.1 percent of foreign residents wish to send their children to senior high. Their actual education continuation rates are considerably lower. Among the first-born children of foreign residents, 14.4 percent actually advanced to junior college or higher education and 36.7 percent went to senior high school (i.e., 51.1 percent in total went to senior high school or higher education) in Japan. The figures among the second-born children are 9.1 percent and 53.2 percent respectively (62.3 percent in total). Foreign residents' state of invisibility in their community life still remains and there are ongoing concerns that the second-generation may be confined to the urban underclass (Tanno 2016).

Furthermore, only 26.7 percent of foreign residents are regular employees despite the tight labor market under Abenomics. A mere 12.3 percent of foreign residents were made regular employees in the past five years (2009–2013) during which the economy was making a rapid recovery. While the foundation of the economy continues to rely on unstable employment, the process of making foreign residents visible from above is unilaterally progressing in the area of public administration. In reality, some foreign residents are consciously and steadily moving toward long-term residency on an individual basis under these conditions. In my opinion, it is unlikely that the visibility of foreign residents would improve without stable employment. It is evident that the foreigner-related problems drawing attention in recent years such as out-of-school children and suspected child abuse cases are closely linked to the problems of the working poor and unstable employment among their parents. My co-authors and I raised the issue of 'invisible residents' as a problem for foreign residents but these days this problem casts a darker shadow on the Japanese side. Why has Japan come to rely on non-regular employment to this extent? 'Invisible residents' is still an effective angle from which to examine this question. A detailed review of the transition from Baba's 'companyism' to 'invisible residents' should elucidate this aspect of change.

# Notes

1. Ruth Benedict, Robert Bellah and James Abegglen are named as some of the leading thinkers in the first phase.
2. Eiji Toyoda, Ōno's boss and the longest-serving executive in Toyota's postwar history, mentioned the efforts made by people besides Ōno in establishing the Just In Time system in his autobiography serialized in *Ketsudan The Nihon Keizai Shimbun Sha* (Toyoda 1985).
3. Examples of overseas studies from this viewpoint include Martin and Florida (1993a, 1993b).
4. It is my understanding that this line of thinking first appeared in *Japan in the Passing Lane: Insider's Account of Life in a Japanese Auto Factory* by Satoshi Kamata (1982).
5. The survey result was published in Yasuo Kuwahara (ed.) (2001).
6. The business contracting firm's labor management cost does not appear in the statement. It corresponds to the balance (71,387 yen) of the amount invoiced to the host enterprise (410,621 yen) minus the amount paid to the worker (283,277 yen) and the amount borne by the firm (55,957 yen), which is effectively the firm's gross profit.
7. In the business contracting industry, the ratio of the worker's hourly wage to the hourly contracting rate (base unit price in Table 6.1) is sometimes called the cost percentage. On a monthly basis, this is equivalent to the ratio of salary the firm pays the worker to the total amount it receives from the host enterprise.
8. The provider of those statements declined to give me permission to publish them. However, the statements contained very similar figures to those in tables 6.1 and 6.2.
9. The shift from Nikkei workers to technical interns/trainees was already observable prior to the GFC. For two decades after the Immigration Act revision in 1990, the rule to limit eligibility for a work permit to the first three generations of Nikkei applicants was not changed and hence Nikkei workers were gradually slipping out of the labor-force age range desired by Japanese industries.
10. Dismissal of technical intern trainees is strictly regulated and if the employer repatriates them as soon as production falls, the company will have difficulty receiving technical intern trainees again next time it needs them.

# The Sociology of 'Foreigners' Human Rights'

## Introduction

This chapter reflects on foreigners' human rights from a sociological perspective based on the four cases discussed in previous chapters: the 'fake Nikkei' case, the foreign juvenile delinquency case, the LGBT foreigner case and the hate speech rally ban case.

In my view, foreigners' human rights need to be understood on a sociological plane because the legal approach as a whole is plagued with contradictions.[1] Foreigners' human rights have thus far been regarded mainly as a legal issue. Constitutional law states the following:

> Persons with nationalities other than Japanese, i.e., foreigners, possess the right to enjoy fundamental human rights. This is because complete denial of foreigners' right to enjoy such rights is found to have no validity in the light of the spirit of international collaboration expressed in the preamble of and throughout the Constitution and increasing protection of human rights under international law, in addition to the idea that fundamental human rights precede statehood. (Ōishi and Ōsawa 2016: 35–36; emphasis added)

In civil law, we find the following interpretation:

> An entity who can be a possessor of rights is, first and foremost, a person (human being) […] upon birth, all persons commence actual enjoyment of the rights to life and health (core personal rights) and acquire capacity to hold various other rights under the interpretation

guideline of Article 2 of the Civil Code ("This Code must be construed so as to honor the dignity of individuals"). And "Unless otherwise prohibited by applicable laws, regulations or treaties, persons with foreign nationalities enjoy private rights" (Article 3-2). (Hironaka 2006: 98)

Thus, foreigners are possessors of human rights from the perspective of both constitutional and civil law.

Even though it is generally recognized that foreigners have human rights, it appears that decisions in individual cases have not been based on this assumption. Yasuo Hasebe calls this 'a paradox raised by Junji Annen', in reference to the Japanese lawyer and jurist who highlighted the issue (Hasebe 2006: Chapter 8). In other words, even though the existence of foreigners' human rights has become an axiom, it has been denied in actual individual cases.

After witnessing fellow human beings wrestling with the state to assert their own rights, I can no longer reduce their situation to the single word 'paradox'. In my view, we can achieve knowledge that differs from a legal understanding if we follow the processes of court action and deportation enforcement from a sociological viewpoint. Along these lines, this chapter examines a common logic underlying the apparently discrete four cases mentioned above. The aim here is to demonstrate that the common logic operating in these cases in fact represents Japanese society's view of resident foreign nationals.

## Why do they have to be deported?

The point of contention in the 'fake Nikkei', foreign juvenile delinquent and LGBT foreigner cases was the enforcement of a deportation order. Each case sought a stay of execution of the deportation disposition, which was essentially the granting of special permission to stay. It is held that the Minister of Justice has a wide-ranging discretionary authority to grant special permission to stay on a case-by-case basis and therefore permission is denied when the minister finds no grounds for granting it. For this reason, the applicant has little chance of winning a favorable ruling if they go to court. However, there still is room to fight the deportation order on the basis of the principle of equality or inadequate consideration of factors requiring consideration and, if the court finds in favor of the applicant and stops the deportation order, the Minister of Justice is obliged to allow the applicant to stay in Japan legally. Consequently, special permission to stay is granted. Yet, the court judgment simply states 'the execution of the deportation order to be suspended for [--] days'. This gives rise to the question of whether or not the immigration authority can deport the applicant once the suspension period has passed. If the applicant has not committed any law violation since, the situation remains the same and therefore a further lawsuit is expected to produce the same judgment. For this reason, the immigration authority issues special permission to stay.[2]

All of the plaintiffs in these cases came to Japan as foreign workers from Latin America. The alleged fake Nikkei, A, arrived from Bolivia in 1991 at the age of thirty-four (and in 1997 for the second time at the age of forty). B in the foreign delinquent case arrived from Peru in 1992 at the age of ten. C, who came out as transgender in Japan, arrived from Brazil in 1997 at the age of nineteen. A and C were foreign workers themselves while B came to Japan as a family member of foreign workers. They all moved from place to place after their arrival. Their unsettled lifestyle suggests that not only the workers but also their dependent family members needed to keep moving in order to make a living in Japan.

All of them were subjected to a deportation disposition but for different reasons: A was falsely accused of faking his Nikkei status and had his visa extension rejected; B was arrested for stealing and a Stimulant Drugs Control Act violation and served prison sentences; and C was arrested for a Stimulant Drugs Control Act violation and her sentence was finalized (she received a suspended sentence and was not imprisoned).

A's and C's cases went to court where the immigration authority's assertions and the courts' judgments stated words to the effect that 'The Constitution stipulates nothing about foreign nationals entering and residing in Japan and imposes no duty on the immigration authority to let foreign nationals enter or reside in Japan. Unless there is a special treaty, a nation is under no obligation to admit foreign nationals into the country. Hence, whether or not foreign nationals are admitted into the country and, if admitted, on what conditions, is to be determined at the sole discretion of the subject nation'. Faithfully echoing the Supreme Court Grand Bench ruling of October 4, 1978 (the so-called McLean judgment), they asserted that any decision made by the immigration authority in individual cases about foreigners' stay in Japan was free from errors.

In recent years, some legal scholars have expressed doubts about this argument. According to one view, the McLean judgment made sense 'because it offered *a valid logic applicable to cases where the broad discretionary authority was available*, but it is reasonable to say that it has lost its validity now that the Administrative Procedure Act has introduced the requirement to establish review standards and disposition standards and that judicial precedents have accumulated' (Abe 2008: 391; emphasis added).

A, B and C were accepted into the country in accordance with the 'long-term resident' status afforded to third-generation Japanese descendants. This residence status was introduced by the Ministry of Justice Public Notice No. 132 issued on May 24, 1990: 'The establishment of status listed in the right column of the section on Long-Term Residents in Appended Table II of the Immigration Control and Refugee Recognition Act, as stipulated in Article 7, Paragraph 1, Item 2 of the same Act' (the so-called Long-Term Residence Notice) typically granting a visa to a Nikkei person. After the abduction and murder of a young girl by a Peruvian citizen of Japanese descent in November 2005 in Hiroshima, the immigration authority instituted criminal record inquiries[3] and the requirement of 'good conduct' was added to the notice in the April 2006 revision (thereafter referred to as the Revised Long-Term Residence Notice). The requirement of good conduct was the main reason for the rejection of C's application for a visa extension.

The Ministry of Justice published the Guidelines on Special Permission to Stay in Japan in October 2006 (as discussed in the Preface). The guidelines were revised three years later and a new version was published in July 2009. The current immigration control operation is administered and regulated via notices and guidelines published by the immigration bureau itself. Although the immigration authority claims to adopt the emic approach of case-by-case decision-making as a matter of form, it does not make decisions on an ad hoc basis. This is obvious from the existence of *Ihan shinpan yōryō* (Guidelines on adjudication of violations), which sets out procedural rules in a very detailed and concrete manner (its 2016 version has 160 pages). In fact, the immigration authority appears to take various measures to ensure that decision-making accords with set patterns as much as possible. It strongly suggests that actual operations are carried out etically despite the theoretical pursuit of an emic approach in administrative control. Nevertheless, it seems that this administrative reality is somehow not taken into account in court deliberations.

## Junji Annen's argument on foreigners' human rights

Now, let us look at what Hasebe called 'Junji Annen's paradox'. According to Annen, in Japan's residence status system, 'in terms of its substance, there is no neutral or colorless general category of residence for foreign nationals; all foreigners possess one of the segmentalized statuses set out under the Immigration Control and Refugee Recognition Act and stay for a limited residence period allowed under their respective residence statuses as long as they stay in Japan legally. This residence status system itself serves as the fundamental constraint on foreigners' human rights'. He argues that 'therefore, asking "to what extent are human rights guaranteed for foreigners living in Japan?" is a seriously misleading way of formulating a question' in the first place (Annen 1993: 167).

The reason for this is that Japan allows the Immigration Act, subordinate to the Constitution, to restrict human freedom of economic activities up-front as well as foreigners' mental/spiritual activities.[4] Annen reasons as follows:

> The system of slicing and dicing an individual and only permitting the undertaking of economic activities in a designated area seems to be premised on the line of thinking that entails a wholesale denial of freedom of economic activities to begin with and the subsequent granting of permission for selected economic activities as a privilege. It is difficult to think that this rule is acceptable under Article 22-1 of the Constitution no matter how broad the lawmaker's discretion over economic freedom may be. In this case, the restriction of foreigners' economic activities under the residence status system must be regarded

as completely different in nature from that of Japanese nationals. (Annen 1993: 172)

It is important to pay attention to a certain assumption Annen refers to in making this argument. As he notes, this line of thinking becomes possible because of the assumption that 'the Constitution takes precedence (over international treaties) in the hierarchy of force and effect between different forms of law and therefore various human rights-related treaties do not change the substance of the constitutional rules', i.e., such treaties and the 'international human rights theory' premised on them have no impact on the Constitution (Annen 1993: 168).

In short, Annen does not believe that the residence status system pays due regard to the human rights demanded by the Constitution. He argues that 'supplementation with human rights does not simply fill the gaps in the existing system; it inevitably destroys the system itself'. If the authority gives resident foreign nationals the same freedoms of residence and movement as the Japanese nationals, it 'will have to grant permanent residency for as long as they wish to stay'. The imposition of a limit on the period of residence means that 'foreign nationals' enjoyment of human rights is recognized only within the scope of their residence status'. Moreover, if it is 'constitutionally unacceptable to make considerations that are disadvantageous' to foreign nationals in their application for visa renewal, 'foreign nationals gain the right to stay once they have entered the country legally'. In other words, once the human rights of foreign nationals are given recognition upon entering the country, 'it will no longer be acceptable to make the non-exercise of all or part of their human rights a condition of residency as the current residence status system does', making the Immigration Act incompatible with the Constitution (Annen 1993: 179–180).

According to Annen, foreigners' human rights become entangled in this predicament because human rights are not established intrinsically within the body of the Constitution. Even the various rights of Japanese nationals provided by the Constitution are the rights of Japanese citizens qualified by the Nationality Act rather than the Constitution because Article 10 of the Constitution provides that 'The conditions necessary for being a Japanese national shall be determined by law'. This structure in which Japanese nationals defined by the Nationality Act enjoy the rights provided by the Constitution means that Japanese nationals' rights are not established under the Constitution. In the case of foreigners who are not citizens under the Nationality Act, the logic of denying all rights up-front and reinstating some of them within the scope permitted by the Immigration Act emanates from here reflexively.

The logic, which is found in both the practical operation of the Immigration Act and the McLean judgment and accepted by the Supreme Court, is built on the logical structure illuminated by Annen. Perhaps it should be called the 'logic for foreigner control'. As a result, this logic creates a situation where the immigration authority can only understand human rights as different for Japanese nationals versus foreign nationals and suffers a mental block when it comes to the question of how to deal with the reality it is facing. Further, the immigration authority is unwilling to explain why the Ministry of Justice and Immigration Bureau do not have to be bound by the notices and guidelines they set down themselves.

## Immigration administration and 'administrative discretion'

Immigration administration is afforded a broad scope of discretion. Nevertheless, it is still part of the administrative actions carried out by public employees. Even if an administrative disposition proceeds with minimal judicial involvement under the law and is accepted by the court, it should be possible to identify where it stands relative to other administrative actions. Let us examine this point based on a series of studies presented by Takayoshi Tsuneoka.

According to Tsuneoka, it was not so long ago that limits were imposed on discretion as an administrative action of the state. This originated in the owner-driver taxi lawsuit that began in the 1960s. The case eventually reached the Supreme Court, which held that concrete procedural standards should be set in selecting a small number of particular people out of a large number of applicants and that such concrete standards 'need to be final and conclusive as to their substance and must not be variable depending on circumstances'. This decision drew a line around discretion by requiring an administrative agency to treat a large number of applicants equally (Supreme Court First Petty Bench Judgment of October 28, 1971)[5] (Tsuneoka 2012a: 150).

Tsuneoka says that the argument was developed over several stages before culminating in the Supreme Court decision in the owner-driver taxi case. The Tokyo District Court judgment of December 20, 1967, held that the setting of assessment criteria was 'one mode of the exercise of discretionary authority conferred on administrative agencies under the governing laws and regulations' and therefore 'the exercise of discretionary authority is constrained by the requirement for reasonableness' and 'the assessment criteria are also constrained by the requirement for reasonableness as to their substance'[6] (Tsuneoka 2012a: 152). The Tokyo District Court judgment of February 22, 1968, held that 'Where the substance of the assessment criteria is found to be unreasonable or the application of the reasonable substance of the assessment criteria is found to be unreasonable, then the resultant disposition is illegal'. Reflexively, however, it meant that 'Where a disposition was made on the basis of reasonable application of the reasonable substance of the assessment criteria, then such disposition is in principle not illegal'[7] (Tsuneoka 2012a: 153). The Tokyo District Court judgment of December 26, 1969, held that 'The possibility of alternatives as to the substance of the assessment criteria in itself does not make such assessment criteria (or a resultant disposition) illegal, but if the assessment criteria themselves are unreasonable, such assessment criteria (or a resultant disposition) are illegal'[8] (Tsuneoka 2012a: 153).

Through the succession of owner-driver taxi lawsuits, the court came to recognize the following:

> It is necessary for administrative agencies to have discretionary authority, due to reasons such as a governing law providing abstract or equivocal conditions for making a disposition, and to adopt a method of determination entailing the establishment and application of standards for the fair and equitable exercise of the discretion. These standards need to be consistent with the intent of the governing law and reasonable in their substance. [...] In selecting a small number of particular individuals from a large number of applicants, an administrative agency

must (1) establish the assessment criteria specifically representing the intent of the governing law provisions on the requirements for making a disposition; and (2) give applicants an opportunity to submit their argument or evidence where the substance of the standards demand a more sensitive or sophisticated ruling. (Tsuneoka 2012a: 155)

Besides the establishment of discretionary disposition standards, there is the problem of how to explain the existence of 'directives (and public notices)' in immigration administration. Limits on directives have also been defined in the course of multiple lawsuits. According to Tsuneoka, there are different aspects to the binding force of directives, but (1) the Supreme Court Third Petty Bench judgment of December 24, 1968, in the 'revocation of directive under the cemetery burial law' case held the following:

In principle, a directive is not a legal rule by nature; it is issued by a higher administrative authority to give its subordinate agencies and their employees instructions about the exercise of their administrative authority and orders regarding their duties. Because such directives are orders to such agencies and employees only within the particular administrative organization, the general public is not directly bound by such directives even if these agencies and employees may be bound by them.[9] (Tsuneoka 2012b: 148)

However, (2) the Supreme Court Second Petty Bench judgment of March 28, 1958 in the 'pachinko ball game machine case' held that if the substance of a directive 'is consistent with the correct interpretation of the law, then a disposition based on such a directive is a legal disposition'.[10] (3) The Supreme Court First Petty Bench judgment of October 29, 1992 in the 'Ikata nuclear power plant case', which was a legal dispute over the decision-making process and criteria for approving nuclear reactor installation, held that 'the specific assessment criteria as the standards for discretionary decision-making are required to be consistent with the intent of the governing law' and 'it is this court's understanding that if the substance of the specific assessment criteria is reasonable, then it has a certain level of legal binding force even though it may not be a full and absolute binding force'[11] (Tsuneoka 2012b: 149–150).

It was confirmed through these court precedents that interpretive standards and directives/notices, which were originally considered to be binding on administrative agencies only, can become guiding principles in a legal action and even bind the court under certain conditions in some cases. Interpretive standards 'can function as guiding principles in a trial as long as they express the correct interpretation of the law. The standards for discretionary decision-making can also function as guiding principles in a trial if their substance is reasonable and consistent with the intent of the governing law and their application is reasonable' (Tsuneoka 2012b: 151). However, reasonable standards for discretionary decision-making do not necessarily receive full respect from the court. There will be some cases in which such standards must not be applied by the court in a trial because they run counter to the intent of the law. 'When the legality of interpretive standards comes under review, such interpretive standards are merely the subject of a judicial review, and the court is able to make its own decision on their legality regardless of the substance of the interpretive standards in question' (Tsuneoka 2012b: 153).

Consequently, standards for discretionary decision-making are 'established as part of the exercise of discretionary authority by an administrative agency' and 'the establishment of such standards is one way or mode of exercise in which an administrative institution exercises its discretionary authority'. As a legal doctrine, the limitations of discretion as an exercise of administrative authority 'can be divided into three categories: substantive standards, procedural standards and decision control standards'. In particular, the substantive standards consist of '(1) significant factual error, (2) contravention of the purpose or motive, and (3) violation of the general principles of law'. The general principles in (3) include 'violations of (i) the principle of equality, (ii) the principle of proportionality, (iii) the principle of good faith, and so on', and 'the standards for decision process control include "not considering factors requiring consideration" and "considering factors not requiring consideration" among others' (Tsuneoka 2012c: 148). This view can be regarded as common sense in court cases involving foreign nationals nowadays and even Judge Jōzuka recommended that attorneys conduct their lawsuits from these points of view as discussed in the Introduction.

Tsuneoka's argument on administrative discretion is also applicable to cases for the stay of execution of a deportation order. In the case of a newcomer Korean overstayer seeking a stay of execution of a deportation disposition after marrying a Japanese national[12] (Tanno 2013: Chapter 10), and in the case in which a Bolivian worker accompanying their family became an overstayer when a long-term residence extension was rejected on the grounds of a car accident and sought a stay of execution of a deportation order (Tanno 2020a: Chapter 6), for example, plaintiffs made their arguments from the viewpoints of substantive standards, procedural standards and decision control standards, which were accepted by the court in allowing them to remain in Japan. The lawsuit that culminated in the Supreme Court Grand Bench judgment of June 4, 2008, which deemed a provision in the Nationality Act unconstitutional, originally began as a case seeking a stay of execution of a deportation order[13] and the logic of Tsuneoka's argument on administrative discretion was used as the starting point of the legal battle for the entire trial (Tanno 2020a: Chapter 4).

## Annen's 'foreigners' human rights' vs. Tsuneoka's 'administrative discretion'

The reason for my examination of Annen's argument on foreigners' human rights and Tsuneoka's argument on administrative discretion at the start of this chapter is that the 'logic for foreigner control (the Ministry of Justice Immigration Control Bureau as the administering agency and the court as the judicial institution for the maintenance of order)' and the 'logic for allowing foreigners' human rights (foreign nationals themselves, their attorneys and the court as the judicial institution for the protection of human rights)' are condensed in them. As we have seen so far, foreigners' human rights have been debated in actual court cases using these two approaches.

From a different angle, Annen's argument is about a logic used in denying foreigners' human rights ('the Supreme Court's logic') and a logic for controlling foreigners in Japan. On the other hand, Tsuneoka's administrative discretion is a logic ('the district courts' and attorneys' logic') that works in favor of allowing foreigners' human rights. The history of Supreme Court judgments up to this point demonstrates that Annen's argument remains very much alive. The use of this logic is not limited to cases involving special permission to stay. As mentioned earlier, the same logic is relied upon in denying the foreigner's right to receive social welfare benefits in court cases over social security for permanent residents. In a way, this means that foreigners are not entitled to raise objections to any decisions made by state authorities in the final phase of dispute on any issues. However, it is impossible to rule out instances when case-by-case consideration becomes necessary as Japan's foreign resident population increases. It appears that these non-excludable cases are dealt with by administrative actions explainable with Tsuneoka's administrative discretion argument or otherwise end in court judgments against state authorities.

So, what kind of cases require case-by-case consideration? All of the attorneys I know told me that this point defies a logical explanation. Some commented that 'even if we think this case is absolutely safe [i.e., winning a stay of execution of a deportation order] because that case was successful, often it doesn't turn out that way'.[14] Yamaguchi recommended that I read two new books: *Zetsubō no saibansho* (Courts of despair; Segi 2014) and *Nippon no saiban* (Justice in Japan; Segi 2015). In these works, Hiroshi Segi, a former court judge and Supreme Court judicial research official, exposes problems pervading Japan's court system today based on his own experience.

According to Segi, the chance of winning a liberal ruling in a court case against state authorities depends on the chance of getting a liberal-minded judge to preside over the case. However, a majority of judges are subjected to personnel control by the Supreme Court in favor of accepting the government's argument and this trend has been accelerated by judicial system reforms. Segi claims that it has become extremely difficult for judges who go against this current to advance to high courts or the Supreme Court. Given Segi's view of the court system, it is understandable that Annen's and Tsuneoka's arguments can coexist. It is probably fair to say that foreign-national plaintiffs have won their cases by relying on the logic of administrative discretion when liberal-minded judges happened to be assigned to their cases. It is also understandable that many of the lower court judgments published in law reports as precedents granting special permission to stay were overturned in higher courts and only a small number of them became the final and binding precedents in reality.

In addition, there is another fact that must not be overlooked—the issue of the family underlying the cases of A and C addressed in this book. Whether or not one exists as a member of a family largely determines the amount of documentary evidence submitted to the court. In A's case, for example, testimonies and evidence supporting his real Japanese ancestry were gathered from not only his brothers, nieces, nephews and cousins living in Japan but also from his relatives in Bolivia. Some of his brothers and cousins worked in his workplace in Japan and made statements about his work attitude.

In C's case, on the other hand, while the plaintiff side could build up strong theoretical arguments in its brief and complaint to the court, it was difficult to gather as much evidence of C's concrete social relationships as in A's case. The situation in juvenile B's stay of execution of a deportation order case was similar to A's, although it did not go to court. Petitions for B's stay in Japan were gathered not only from the people with whom he had direct relationships such as his mother, uncles and cousins, his long-term probation officer and his former Japanese girlfriend, but also from his mother's doctor and his family's associates, and these were submitted as evidence of B's social relationships.

As the granting of special permission to stay is assessed on a case-by-case basis, the more the information available, the easier the assessment becomes. It is as if the probability of obtaining special permission to stay can be expressed as a function of the amount of evidence demonstrating social relationships in Japan (i.e., $F(X) = f(x)$). Consequently, it becomes inevitable that someone like C, who lives as a transgender person away from her family, is structurally excluded from the special permission to stay mechanism.

## Foreigners replacing imperial subjects

Contrary to the argument I have presented so far, the view that the protection of foreigners' human rights has greatly improved in Japan has emerged in recent years. This view seems to have been advanced by legal scholars in particular. For example, Kōichi Aoyagi described the Supreme Court Grand Bench judgment of June 4, 2008 (about the unconstitutionality of the Nationality Act) as 'the Supreme Court has been dancing [towards rights protection] lately' (Aoyagi 2009). The opinion that the logic in the McLean judgment can no longer be the mainstream theory is perhaps part of this way of thinking. Certainly, when a previously rejected right is given recognition by the court, it appears as if foreigners' rights have been broadened. However, as cases involving foreign nationals are deliberated on a case-by-case basis, a newly given recognition in one case does not mean that it will be recognized in similar cases. In this sense, standards have not changed. This is clear from the Ministry of Justice's stated position that it is not bound by the guidelines pertaining to special permission to stay despite publishing them itself.

Foreigners' rights are different from Japanese nationals' rights. So, what are the rights of foreigners in Japan? In his essay on Japanese constitutional history, Katsutoshi Takami states:

> The Meiji Constitution [...] provides for various rights and freedoms [...] as seen in a catalogue of the human rights declarations in Western nations [...] such as "freedom of residence and movement" (Article 22), "the right of access to the court" (Article 24), "physical freedom" (Article 23), "secrecy of correspondence" (Article 26), "guarantee of ownership" (Article 27), "religious freedom" (Article 28), "freedoms of speech, the press and association" (Article 29), "the right of petition" (Article 30) and so on. However, <u>the constitution guaranteed them as the rights the emperor conferred upon his subjects as privileges, not as "inalienable fundamental human rights". It was therefore considered that constitutional rights could only be asserted if they did not contradict the status of the subject people.</u> (Takami 2006: 49–50; underline in original)

If we substitute 'the emperor' with 'the state' or 'the Japanese government', 'subjects' with 'resident foreign nationals', and 'the status of the subject people' with 'the status of their residence', the underlined passage then reads: 'the constitution guaranteed them as the rights the state or the Japanese government conferred upon its resident foreign nationals as privileges, not as "inalienable fundamental human rights". It was therefore considered that the constitutional rights could be only asserted if they did not contradict the status of their residence'. This corresponds to Annen's argument on foreigners' human rights. In other words, the foreigners' standing in Japan today comes very close to the status of subjects under the Constitution of the Empire of Japan.

Takami continues: 'The restricted nature of rights protection is expressed by the reservation clause in the law. In other words, constitutional rights were guaranteed only "within the scope of law" in principle. This meant that constitutional rights and freedoms could be restricted in any way as long as it was effected by law' (Takami 2006: 50). Takami's explanation of the nature of imperial subjects' rights perfectly captures the constitutional rights of foreigners in contemporary Japan. Foreigners' rights contain the remains of 'the logic of subjects' rights' and therefore are given limited protection. *As the people of postwar Japan transitioned from imperial subjects to Japanese citizens under the new constitution, resident foreign nationals were thrown into the preserve of the logic of imperial subjects as if to fill the void.*

Nevertheless, there are some signs of a breakthrough. The presence of the family is a major factor in determining whether or not to grant resident foreign nationals special permission to stay these days but this was not the case in the past. As far as precedents from the 1960s show, no consideration was given to the family circumstances of Korean residents in Japan, who were treated as Japanese until the San Francisco Peace Treaty came into operation on April 28, 1952 and subsequently became foreign nationality holders following the liberation and independence of Japanese-occupied territories (Zainichi Chōsenjin no jinken wo mamoru kai 1968).

The situation has changed since then. Today, special permission to stay is granted in a large number of cases albeit by case-by-case assessment, and many cases are brought to court. The immigration authority has published guidelines despite claiming that it is not bound by them in implementing immigration administration. Administration is carried out in line with a certain policy direction. It is abundantly clear that the immigration authority considers the presence of the family as an important factor because the list on the Ministry of Justice website showing examples in which special permission to stay has been granted does not include any cases that involve a single person.

This consideration was further expanded in hate rally regulations. While 'the dignity of persons with countries of origin other than Japan' is not mentioned in the text of the Anti-Hate Speech Act, that expression as well as 'the dignity of foreigners' was used numerous times in debates on legislation in the National Diet. All of the past cases brought to court by foreigners were about the treatment of individual foreign nationals. However, the hate rally injunction case in Kawasaki was about the act of defamation and abuse targeting Zainichi Koreans in general or the local community of Sakuramoto rather than a particular individual.

The opening passage in the preamble of the Anti-Hate Speech Act states:

> In recent years in Japan, unfair discriminatory speech and behavior has been used to incite the exclusion of persons with countries of origin other than Japan, or their descendants, who are legally residing in Japan, from local communities, on the grounds that they are from countries or regions outside of Japan. This has caused great suffering to persons of the [sic] origin or their descendants and serious rifts in the local communities. (Japanese Law Translation Database System [Ministry of Justice], https://www.japaneselawtranslation.go.jp/ja/laws/view/4081/je)

It recognizes that not only the targeted individuals but also the community in which they live suffer as victims. As mentioned earlier, however, the Anti-Hate Speech Act's deterrent element was questioned because the law contained no specific provision to prohibit hate speech and behavior.

Then, the Yokohama District Court Kawasaki Branch ruled that the right of resident foreign nationals to live peacefully in the local community was protected by Article 13 of the Constitution on the basis of the Social Welfare Act. This was an unthinkable development given that the Japanese courts had been deploying Annen's foreigners' human rights argument as soon as foreigners asserted their right to pursue happiness under Article 13 of the Constitution and claiming that foreigners were not in a position to demand constitutional rights.[15]

Why was the Yokohama District Court Kawasaki Branch able to invoke the Constitution in making that decision and why was the Ministry of Justice Human Rights Bureau able to issue an advice following the court ruling? A first-generation Zainichi woman and a third-generation Zainichi woman and her spouse individually lodged complaints for human rights violations. They raised the issue of their right to protect their personal lives as well as the lives of their families, including a child with dual citizenship. In the application for a temporary injunction prohibiting a hate speech rally that followed, a social welfare corporation operated jointly by Japanese and resident foreigners complained that the hate speech rally would impede the delivery of service to members of the local community. The right to live peacefully, which was recognized on the basis of Article 13 of the Constitution in the injunction case, covers not only families or organizations consisting of foreign nationals but also local communities consisting of both foreign and Japanese residents. In this sense, the court ruling protected 'the dignity of foreigners' and 'peaceful community life' according to the legislative purpose of the Anti-Hate Speech Act (Tanno 2020b). Resident foreign nationals as individuals may remain in the category of imperial 'subjects' but now their rights are institutionally guaranteed in cases where they are members of a family or community.

## Conclusion: The future of the remnants of the Empire of Japan (i.e., resident foreigners)

The study of legal precedents is carried out on the assumption that the rights won in past court cases would be applicable to other people in the same society and hence any progress made with regard to the social issue in question is expected to be seen as the minimum standard accepted by the state. For example, when litigation over the minimum standards of livelihood protection (the so-called Asahi case) was fought as the question of 'the right to maintain wholesome and cultured living', the outcome had influence on a broader societal level beyond individual court cases. Setting a precedent by bringing an issue to the court has society-wide implications. However, this does not apply to foreigners' issues. In fact, unsuccessful lawsuits can reveal the administrative agency's understanding of the exercise of its authority against foreigners as well as the court's perception of the way the administrative agency uses its authority with respect to foreigners' human rights. In a way, close scrutiny of unsuccessful cases can uncover the state's logic of control over minorities better than successful cases can.

A case in point is that of the LGBT foreigner discussed in chapters 3 and 4. The very thing that stopped the state from finding grounds for granting her permission to stay in Japan reveals the problem facing foreigners and sexual minority people in Japan. This way of approaching an issue is not exceptional in the study of foreigners and has been used in discussions about Zainichi Koreans' human rights and social security.[16]

The necessity of this approach in researching how the state exercises its power over resident foreign nationals is associated with the fact that foreigners' legal status in Japanese society is no different from that of 'subjects' under the Constitution of the Empire of Japan. Even under the Postwar Constitution, Japan recognizes foreigners' 'personal rights' only as 'privileges' as if to force them to remain in the space left behind by the Imperial Constitution. This situation has been allowed to persist under the Postwar Constitution. Why has no one called this into question?

Drawing on Waldron's argument, Tsunemasa Arikawa states:

> A society respectful of "human rights", an "equitable" society, means a society in which all members are supposed to be treated with "dignity". Because the concept of "dignity" is inseparably tied to "high rank" and "public office" in the first place, there is an understanding that it is more appropriate to describe a society treating all its members with "dignity" as a society in which "high rank" has been universalized, i.e., a society in which all its members have acquired "high rank", rather than a society in which a status system has been abolished.[17] (Arikawa 2016: 5–6)

In the light of Arikawa's argument, and given that 'the dignity of individuals' under the current constitution plays a major role in the transition from subjects to citizens, the main question in the foreigners' human rights issue is whether or not 'the dignity of foreigners' exists in Japan. When I state that 'foreigners do not have human rights', I mean that the Constitution provides for 'foreigners' human rights' but not 'the dignity of foreigners'.[18]

The special permission to stay system was essentially a form of alternative justice for the immigration law under the Postwar Constitution. Despite the enforcement of a deportation order, the Minister of Justice and the directors of regional immigration bureaus with delegated authority can suspend the administration of law when they discover grounds for conferring a 'favor' and issue special permission to stay followed by the granting of new residence status. Because of this structure, deportation is the only option for individual foreigners, but special permission to stay is granted if the immigration authority decides that a particular foreigner's continued presence in Japan is preferrable from the viewpoint of their social relationships as a whole. As we have seen, the foreigner's chance of receiving special permission to stay largely depends on their ability to gather a large amount of supporting evidence, and the scope of admissible supporting evidence has changed over time. The current scope appears to be 'the legal family and its social relations'. When the foreigner's removal from Japan (i.e., social death) is expected to cause a considerable loss to people within the scope of 'the legal family and its social relations', a decision is made from the viewpoint of their social existence rather than as an individual matter. Alternative justice is served by shifting the plane of reasoning behind decision-making.

The same logic was at work when the dignity of foreigners was raised under the Anti-Hate Speech Act. To prevent a rift in a family or community containing non-Japanese members, it recognizes the dignity of foreigners as people living in the local community. In my view, this thinking (i.e., something that is not recognized for an individual can be recognized for a group/community to which the individual belongs by shifting the plane of reasoning from the individual to the group/community) echoes the approach used for the special permission to stay mechanism.

Based on his experience as a judge, Tokiyasu Fujita discusses a change of precedents by the Supreme Court from the perspective of change in the 'court judge's view'.

> The Supreme Court justices draw a line ultimately by reference to their own "good sense" as Supreme Court justices and in each age each justice found a standpoint that she/he considered fair and impartial (at least subjectively). [...] The "judge's view" here refers to things like which way they direct their gaze, what to look at, how deep they look and so on in the said act of line-drawing in a trial. In other words, it is a question of what and how to examine and what and how to assess, and in the case of administrative disposition by an administrative agency,

for instance, it can be regarded as an intellectual activity for so-called "control and review of the decision-making process" (which is familiar to administrative law scholars). (Fujita 2016: 111–112)

When the 'judge's view' changes, something that was constitutional at the time of legislation or for a long time after that can be ruled no longer constitutional.

The McLean judgment has not been replaced as a precedent, so the judge's view on 'foreigners' human rights' has not changed since October 4, 1978. Nevertheless, 'foreigners' dignity' has now been injected from another direction into the issue of foreigners' human rights under the Immigration Act, into which the addition of the human rights concept was said to punch a hole in the logic. Once a person's 'dignity' has been recognized, continuing to deny that person basic human rights may be possible for a short time but, in my opinion, is impossible in the long run. Society's view has changed.

When the hate speech rally was banned, Choe Gangija, one of the parties who lodged human rights violation complaints, commented, 'We have come to be protected by this law'. Now the national and municipal governments have the responsibility to protect residents with foreign nationalities so that they can live in the community with dignity. They still cannot demand their constitutional rights as individuals but they are able to access human rights in another way. Things can change. It has been shown that there is light at the end of the tunnel for people struggling for freedom.

# Notes

1 This view can also be found in a court judge's criticism of scholars who have studied law solely in an academic setting. Tokiyasu Fujita, who made the transition from law professor at Tohoku University to Supreme Court judge, argued: 'To legal interpretation scholars, what the Constitution says is the most important question, which serves as the fundamental starting point for legal interpretation from which all forms of law (acts of the state) are supposed to derive' but 'on the other hand, the fundamental task above all others for a judge is to decide which of the parties in an actual dispute before court wins, and to do so as promptly as possible. The primary criterion for decision-making is whether it is a "fair resolution of conflict", so to speak' (Fujita 2012: 136).

2 If the applicant commits a violation of law, however minor, between the stay of execution and the issuance of special permission to stay, the stay of execution is cancelled immediately and the applicant is deported.

3 This incident has been covered in press reports such as 'Hiroshima joji satsugai jiken, Perūjin taiho! "Akuma ga yatta"' (The Hiroshima girl murder case, a Peruvian arrested, claims 'The devil did it') by Masao Awano and Shōko Okuda (*Yomiuri Weekly*, December 18, 2005) and others. Early reports speculated that the crime had been committed by a fake Nikkei person because the perpetrator had used a forged passport to enter Japan. These reports were later found to be incorrect and it was established that he was a real Nikkei person who had used the forged passport in order to hide his criminal history in Peru.

4 For foreigners to conduct religious activities occupationally, they must obtain 'religious activities' residence status (a so-called missionary visa), meaning that they must obtain permission from the Japanese government if they wish to practice religion as an occupation beyond their private faith. Moreover, this 'religious activities' residence status is applicable to foreign nationals dispatched by foreign religious organizations to Japan-based entities and therefore individual religious practitioners who wish to establish a religious organization in Japan fall outside the scope of its applicability.

5 *Saikō saibansho minji hanreishū*, vol. 25, no. 7: 1037–1068.

6 *Gyōsei jiken saiban hanreishū*, vol. 18, no. 12: 1713–3194.

7 *Shōmu geppō*, vol. 14, no. 3: 300–311.

8 *Shōmu geppō*, vol. 16, no. 4: 404–409.

9 *Saikō saibansho minji hanreishū*, vol. 22, no. 13: 3147–1068. The meaning stays the same when 'directives' is substituted with 'notices'. Nevertheless, Hiroshi Shiono indicates that this judgment has not become a doctrine by stating, 'A directive as an interpretive criterion binds subordinate administrative agencies.

However, its effect is limited to that extent, and it is not used by the court as a standard in relation to the people. In this sense, it does not have an external effect' (Shiono 2005: 94).

10 *Saikō saibansho minji hanreishū*, vol. 12, no. 4: 624–648.
11 *Saikō saibansho minji hanreishū*, vol. 46, no. 7: 1174–2579.
12 *Hanrei jihō*, 1771: 76–83.
13 Shortly after the Tokyo District Court ruled that the act was unconstitutional in the first trial, I had a chance to celebrate the win with the case's lead attorney Gen'ichi Yamaguchi, administrative specialist Madoka Majima of the secretariat, and attorney Emiko Miki in Yokohama. Yamaguchi said, 'I didn't understand why they would not grant special permission to stay because matters in this case were within the scope indicated by the Immigration Bureau notices in the first place. So, I had no choice but to take it to court. I realized on the way that we could fight over the Nationality Act as well and we decided to do it. When it became clear that the immigration side might lose, they approached us with an overture to the effect that they would grant special permission to stay if we dropped the case'.
14 Two attorneys (Gen'ichi Yamaguchi and Yuki Maruyama) and staff at ALT Law Firm where I conducted my case research continued: 'The situation was better in the 1990s. In the 2000s, it looked as if much progress had been made, on the surface, with directives, notices, releasing case summaries on the immigration bureau's website etc., but it actually got harder to predict what the court would decide. I believe we have more wins than losses, but it is more difficult to predict the outcomes of individual cases. Results were more predictable before (until the end of the 1990s)' (interviewed on April 17, 2017).
15 Emiko Miki, the leading attorney for the Sakuramoto hate rally injunction application, once told me, 'Mr. Tanno, I became so emotional that I made a slip of the pen in that instance. We wouldn't normally raise Article 13, you know. Actually, I thought "Oh dear" after raising it'.
16 This type of study has been reported in Zainichi Chōsenjin no jinken wo mamoru kai (1968), Yoshioka (ed.) (1978) and Yoshioka (ed.) (1980), among others.
17 See Waldron (2012b) for the relationship between rank and dignity.
18 Arikawa argues: 'Assuming Waldron's understanding that "dignity" has not completely lost its association with "high rank" or "public office" to date, if the overthrowing of the traditional status system takes the form of the abolition of "rank" itself in law, then it is easy to imagine that such law will not directly culminate in protection of the "dignity" of the "ordinary people" subjected to it' (Arikawa 2016: 18) and 'Waldron mentions, for example, guaranteeing

access to a hearing before a court. While the process involving the submission of evidence and presentation of arguments by the opposing parties before the court is able to rule on a disputed right indicating that the contemporary court system is a dispute resolution method built on respect for both parties, this is not a mechanism protecting the parties to the dispute merely as people in need of protection. Law respects each party as an entity who is capable of defending (assertions of) themself and in doing so respects "the dignity of the person subjected to law"' (Arikawa 2016: 18–19). The first comment points to the need to think about the relationship between the question of whether foreigners can become public officials in Japan and the question of whether foreigners are treated as individuals with 'dignity' under Japanese law. The second comment is helpful in understanding why courts do not get involved in deportation procedures and why the adversarial model is thought to be unnecessary for deportation procedures.

# Re-examining 'Foreigners' Human Rights': Approaching 'Long-Term Residence' from the Historical Sociology of Residence Status

## Introduction

This chapter is based on the written opinion I submitted to the Tokyo District Court Second Civil Division. In my view, it is possible to relativize the McLean judgment, a precedent limiting the human rights of foreigners, by examining the 'long-term residence' status from a historical sociological perspective. The LGBT foreigner case involving the issuance of a deportation order is used as a concrete example, in which same-sex marriage to a Japanese partner becomes another point of contention. The question of the legalization of same-sex marriage aside, there still remains the possibility of giving appropriate protection to mixed-nationality families, including those involving same-sex marriage. Based on this idea, the following written opinion addresses the overstepping or abuse of the scope of discretion of the Minister of Justice and others in decision-making regarding special permission to stay.

## Residence of foreigners in prewar Japan

At the beginning of the Meiji era, what we now call 'citizens' rights' had not yet been established. In 1869, lands and people were taken from feudal lords and returned to the emperor and feudal domains were replaced by prefectures. The Family Register Law of 1871 created the first residence-based unified household register that replaced the social status-based register.[1] As shown by the abolition of hereditary stipends in 1876, however, the status hierarchy was still taken for granted in society.

How were foreigners treated at that time? The Meiji government inherited the Ansei Five-Power Treaties, the first of which was the Treaty of Amity and Commerce between the US and Japan signed by the Tokugawa shogunate in 1858. Treaty ports became enclaves for foreign residents, who were permitted to stay as long as they were engaged in commerce with no restriction on change of occupation. While Japanese people were still subjected to a social status system, foreigners were entitled to freedom of occupational mobility.

In 1894, the Meiji government successfully negotiated the signing of revised treaties, which superseded the unequal treaties from 1900. Article 1 of the revised treaty with the US stated as follows: 'The said subjects may freely and easily take their cases to court for the expansion or defense of their rights, and in doing so they are entitled to select and use an advocate, defense counsel or proxy as are Japanese nationals and enjoy the same rights and privileges as those enjoyed by Japanese nationals in relation to all matters concerning dealings with the judiciary in addition to the foregoing'.

Given this history, it was no wonder that Article 3-2 of the Civil Code as a general law, which came into operation when the Act for Enforcement of the Civil Code (Act No. 11 of 1898) was promulgated, stated that 'Foreigners enjoy private rights except when prohibited by a law, regulation or treaty'. The Civil Code was promulgated during the period between the revision of the unequal treaties in 1894 and the enforcement of the revised treaties in 1900.

Restrictions on foreigners' freedom to choose their occupation already existed before the promulgation of the Civil Code. The Regulation of National Banks (Grand Council of State Proclamation No. 106 of 1876) prohibited foreigners from setting up a national bank. The Press Regulations (Imperial Decree No. 75 of 1887) barred foreigners from becoming newspaper publishers or editors. The Mining Regulations (Act No. 87 of 1890) prohibited foreigners from operating a mining business or becoming mining union members or mining company shareholders. The Attorney Act (Act No. 7 of 1893) rendered foreigners ineligible to become attorneys while the Ship Act (Act No. 46 of 1899) barred foreigners from becoming marine pilots. The occupations closed to foreigners were defined in the manner of a negative list.

Once consular jurisdiction was abolished after the promulgation of the Meiji Civil Code, foreigners began living outside of designated enclaves and this necessitated the creation of a legal system to place generalized restrictions on foreigners. Typical examples include Home Affairs Ministry Ordinance No. 32 of July 8, 1899, on 'lodging notification and other matters' and Imperial Decree No. 352 of July 17, 1899, on 'matters concerning the residence and commercial activity of foreigners who have no freedom of residence under a treaty or convention'. The former introduced the residence registration requirement for foreigners in general while the latter imposed restrictions on foreign general workers regarding their residence and employment.[2]

A generalized control of foreigners' entry began with the enactment of Home Affairs Ministry Ordinance No. 1 promulgated on January 24, 1918, on 'matters concerning foreigners' entry'.[3] The focus of control at the time was on the period of stay. Article 4 gave prefectural governors the power to deport or refuse entry of foreigners by providing that 'a person who is found to have violated the provision of the preceding article, or used a passport or nationality certificate in another person's name, or obtained a visa on a passport or nationality certificate in a fallacious way, may be barred from entering or expelled from the imperial territory by order of the prefectural governor'. This was because the system looked at foreigners in terms of their 'period of stay' rather than their 'residence status', based on their activities. The period-of-stay viewpoint leads to a mechanism of control in the place of residence whereas emphasis on residence status necessitates control at the time of entry. Consequently, prefectural governors were authorized to enforce denial of landing and deportation.

## Foreigners' residence under occupation and system change

The Office of the Supreme Commander for the Allied Powers (hereafter referred to as 'GHQ') took away border control powers from the Japanese imperial government and issued a memorandum entitled 'Entry and

Registration of Non-Japanese Nationals in Japan' (SCAPIN-852) on April 2, 1946.[4] Article 1 states: 'From time to time non-Japanese nationals, not part of the Occupation Forces, will be granted permission to enter Japan. These persons will reside in Japan on a semi-permanent basis. The absence of Japanese consuls abroad and the consequent impossibility of obtaining visas, necessitates the establishment of a procedure for legal entry and residence' (Saikō saibansho Jimu-sōkyoku Shōgai-ka 1950b: 362). Imperial Decree No. 207 for 'alien registration' was announced on May 2, 1947, based on this memorandum.

On February 25, 1947, prior to the promulgation of the alien registration decree, the General Headquarters Legal Section issued a memorandum titled 'Registration of Chinese Nationals' (SCAPIN-1543). Following the division of the Korean Peninsula, the General Headquarters Diplomatic Section issued a directive on the 'Use of name for Korea in forthcoming registration of aliens' to deal with former colonial residents (Saikō saibansho Jimu-sōkyoku Shōgai-ka 1950b: 363–366). This was because former colonial residents were the main target of the alien registration law.

In the early phase of occupation, the definition of 'alien' fluctuated. The GHQ memorandum titled 'Repatriation' (SCAPIN-927) issued on May 7, 1946, stated as follows: 'The provisions for repatriation of all other individual Japanese nationals and displaced persons in Japan formerly domiciled in China, Formosa, Korea, and the Ryukyus, insofar as these provisions are not covered by other directives of the Supreme Commander for the Allied Powers'. After paragraph two, 'Repatriation to Korea', paragraph three, 'Repatriation to Ryukyu' contained a directive for dealing with Okinawans, treating them as part of the former colonial population. Incidentally, the status of the Formosan people was complicated (Saikō saibansho Jimu-sōkyoku Shōgai-ka 1950a) because the government of the Republic of China (ROC) granted ROC nationality to the people of Taiwan province from October 25, 1945. Kenta Hiraga noted, 'As for criminal jurisdiction, Taiwanese people who received their registration certificates from the ROC mission in Japan were regarded as people from the Allied Powers over whom the Japanese courts had no jurisdiction. However, this restriction on criminal jurisdiction did not apply to Koreans' (Hiraga 1950: 164).

The GHQ gradually handed over border control powers to the Japanese government as the country moved closer to its return to international society. The GHQ issued a memorandum entitled 'Establishment of Immigration Service' (SCAPIN-2019) on June 22, 1949, stating as follows: 'The immigration officials will be under the direct supervision of the Commanding General, Eighth Army' and 'The Japanese Government will establish a central office of record for all clearances granted by the Supreme Commander for the Allied Powers to individuals entering or departing Japan, except occupation force personnel travelling under official orders'. Based on this directive, the Japanese government issued Cabinet Order No. 299 concerning immigration service on August 10, 1949 and established the immigration control department within the Ministry of Foreign Affairs Administration Bureau. The GHQ directed the Japanese government to correct weaknesses in its immigration control administration by stating in a memorandum titled 'Immigration' (SCAPIN-2122) on September 15, 1950, 'The Supreme Commander for the Allied Powers in letter referenced in paragraph 1d called attention to certain weaknesses in governmental structure with respect to the control of unlawful immigration activities and enumerated certain measures to be taken to correct these weaknesses'. In response, the Japanese government promulgated Cabinet Order No. 295 for the 'Establishment of the immigration control agency' on September 30, 1950, to take over the process for controlling entry, departure and residency of foreign nationals other than occupation force personnel.

Prior to the memorandum on immigration, however, the GHQ specified certain entry application procedures in Circular No. 3 on 'Control of entry and exit of individuals, cargo, aircraft, and surface vessels into and from Japan' (GHQ/SCAP-3) on February 3, 1950. It categorized foreigners according to their period of stay.

1  Intransit—authorizes individual to remain in Japan for a specified period of stay not to exceed 15 days.

2  Tourist—authorizes individual to remain in Japan for not to exceed 90 days.

3   Temporary visitor—authorizes individual to remain in Japan for a period of stay not to exceed 180 days.

4   Semipermanent resident—authorizes individual to remain in Japan for an indefinite period.

5   Permanent resident—authorizes individual to remain in Japan for permanent residence.

6   Occupation force personnel—indefinite unless otherwise specified. (Saikō saibansho Jimu-sōkyoku Shōgai-ka 1950b: 421)

There was a major change in the nature of deportation orders during this period. In the Alien Registration Decree of May 2, 1947, Article 13 provides that 'the prefectural governor may order the deportation of a foreign national falling under one of the following items out of Japan' and Article 14 provides that 'a foreign national falling under one of the following items may be deported as provided for by the Minister of Home Affairs'. The prefectural governor was responsible for issuing deportation orders under Article 13 and the Minister of Home Affairs enforced them under Article 14. In the revision by Cabinet Order No. 381 of 1949, the deportation rules were merged into Article 16, stating that 'a foreign national who falls under one of the following items may be deported from Japan as provided for by the Attorney General'. This change has been regarded as a shift from 'the compulsory-execution-type expulsion of foreigners practiced in Europe' to the 'immediate execution' type in American law (Hatano, Kurashima, Tanaka, Shigemi and Ishizaki 2000: 90).[5]

The Japanese government subsequently promulgated Cabinet Order No. 319, 'Immigration Control Order', on October 4, 1951, of which Article 4 provided that 'A foreign national is permitted to land in Japan only when possessing a status of residence under one of the following items unless otherwise provided for by this order', marking a transition to the residence status system. The Immigration Control Order was revised by the Act on Measures for Ministry of Foreign Affairs Orders Issued pursuant to the 'Imperial Ordinance on Orders Issued Incidental to Acceptance of the Potsdam Declaration' (Act No. 126 of April 28, 1952). It included the following revisions: 'Article 2 (ii) the term "foreign national" means a person who does not have Japanese nationality' and the addition of the article '(Acquisition of Status of Residence)' after Article 22 in Chapter IV, Section 1. The categorization of foreign nationals' residence was changed from the European-type based on the period of residence to the US-type based on the purpose of residence upon entry into the country.

## 'Long-term residence' status

Hidenori Sakanaka and Toshio Saitō describe the lack of article-by-article commentaries on the Immigration Act as follows: 'No manual with article-by-article commentaries has been published so far. The likely reasons include the specific nature of the law mainly targeting foreigners, a paucity of materials relating to legislation due to its enactment as a Potsdam Order, and a lack understanding of the US immigration law on which the act was based' (Sakanaka and Saitō 2007: vi). However, they do not clarify which part of the act derives from the US law.

Regarding the addition to the Nationality Act of Article 4 (vi), which mandates 'on or after the date on which the Constitution of Japan comes into effect, not having planned or advocated the destruction of the Constitution of Japan or the government established thereunder with force, and not having formed or joined a political party or other organization planning or advocating the same' as a condition for naturalization of a foreign national, Kenta Hiraga, the author of the postwar Nationality Act, explains as follows: 'This condition did not exist in the old nationality act and has been added to the new act; the wording followed the example of Article 38 (v) of the National Public Service Act but the concept is modeled on Article 205 of the US Nationality Act of 1940' (Hiraga 1951: 307). On the other hand, Article 5 (xi) of the Immigration Control Order provides for 'a person who schemes or advocates the overthrow of the Constitution of Japan or the government formed thereunder by means of force or violence, or who organizes or is a member of a political party or any organization which schemes or advocates the same'. The provision's intent is the same as that of Article 4 (vi) of the Nationality Act.

Chapter 8

Article 4-1 of the Immigration Control Order set out sixteen residence statuses. Statuses in items 14, 15 and 16 did not relate to any activity. Status 4-1-14 was 'a person intending to reside in Japan permanently', 4-1-15 was 'the spouse of a person falling under one of the items from 5 to 13 and the person's child who is a minor and unmarried', and 4-1-16 was 'a person particularly specified by an ordinance of the Ministry of Foreign Affairs, except those falling under any of the foregoing items'. These items, represented by respective article-item numbers under the old system, remained until the 1989 revision and were replaced with 'permanent resident' (former 4-1-14), 'dependent' (former 4-1-15), 'spouse or child of Japanese national' (former 4-1-16-1) and 'designated activities' (former 4-1-16-3) under the new system.

Article 2-6 of Act No. 126 of April 28, 1952, mentioned in the previous section, was provided for in the Immigration Control Order as Status 4-1-16-2: 'A person who has lost Japanese nationality pursuant to the provisions of the Treaty of Peace with Japan, on the date on which that treaty came into effect, and has been residing in Japan continuously since before September 2, 1945 (including those who were born in Japan in a period from September 3, 1945 to the date on which this law first took effect) may continue to reside in Japan without a residence status until such time as the person's residence status and period of residence are provided for separately by law'.[6] In the 1989 revision of the Immigration Control Act, 4-1-16-2 was replaced by 'the children of those who have lost Japanese nationality pursuant to the peace treaty with Japan'.

The 1989 revision of the Immigration Control Act also instituted ten new residence statuses and listed all residence statuses in Appended Table I according to 'designated activities' and Appended Table II according to 'personal status or position for which residence is authorized'.[7] The new resident statuses in Table I were 'those which had been dealt with by the flexible application of the residence status of "a person whose residence is specifically requested by the Minister of Justice" in order to resolve their previous entry issues' and the new statuses in Table II were set out based on the same logic. Therefore, 'the resident statuses of "designated activities" (activities that are specifically designated by the Minister of Justice for foreign nationals) and "long-term resident" (those who are authorized to reside in Japan with a period of stay designated by the Minister of Justice in consideration of special circumstances) are granted to people who are authorized for specific activities or positions designated by the Minister of Justice in a public notice' (Sakanaka and Takaya 1991: 12).

Incidentally, the Immigration and Nationality Act of the US provides for two residency categories: immigrant visas for people wishing to live in the US permanently and non-immigrant visas for those who wish to stay in the US for specific activities such as work and study.[8] *The US categorization is essentially identical to the Japanese categorization used for appended tables I and II and, given that the US law is the parental law of the Japanese immigration law, the immigrant visas category of the US law corresponds to Appended Table II under which the plaintiff's residence status of 'long-term resident' was newly established.*

## Special permission to stay and family

The family always received consideration in the process of transition to the residence status system. Attorney-General's Office Prosecution Administration Bureau Notice No. 24448 of July 31, 1950, on 'Revision of the Alien Registration Order and its Enforcement Regulations' indicated the policy direction for deportation by stating the following:

> Pursuant to Supplementary Provision Paragraph 3 of the Emergency Measures Order pertaining to the Restriction on Travel by Persons Who Have Their Registered Domicile in the Nansei Shotō below the 30th Parallel North (Cabinet Order No. 227, 1950), which was promulgated and took effect on July 11 this year, the Alien Registration Order was partially revised, and the Alien Registration Law Enforcement Regulations was also partially revised as Appended Sheet 1 (Legal Affairs Office Order No. 83 of 1950) on 21 July and took effect on the same day. The purpose of this round of revisions was to eliminate uncertainties by clearly setting forth in the said order matters relating to the procedures to deport foreigners from Japan previously envisaged in the Alien Registration Order Enforcement Regulations and to make

relevant procedural modifications. (Saikō saibansho Jimu-sōkyoku Shōgai-ka 1950b: 270)

The notice included the following instructions.

1 When requesting the prefectural governor to issue a deportation order against a person falling under one of the items from 2 to 4 of Article 16 of the Alien Registration Order, the public prosecutor must include the following additional information: (1) date of entry (in particular, any suspicion of illegal entry); (2) the person's character and personal history (in particular, history while residing in Japan); (3) family relations (in particular, any risk of the person's deportation destroying the family); (4) past convictions and other crimes (and summary of facts of each crime, where possible); (5) guarantors; and (6) other positive and negative grounds for making a deportation decision.

2 Where it is considered appropriate to allow a person who committed a crime specified in Article 12 of the Alien Registration Order to stay in Japan with the special approval of the Supreme Commander of the Allied Powers, the public prosecutor is advised to collect a petition for special approval to stay (or a similar document; the same applies hereinafter) from the person to be deported (hereafter called the deportee) or a concerned party if possible, to conduct an investigation of the case, in particular about the circumstances relating to the aforementioned items from (2) to (6), by liaising closely with the police and other authorities, irrespective of whether the deportation order has been issued or not, then to submit the outcome of the investigation and the public prosecutor's opinion together with the aforementioned petition to the prefectural governor. The public prosecutor is instructed to request a deportation order nevertheless even in this case. In cases other than the above, the aforementioned procedures must be followed when the deportee or a concerned party presents a petition. (Saikō saibansho Jimu-sōkyoku Shōgai-ka 1950b: 270–271)

The Alien Registration Order performed the role of the immigration law until the Immigration Control Order came into effect. *Attorney-General's Office Prosecution Administration Bureau Notice No. 24448 of July 31, 1950, on 'Revision of the Alien Registration Order and Its Enforcement Regulations'* was a prototype of today's special permission to stay. *The decision-making process involving an investigation of circumstances relating to items from '(2) the person's character and personal history' to '(6) other positive and negative grounds for making a deportation decision' together with the person's petition is particularly noteworthy. Further, the order requires the public prosecutor to investigate '(3) family relations (in particular, any risk of the person's deportation destroying the family)' specifically to find out the impact of a person's deportation on the family left behind in Japan. It indicates that the effect of the person's removal from Japan on the people left behind has been an important factor in granting special permission to stay from the start.* The level of 'assimilation into Japanese society' gauged by these specific indicators was used as a measure of assimilation (or incorporation) into Japan through the family.

Article 2-6 of Act No. 126 of April 28, 1952, was repealed when the Special Act on the Immigration Control of, inter alia, those who have lost Japanese nationality pursuant to the Treaty of Peace with Japan (Act No. 71 of May 10, 1991) (hereafter referred to as 'the Special Act on Immigration Control') came into operation. Article 22 of the Special Act on Immigration Control provides that 'Insofar as a special permanent resident is concerned, a deportation pursuant to the provisions of Article 24 of the Immigration Control Act may be carried out only if one of the following items applies to that person'. The items include: (1) a person who was sentenced to imprisonment without work or a heavier punishment without a suspension of sentence; (2) a person who was sentenced to imprisonment without work or a heavier punishment, for an offence against the head of state or a diplomatic mission, and whose criminal act was determined as having significantly harmed the interests of Japan; or (3) a person who was sentenced to imprisonment for more than seven years or for life, and whose criminal act was determined as having significantly harmed the interests of Japan. In short, special permanent residents are not deported for a minor crime.

When the Immigration Act was revised in 1989, the aforementioned Article 22 was modified as follows:

Article 22(1) Any alien who wishes to change his/her status of residence to that of "Permanent Resident" shall apply to the Minister of Justice for permission for permanent residence in accordance with the procedures provided for by a Ministry of Justice ordinance. Article 22(2) [...]. However, the following items do not have to be conformed to in cases of the spouse and children of Japanese nationals, of residents with permanent residence status or the spouse and children of a person who resides in Japan pursuant to the provisions of Article 2-6 of the Act on Measures for Ministry of Foreign Affairs Orders Issued pursuant to the Imperial Ordinance on Orders Issued Incidental to Acceptance of the Potsdam Declaration (Act No. 126 of April 28, 1952).

(i) The alien's behavior and conduct must be good.

(ii) The alien must have sufficient assets or skills to make an independent living.

Under the provisions, the Minister of Justice may grant permanent resident status to a foreign national who is the spouse or child of a Japanese national or a permanent resident irrespective of the person's conduct or assets or ability to make a living. According to a former official involved in immigration affairs at the Ministry of Justice, 'Its intent was to give consideration to complementing special measures for the residence permit as the ministerial act for those who fall under Article 2-6 of Act 126 and certain descendants of theirs in the aforementioned supplementary provisions and to incorporate a new way of thinking for facilitating a stable residency as a family unit for Japanese and permanent residents whose life is based in Japan' (Hatano, Kurashima, Tanaka, Shigemi and Ishizaki 2000: 154).

Article 22 of the revised Immigration Act of 1989 was all about the residence statuses listed in Appended Table II. *The residence statuses in Table II 'incorporate a new way of thinking for facilitating a stable residency as a family unit' while trying to balance the people who were subsequently dealt with in the Special Act on Immigration Control. 'The spouse and children of a Japanese national' and 'permanent resident' were the direct results of that thinking and 'the spouse and children of a permanent resident' and 'long-term resident' were also created based on the same thinking.*

The practical operation of the 'long-term resident' status was provided for by Ministry of Justice Public Notice No. 132 issued on May 24, 1990: 'The establishment of status listed in the right-hand column of the section on Long-Term Residents in Appended Table II of the Immigration Control and Refugee Recognition Act, as stipulated in Article 7, Paragraph 1, Item 2 of the same Act' (hereafter called Long-Term Resident Notice). 'Children of children' of a Japanese national and 'children of a Japanese national with dual citizenship' (third-generation Japanese descendants) were provided for in Long-Term Resident Notice No. 3, dual-citizen 'children of children' of a Japanese national in Long-Term Resident Notice No. 4, the spouse of a third-generation Japanese descendant under Notice No. 3 in Long-Term Resident Notice No. 5, and 'unmarried minor dependent children' of children of a third-generation Japanese descendant under Notice No. 3 (fourth-generation Japanese descendants) in Long-Term Resident Notice No. 6. These people were made eligible for the 'long-term resident' status by submitting the required documents to the authority.

Following the abduction and murder of a Japanese girl by a Nikkei man in 2005, the Long-Term Resident Notice was revised on March 29, 2006, with the addition of the 'good conduct and behavior' requirement, which took effect one month later. Good conduct was not a requirement for long-term residence status for sixteen years from 1990. This was because the status was created for the purpose of facilitating people's stable residence as a family unit which was completely different from that of pre-existing resident statuses.

## 'Long-term resident' status and family

Long-Term Resident Notice nos. 3–6 for Japanese descendants were designed to allow a third-generation Japanese descendant and their spouse and children to reside in Japan with the same residence status while providing separate definitions for them. *By design, the system treats family members under the same category because they reside in Japan as a family.*

Long-term residence status is granted to 'those who are authorized to reside in Japan for a period of stay designated by the Minister of Justice in consideration of special circumstances' on a case-by-case basis. It is not the case that all 'long-term residents' are assumed to live with their family. Only the 'activities specified through public notice' allow decision-making according to set patterns. People who plan to live with their family are those who are dealt with through the long-term resident notice. In 1990, Vietnamese refugee families were dealt with in Long-Term Resident Notice nos. 1 and 2, Japanese descendants in nos. 3–6, and unmarried minor dependent adopted children irrespective of descent in no. 7. In addition to Japanese descendants, the current Long-Term Resident Notice (as of April 2022) covers Vietnamese refugees, Myanmar refugees in Thailand and the Japanese wartime orphans left behind in China. *The Long-Term Resident Notice is a list of categories of people whom the Japanese government is committed to accept as a family unit from time to time.*

People with long-term residence status are eligible to receive public assistance, child support and other social security benefits. Regarding special permission to stay, Part III, 'Major issues and guidelines on the immigration control administration service', of the Basic Plan for Immigration Control (The 2$^{nd}$ Edition) states:

> Upon judging the grant of this special permit to stay, Minister of Justice shall consider various aspects in each case comprehensively, such as the reason of application for the special permit to stay, the foreigner's family condition, living condition, behavior and other circumstances, necessity of humanitarian consideration for the foreign national and influence to other illegal residents. The special permit is granted basically when the foreign national has a deep connection with the Japanese community and when there arises a serious problem especially from the humanitarian point of view, if the said foreigner is deported. [...] [A]s for an illegal resident who is recognized to have a civil status or position with a Japanese national, a permanent resident or a special permanent resident and has close connection with the Japanese community, appropriate measures shall continue to be taken in individual cases with humanitarian consideration.[9]

Article 24-4-2 of the Immigration Control Act stipulated grounds for the deportation of a person with a residence status listed in Appended Table

I who had been convicted of involvement in foreign crime syndicates. The 'action for the revocation of a deportation disposition' case (Tokyo District Court judgment of July 4, 2003) states: 'The provision of Article 24-4-2 of the Immigration Control Act [...] limits its application to residents with a residence status listed in the left-hand column of Appended Table I (so-called activity-based statuses); it is understood that this is because residents with residence statuses listed in the left-hand column of Appended Table II (so-called personal position-based statuses) have by their nature a deeper connection with Japanese society in comparison with those with activity-based statuses and hence it is not appropriate to subject them to a deportation disposition when they receive a suspended sentence'. Kazuteru Tagaya argues that this is because Appended Table II is regarded as a list of people whose deep connection with Japan should be protected in the actual practice of court trials (Tagaya 2016: 75).

In the 'action for the revocation of a disposition to deny change of residence status' case (Supreme Court First Petty Bench judgment of October 17, 2002), the court held that a foreign national was qualified to have the 'spouse of a Japanese national' residence status by stating as follows: 'It is the court's understanding that a foreign national intending to carry out activities according to the personal status of the spouse of a Japanese national may obtain the "spouse of a Japanese national" residence status because the said foreign national intends to engage in activities in Japan as a person in the special family relationship of a marriage with a Japanese national which is essentially a communal life sincerely committed by two persons of different sexes for the purpose of permanent mental and physical union' (*Saikō saibansho minji hanreishū*, vol. 56, no. 8: 1823–1902). In the 'action for the revocation of a deportation disposition' case (Tokyo District Court judgment of June 14, 2007; hereafter called 'the 2007 Tokyo District Court judgment'), the court held that a de facto relationship equivalent to a substantive and sincere marital relationship for three years and ten months deserved protection by referring to the aforementioned Supreme Court First Petty Bench judgment of 2002 and stating as follows: 'Despite the absence of a concrete agreement on when they would lodge a marriage notification, they were living a communal life equivalent to a marital relationship which is considered a de facto relationship. This court finds that the relationship was considerably stable as it continued for approximately three years and ten months until the plaintiff was arrested for the alleged immigration law violation'.

In the LGBT foreigner case at hand, C's sincere and substantive communal living with her Japanese partner was equivalent to a marital relationship as described in the 2007 Tokyo District Court judgment and continued for a longer period than three years and ten months. C deserved protection according to her long-term resident status as well as consideration for her substantive and sincere communal life with her Japanese partner.

## The McLean judgment and special permission to stay in the 2020s

Special permission to stay is granted at the discretion of the Minister of Justice. The McLean judgment initially drew attention to the ruling in the following manner:

> It should be understood that the guarantee of fundamental rights included in Chapter Three of the Constitution extends also to foreign nationals staying in Japan except for those rights, which by their nature, are understood to address Japanese nationals only. This applies to political activities, except for those activities which are considered to be inappropriate by taking into account the status of the person as a foreign national, such as activities that have influence on the political decision-making and its implementation in Japan. (*Saikō saibansho minji hanreishū*, vol. 32, no. 7: 1233)

More recently, however, emphasis has been placed on the following part: 'Guarantee of fundamental rights to foreign nationals by the Constitution should be understood to be granted only within the scope of such a system of the sojourn of foreign nationals and does not extend so far as to bind the exercise of discretionary power of the state'.

Moreover, the McLean judgment was handed down on October 4, 1978, before the international laws guaranteeing foreigners' social rights came into operation in Japan. The International Bill of Human Rights (the

International Covenant on Economic, Social and Cultural Rights is Treaty No. 6 of 1979 and the International Covenant on Civil and Political Rights is Treaty No. 7 of 1979) took effect on September 21, 1979; the Convention relating to the Status of Refugees on January 1, 1982; the Convention on the Elimination of all Forms of Discrimination Against Women on July 25, 1985; and the Convention on the Rights of the Child on May 22, 1994. The residence status of 'long-term resident' was developed in this international context. The plaintiff in the McLean case entered and conducted activities under Residence Status 4-1-16-3. While Residence Status 4-1-16 covered sub-categories involving family members (4-1-16-1 'the spouse and children of a Japanese national' and 4-1-16-2 'child of persons who have lost Japanese nationality under the Treaty of Peace with Japan'), 4-1-16-3 was for 'designated activities' and was considered the residual sub-category for all other types, although some residents with this status might live with their family. McLean fell under this residual sub-category.

After the revision of the Immigration Act in 1989, the number of special permissions to stay increased significantly and the decision-making authority was delegated from the Minister of Justice to the directors of regional immigration bureaus through circular notices. The role of administrative circular notices and special permissions to stay were debated in the 'action for the revocation of a deportation disposition' case (Tokyo District Court decision of December 27, 2001). The case has been described as '(1) an example in which execution based on a deportation order, including detention, was suspended' and '(2) an example in which it is highly likely that the issuance of a deportation order is illegal due to an abuse of discretionary authority or a violation of the proportionality principle despite the existence of grounds for deportation' (*Hanrei jihō* 177: 76–83).

This Tokyo District Court decision ruled that the execution of the deportation disposition was outside of the bounds of 'the Justice Minister's discretion' and noted as follows:

> [T]he issuance of a written deportation order by a supervising immigration inspector is prescribed as an administrative disposition to make the deportation order against the foreign national in question final and binding (Articles 47-4, 48-8 and 49-5 of the Act); in practice, discretion

under Article 24 of the Act, which is the substantive provision for deportation, is delegated to the supervising immigration inspector through the aforementioned procedural provisions for deportation and consequently the supervising immigration inspector may exercise this discretion in deciding whether or not to issue a deportation order (discretion as to effect) and, if issuing, when to issue it (discretion as to time), and therefore it is expected that the rule against violation of the proportionality principle also is passed on to the supervising immigration inspector.

The decision went as far as referring to the 'supervising immigration inspector's discretion'.

The presiding judge, Masayuki Fujiyama, used the notion of the 'supervising immigration inspector's discretion' in his ruling because by then the number of cases seeking special permission to stay had become constantly high. This was a recognition that, in the act of routine decision-making governed by administrative notices, the actual exercise of administrative discretion took place in the actions of the supervising immigration inspector. It is understandable that the judge made the seemingly unusual reference to the 'supervising immigration inspector's discretion' given the actual situation where regional immigration bureaus were taking on decision-making for increasing numbers of such cases.

The 'action for the revocation of a decision denying change of residence status' case (Nagoya District Court judgment of February 17, 2005) held as follows:

> A decision on whether or not to approve a foreign national's application for changing residence status, upon logical analysis, consists of two components—(1) determining whether the activities that the foreign national in question intends to conduct after the change of residence status fall under the category of residence status requested in the application (hereafter referred to as 'eligibility for residence status'), and (2) determining whether it is appropriate to allow the change of residence status in consideration of other circumstances—both of which need to be affirmed before a permission is granted, and, *as (1) is*

> *fundamentally a determination of facts, it is reasonable to find that the Justice Minister's broad discretionary power is applicable only to (2) in a strict sense* (except that the question of how the determined facts should be evaluated would be part of (2)). In determining the eligibility for residence status, *it is necessary to establish that the applicant has the true intent to conduct the activities falling under the residence status category related to the application on the basis of the applicant's past activities during the period of residence in addition to the planned activities under the new residence status described in the application form.* (*Hanrei taimuzu* 1209: 101–112; emphasis added)

It was the court's view that the scope of the Minister of Justice's discretion and of the directors of regional immigration bureaus' delegated discretion were also restricted in decision-making regarding change of residence status and that the verification of the applicant's activities was necessary.

Given these opinions and interpretations, the decision not to grant C a special permission to stay and the execution of her deportation order could not be satisfactorily explained by the mere case-by-case exercise of the discretion delegated by the Minister of Justice. Decisions made by directors of regional immigration bureaus and those made by the Minister of Justice are qualitatively different. This is evident from the fact that the Minister of Justice has not delegated authority to these directors on matters such as the recognition of refugees and the revocation of refugee status. Routinized decision-making under directives and notices requires observance of the principle of proportionality and a balance between the case at hand and other cases in which special permission to stay has been granted (the principle of equality).

As far as the treatment of foreign nationals who reside with their family and those who reside in Japan under resident status categories that assume residence as family members is concerned, it is unreasonable to claim that a special permission to stay could not be granted to C on the basis of the McLean judgment, a court precedent from a completely different era in terms of the social situation and the international environment presupposed by the legal and residence status systems.

Chapter 8

# A mandamus action for special permission to stay and the avoidance of deportation

C's case became a mandamus action for the revocation of a decision to deny special permission to stay because her petition for reconsideration on grounds of a change of circumstances subsequent to the issuance of a deportation order (i.e., stable cohabitation, providing mutual assistance and cooperating with a Japanese partner) was rejected.

C is transgender. Her relationship with a Japanese male partner with whom she was living, cooperating and providing mutual support was legally a same-sex marriage. Brazil, the country of her nationality, has legally recognized same-sex marriage but in a unique way: 'although Brazil steered itself in the direction of recognizing same-sex marriage prompted by two court rulings in 2011, it has not enacted a law recognizing same-sex marriage, at least to date' (Ōmura 2018: vi).

According to Daniel Machado, 'Brazil has become the only country in the world which gives same-sex couples the same level of legal protection as opposite-sex couples' (Machado 2018: 4). The reason for Brazil's recognition of same-sex marriage is explained as follows:

> In consideration of social conditions such as the presence of a large number of unmarried couples and a rising number of single-mother families, the 1988 Federal Constitution expanded the scope of "special protection by the state". A provision limiting the "family" under protection by the state to the family formed by a marriage was revised and elevated the "stable union between a man and a woman" (Article 226-3 of the Constitution) and the "single-parent family" (*familia monoparental*) (226-4) to the status of the "family entity" (*entidade familia*) eligible for "special protection by the state". What used to be called an extramarital relationship between a man and a woman (*concubinato*) was divided into two categories—"*concubinato puro*" with no bar to marriage eligible for protection under a judiciary-created doctrine and "*concubinato impuro*" with bar to marriage not eligible for protection—and Article 226-3 about "stable union between a man and a woman" was understood to offer protection only to the former. Subsequently, Law No. 1971 of 1994 changed the

term "*concubino(a)*" with a discriminatory connotation to "partner" (*companheiro*) and included provisions for the rights and duties of the *concubinato puro* spouse. In 1996, a law corresponding to Article 226-3 of the Constitution was finally enacted (Law No. 9278 of 1996) and "*concubinato puro*" itself came to be called "stable union" (*uniao estavel*) and a spouse in such a union "*convivente*" (cohabiting/domestic partner). It provided for "the rights and duties of the companions" (Article 2) and "the rights and duties related to property" (Article 3) in "a durable, public and continuous relationship between a man and a woman with the purpose of forming a family" (Article 1) as well as the procedures to have this relationship converted into a marriage (Article 8 and Federal Constitution Article 226-3) and the jurisdiction of the Family Court (*vara de familia*) and confidentiality (Article 9). This legislation explicitly strengthened legal protection for *concubinato puro*/stable union. The conventional "*concubinato* relationship" was institutionalized as a legal "de facto marriage" (*casamento de fato*) and positioned as a family relationship based on a marital relationship rather than a property relationship. (Machado 2018: 42–43)

Consequently, Brazil included the same-sex partner in the definition of partner, changed the concept of the family from the parent-child relationship formed by an opposite-sex couple protected by the marriage law to the stable union of a couple bonded by love (regardless of opposite-sex, same-sex, legal or de facto marriage) protected by the family law, and recognized that the family formed by a same-sex marriage deserved legal protection (Machado 2018: Chapter 3).

The Ministry of Justice Immigration Control Bureau issued a notice on 'residence status for same-sex spouse' (June 2017) and claimed to afford same-sex spouses a residence status on humanitarian grounds by announcing as follows: 'In light of the recent development of laws relating to same-sex marriage in other countries, the bureau has decided to make consideration for so-called same-sex couples who are legally married in their home countries from a humanitarian point of view so that they can lead a stable life in Japan just as they do in their countries, and hence our policy is to permit their entry and residence under the "designated activities" residence status'.[10]

A deportation disposition is an administrative penalty. Yet, a deportation order includes detention of a suspect.

> Detention may be meted out other than in criminal proceedings. The following situations are provided for by law: (1) the Immigration Control and Refugee Recognition Act, Article 39 (detention) and Article 43 (emergency detention); (2) the Narcotics and Psychotropics Control Act (forced hospitalization and isolation); (3) the Act on Mental Health and Welfare for the Mentally Disabled, Article 29 and 34 (forced hospitalization); (4) the Act on the Prevention of Infectious Diseases and Medical Care for Patients with Infectious Diseases, Article 7 and 8 (forced hospitalization and isolation); (5) the Venereal Disease Prevention Law, Article 15 (hospitalization order without penalty for noncompliance); (6) the Police Duties Execution Act, Article 3 (temporary protection of drunken or deranged persons). Although these are not criminal procedures, they should be subjected to the said article because detention has serious implications for the detainee's interest. The most important intent of Article 33 [of the Constitution of Japan] is that the lawfulness of detention is in principle determined by the court in advance. In the case of administrative proceedings, some situations may be unsuited for supervision by the court. Nonetheless, there is the need for a neutral adjudicating institution equivalent to the court. (Takahashi 2006: 403)

It is argued that 'As for the provision that "The written detention order set forth in the preceding paragraph shall be issued upon application by an immigration control officer or by a supervising immigration inspector of the office to which the former is attached" (Article 39-2), it is doubtful that the adjudicator can be regarded as neutral' (Takahashi 2006: 404).

In the 'appellate case in an action seeking the revocation of a detention disposition' (Tokyo High Court judgment of February 24, 1958), the fact that 'Although Article 51 of the Immigration Control Order requires that the form of a written detention order shall contain the nationality of the deportee and the reason for the deportation, these items were not contained in the written detention order issued in the case at hand' was found problematic but not illegal (*Gyōsei jiken saiban hanreishū*, 9(4): 1003–1013). In the 'obstruction of performance of a public duty case under public prosecution' (Tokyo High Court judgment of April 15, 1972), it was held that 'detention under the Immigration Control Order is an administrative disposition and not a criminal penalty, and therefore even if an illegal entrant may be deprived of liberty under the said order, that in itself does not automatically constitute a violation of Article 31 of the Constitution' (*Hanrei taimuzu* 279: 359–361).

These rulings are occasionally referred to as precedents even today. In both cases, the question of violation of Article 31 of the Constitution was raised and rejected in relation to the execution of an administrative disposition under the Immigration Control Order. As both rulings are older than the McLean judgment and well before Japan's ratification of the International Bill of Human Rights, the Convention relating to the Status of Refugees, the Convention on the Elimination of all Forms of Discrimination Against Women and the Convention on the Rights of the Child, there is no reason that today's courts have to be bound by these precedents.

In fact, the rulings for the 'action for the declaration of nullity of a deportation disposition (first case)' (Tokyo District Court judgment of May 27, 2004) and the 'action for the revocation of the portion of nonrecognition of refugee status (second case)' (Tokyo District Court judgment of May 27, 2004) confirmed that a disposition by the issuance of a written deportation order with incorrect or omitted entries is invalid:

> Indeed, according to Article 51 of the act and Article 45 of the enforcement regulations of the same act, the destination is not a legally required entry for a written deportation order, which is essentially issued to its addressee as a declaration of intent to deport from Japan, and the destination may be entered in order to facilitate the execution of the order and not as an entry relevant to the validity of the disposition itself; based on this interpretation, there is some doubt that the incorrect entry of the destination immediately renders the entire deportation disposition illegal. However, according to the entire import of the oral arguments, *it is found that not only deporting the deportee out*

*of Japan but also transporting the same to the destination specified in the written order are treated as essential components of a valid deportation order in the actual deportation operation today; for these reasons, if the entered destination was found to be incorrect, there was no means to stop the deportee's deportation to the incorrect destination at that point of time other than to render the entire deportation order illegal and invalid. Consequently, despite the aforementioned interpretation, the court has no option but to accept that the written order as a whole had at least a serious defect and was invalid.* (emphasis added)

Incidentally, the plaintiff in the case at hand fought against her deportation, not detention. Deportation would not only remove her existence from Japan but also bar her from re-entering Japan under the current immigration law (a deportation order under Article 24-4(iv)(h) of the Immigration Control Act is one of the reasons for denial of landing). From the viewpoint of C's partner, this meant that he would never be able live with, cooperate with and provide mutual assistance to C. This is another reason why the deportation order against the plaintiff should comply with the principles of equality and proportionality of crime and punishment, and moreover, why recognition should be given to the ultimate destruction of the Japanese partner's existing life caused by C's deportation, which would be irreparable no matter what compensation he might receive.

As discussed earlier, the special permission to stay system has been operated by giving consideration to the deportee's family and social relationships rather than the subject of the deportation order since the Attorney-General's Office Prosecution Administration Bureau Notice No. 24448 of July 31, 1950, on 'Revision of the Alien Registration Order and Its Enforcement Regulations' introduced its prototype under the rule of the occupation forces. Special permission to stay is granted when the former (the deportee's family and social ties) is found to be worthy of preservation. This is another reason why the mandamus action for special permission to stay would contribute to the welfare of those in social relationships with C in Japan, including her Japanese partner.

## Residence status and the family Japan wants to protect

Special permission to stay has been granted in some cases even when there were grounds for denial of landing according to the letter of the law. Since the government started publishing 'permitted cases' in 2003, examples of people with narcotics-related convictions have continued to appear on the list. Special permission to stay has been granted even to perpetrators of human trafficking, which seems to be far more harmful to society than minor drug offences.

The family seen through the lens of special permission to stay is analogous with the family over which the constitutionality of the Nationality Act was fought. The 'unconstitutionality of the Nationality Act' case (Supreme Court Grand Bench judgment of June 4, 2008) argued as follows:

> The primary reason that this provision was included in the Act can be construed as that in the case of a child acknowledged by a Japanese father after birth, when the child has acquired the status of a child born in wedlock as a result of the marriage of the parents, the child's life is united with the life of the Japanese father and the child obtains a close tie with Japanese society through his/her family life, and therefore it is appropriate to grant Japanese nationality to such a child. […] It is construed that Article 3, para.1 of the Nationality Act, while keeping the basic principle of the Act, the principle of jus sanguinis, provides for certain requirements that can be the indexes by which to measure the closeness of the tie between the child and Japan, in addition to the existence of a legal parent-child relationship with a Japanese citizen. (www.courts.go.jp/app/hanrei_en/detail?id=955)
>
> Furthermore, according to the socially accepted views and under the social circumstances at the time when the provision of Article 3, para.1 of the Nationality Act was established, there may have been adequate reasons to consider that in the case of a child born to a Japanese father and a non-Japanese mother, the fact of the legal marriage of the parents *would show the existence of the child's close tie with Japan developed through his/her family life* with the Japanese father. In light of the aforementioned trends in the nationality law

systems enforced in foreign states at the time of introduction of the provision of said paragraph, a certain reasonable relevance can be found between the provision that requires legitimation in addition to acknowledgment for granting Japanese nationality, and the legislative purpose mentioned above. However, [...] it does not always match up to the realities of family life of today to determine that a child born to a Japanese father and a non-Japanese mother has a close tie with Japan to a sufficient extent for granting him/her Japanese nationality only after the Japanese father became legally married to the non-Japanese mother. [...] In addition, it seems that other states are moving toward scrapping discriminatory treatment by law against children born out of wedlock, and in fact, the International Covenant on Civil and Political Rights and the Convention on the Rights of the Child, which Japan has ratified, also contain such provisions to the effect that children shall not be subject to discrimination of any kind because of birth. [...] [M]any states that had previously required legitimation for granting nationality to children born out of wedlock to fathers who are their citizens have revised their laws in order to grant nationality if, and without any other requirement, it is found that the father-child relationship with their citizens is established as a result of acknowledgement. (www.courts.go.jp/app/hanrei_en/detail?id=955; emphasis added)

Based on these reasons, the court ruled that the particular provision in the Nationality Act was unconstitutional.

This Supreme Court judgment was drafted by Hideaki Mori, who was the Supreme Court judicial research official in charge of each case tasked with writing *Saikō saibansho hanrei kaisetsu* (Commentary on the decisions of the Supreme Court) at the time. Mori happened to be the presiding judge in the case at hand. The Supreme Court judgment concluded that the provision was constitutional at the time of the Nationality Act revision in 1984 but that it was unconstitutional when the plaintiff sought 'acquisition of nationality by notification' due to changes in the socially accepted views and social circumstances since the revision. According to Kiyoshi Hosokawa, who was the head of Civil Affairs Fifth Division of the Ministry of Justice at the time of the 1984 revision,

The formation of a close tie with Japan through a parent-child relationship is based on the child's becoming a constituent member of Japanese society by inclusion in a Japanese national's family, and therefore, it is appropriate to grant Japanese nationality to the child born in wedlock to a Japanese national regardless of whether the Japanese national is the father or the mother of the child. On the other hand, a child born out of wedlock is a child in an abnormal family relationship and therefore cannot be expected to form the same level of parent-child relationship as children born in wedlock in every case. For this reason, such a child needs to be considered separately. (Hosokawa 1984: 11)

The description that a child born out of wedlock is in an abnormal family relationship is in itself considered discriminatory in contemporary Japanese society.

Japan's *jus sanguinis* has been 'becoming Japanese by becoming part of the family' even in the postwar period. The same logic underpins special permission to stay. The granting of special permission to stay to foreign nationals who are in a family relationship with a Japanese national or a permanent-resident foreign national is the logic of the Nationality Act in a different form. The scope of the family in relation to the granting of special permission to stay is broader than that under the Nationality Act and hence it is not denied even in a case that cannot be dealt with under the Family Register Act.

# Conclusion

In recent years, former Supreme Court justices have started opening up about the court cases in which they were involved (Takii 2009; Takii 2017; Fujita 2012; Fujita 2016; Izumi 2013; Izumi, Watanabe, Yamamoto and Niimura 2017; Izumi 2019; Ishikawa, Yamamoto and Izumi 2019; Chiba 2017; Chiba 2019). It is said that the judgment on the unconstitutionality of Article 3 of the Nationality Act was made based on (1) the view that the provision was constitutional at the time of its formulation but subsequently became unconstitutional by the time the foreign national in question raised the issue; and (2) an examination within the 'framework of rational decision-making by comprehensively balancing' various conditions.

The first reasoning above was adopted because 'based on the presumption of the legislature's discretionary power, the court accepts what the legislature has determined reasonable as constitutional in principle; the court finds it unconstitutional only when the scope of legislative discretion is clearly exceeded or abused; the standard is tied to the presumption of constitutionality and the doctrine of obviousness and founded on the doctrine of separation of powers in a democracy to honor and respect the legislature' (Izumi 2019: 372). As for the second reasoning, 'The "framework of rational decision-making by comprehensively balancing" does not explain the criteria or the approach and standard to be used for an examination of unconstitutionality. After all, it only means that the constitutionality of a restriction or discrimination is judged by the measure of "rationality". And judging the measure of "rationality" by comprehensively balancing various factors means, in the end, that the judge makes a subjective decision' (Izumi 2019: 347).[11]

Nevertheless, decision-making regarding special permission to stay has to be done within the 'framework of rational decision-making by comprehensive balancing' because it is granted when the Minister of Justice and authorized officials think it appropriate to grant it after a comprehensive consideration of the foreign national's circumstances. This is a way to deal with unanticipated cases. The comprehensive balancing framework enables the decision-maker to grant special permission to stay to someone with grounds for refusal of entry or, depending on the notices in operation at the time, to someone who marries after an arrest or detention.

In the judgment on the unconstitutionality of Article 3 of the Nationality Act, justices Kazuko Yokoo, Osamu Tsuno and Yūki Furuta provided the following dissenting opinion that there were no objective indicators proving the alleged change in the public consciousness about family.

> However, although it is true that the views regarding family lifestyles and parent-child relationships have changed to some extent, in what form and to what extent these views have changed, or whether or not

there has been a significant change in the public consciousness of these matters, cannot be deemed to be specifically clarified.

We do not think that there has been an outstanding change in the realities of family lifestyles. According to the statistics, the number of children born out of wedlock increased from 14,168 (1.0%) in 1985, the year following the year of enactment of Article 3, para.1 of the Nationality Act, to 21,634 (1.9%) in 2003, and the number of children born to Japanese fathers and foreign mothers also increased from 5,538 in 1987, the first year when statistical data were available, to 12,690 in 2003, but the increase in these numbers is small.

Thus, contrary to the argument presented by the majority opinion, it is sufficiently possible to regard the fact that the increase in the number of children born out of wedlock over the past 20 years is so small, as proof to show, at least, that there has been no significant change in the public consciousness with regard to the desirable form of a family with a child. (www.courts.go.jp/app/hanrei_en/detail?id=955)

On the other hand, Mori argues as follows in footnote 36 of the research official's report of the Nationality Act unconstitutionality judgment. Regarding 'A change in the consciousness about the different legal treatment of children born out of wedlock', (1) 'The provision of the stipulation of Article 900-4 of the Civil Code limiting the share in inheritance of a child born out of wedlock to one half of that of a child born in wedlock was commonly accepted as conformable to Article 14-1 of the Constitution but support for the view that it is unconstitutional has been growing since the late Shōwa era'; (2) 'the Legislative Council's 1996 report to the Minister of Justice, "The outline of a legislative bill for partial revision of the Civil Code", states that the share in inheritance of a child born out of wedlock shall be the same as that of a child born in wedlock'; (3) 'distinction in the treatment of children born in wedlock and those born out of wedlock was found in the method of entry for the relationship between the head of a household and children in a residence certificate (Guidelines for Administration of the Residential Basic Book) and the method of entry for the relationship between parents and children in a family register (Ordinance for Enforcement of the Family Registration Act Appendix 6 etc.) but the 1994 revision of the former and the

2004 revision of the latter eliminated the distinctions'. Instead of an increase in the number of de facto marriages or children born out of wedlock, he rates a change in the institutional aspect as a change in social consciousness (Mori 2011: 318–319).

The 'action for partition of property' case (Supreme Court Grand Bench judgment of April 22, 1987; hereafter referred to as the 'unconstitutionality of the Forest Act case') was fought over Article 186 of the Forest Act. Although it was ruled unconstitutional, there was no change of precedent. The court found it unconstitutional based on a dramatic change in the social and economic environment assumed by the Forest Act when it was legislated in 1907.

After the war, the Nationality Act was revised in 1950 (Shōwa 25), 1984 (Shōwa 59) and 2008 (Heisei 20). The interval between the changes in the Shōwa era was thirty-four years and that between Shōwa and Heisei was twenty-four. The shorter interval indicates an accelerating speed of change in the postwar Japanese family. On the other hand, foreigners' human rights continue to be restricted based on the McLean judgment of October 4, 1978. The plaintiff in question was accepted into Japan with the 'long-term resident' status newly established in the 1989 revision of the Immigration Control Act and her circumstances are incomparable with those of McLean's. Her case should be considered to be different from the much older case as the court did in the unconstitutionality of the Forest Act case. *Decision-making needs to be premised on the following factors: In the context of the historical transition of Japan's residence status system discussed in Sections 2–5 of this written opinion, the primary consideration should be given to (1) how Japan intended to accept people with the qualifications equivalent to the current residence statuses from time to time. Next, (2) the case should be compared with prior cases in which special permission to stay was granted despite a court conviction and assessed accordingly. Then, (3) the family life of C's Japanese partner, which would be lost if C was deported from Japan, needs to be weighed up.*

# Notes

1. Japan first introduced the principle of *jus sanguinis* with Grand Council of State Proclamation No. 103 of 1873 on 'rules for marriage to foreigners' requiring people registered in the Jinshin family register from 1872 to obtain a permit from the government if they wished to marry a foreign national. Aritsugu Tashiro considers that 'Japan before its opening in the Meiji era was a pre-modern state but it as a state must have had a substantive nationality law (as a common-sense canon or an unwritten code) and such a law would have been based on the idea of "non-differentiation of residents and nationals"' (Tashiro 1974: 55).

2. The system of foreigner registration for particular nationalities was introduced by Imperial Decree No. 137 of August 4, 1894, on 'matters concerning the Qing subjects residing in the Empire of Japan'. This decree is said to be Japan's first national law concerning immigration control. Article 4 states as follows: 'The Qing subjects registered under Article 2 shall be permitted to move their residence provided they have their registration certificate endorsed by the prefectural governor of their current address first and submit the same to the prefectural governor of their new address for registration under Article 2 within three days of arrival in the new residence'. Then, Article 5 states, 'Prefectural governors may expel from their territories any Qing subjects who fail to complete registration as required by this decree'. We can see the inception of a law, including the foreigner registration and deportation rules (a substantive immigration law), after the Sino-Japanese War.

3. Yasuaki Ōnuma characterizes the immigration law, including this ordinance, under the Meiji Constitution as follows: 'The statutes concerning immigration control always relied on imperial decrees and home affairs ministry ordinances in order to legislate administrative authority instead of acts legislated with the support of the Imperial Diet. Their contents were markedly simpler than contemporaneous immigration laws of other countries or Japan's postwar immigration law' (Ōnuma 1978: 262).

4. According to the bilingual English and Japanese document in Saikō saibansho Jimu-sōkyoku Shōgai-ka (1950b: 361–362). The original documents with Supreme Commander for the Allied Powers Index Numbers (SCAPIN) referred to hereafter can be accessed via the National Diet Library Digital Collection.

5. Ōnuma points out that in addition to the immediate-execution-type deportation, the revised alien registration decree entailed (1) substantially heavier penalties and (2) the exclusion of protection for the rights of the accused provided for by the Code of Criminal Procedure (Ōnuma 1978: 310).

6   However, third-generation Koreans in Japan were dealt with separately under Status 4-1-16-3.
7   New categories in Table I include 'legal/accounting services', 'medical services', 'researcher', 'instructor', 'specialist in humanities/international services', 'intra-company transferee', 'cultural activities' and 'pre-college student'. 'Spouse or child of permanent resident' and 'long-term resident' were added to Table II.
8   Section 101(a)(15)(B) of the Immigration and Nationality Act states as follows: 'An alien (other than one coming for the purpose of study or of performing skilled or unskilled labor or as a representative of foreign press, radio, film, or other foreign information media coming to engage in such vocation) having a residence in a foreign country which he or she has no intention of abandoning and who is visiting the United States temporarily for business or temporarily for pleasure'. Those described in the brackets fall under the non-immigrant visas category.
9   The provisional English translation of the Basic Plan Second Edition can be accessed at https://www.moj.go.jp/isa/content/001342292.pdf.
10  Prior to this, the Ministry of Justice issued Immigration Services Agency Notice No. 5357 of October 18, 2013, on 'the entry and residence examinations of same-sex spouses (notice)'. This was issued by the head of the immigration and residency division to the directors of regional immigration bureaus and branches. The notice stated, 'When a spouse in a same-sex marriage legally recognized in their home country applies for a change of residence status to "designated activities" so that the applicant can live together with the spouse as a dependent, the application, together with the officer-in-charge's opinion on grounds for humanitarian consideration, must be referred to the ministry for instructions'. It shows that the decision to grant same-sex spouses a residence status under the designated activities category is made by the Ministry of Justice.
11  This is not the only explanation offered by all of the former Supreme Court justices. Katsumi Chiba states, 'Just as in precedents on constitutionality, as [judges] are making a decision on a very polarizing subject, socially and politically, they need to consider various circumstances in light of the "standpoint of the judicial branch", make a prudent decision taking account of the overall social trend, changes in people's attitudes, expectations and opinions about the judicial branch and so on and handle the case in a way appropriate for the situation; in other words, to draw a conclusion by considering all the important factors to consider comprehensively from multiple angles' (Chiba 2019: 7). Chiba explains that comprehensive balancing is inevitable when judges make a decision while avoiding judicial legislation and considering political and social conflicts.

# Discovering Justification for Special Permission to Stay: A Constitutional Order Approach

## Introduction

Part of the written opinion I submitted to the Tokyo District Court, on which Chapter 8 is based, found its way into the judgment at the first trial. However, the plaintiff was unable to secure special permission to stay and decided to appeal to the Tokyo High Court. On that occasion, I made two written submissions of my opinion. This chapter is based on the first of them.

Let us first review the Tokyo District Court's judgment. This case was a 'mandamus action for the revocation of a determination' because the plaintiff's petition for reconsideration had been rejected. It took this form because this case sought an order to revoke the determination not to grant special permission to stay made by an adjudicating administrative agency (i.e., the director of the Tokyo Regional Immigration Bureau). This constituted an action for a judicial review of an administrative disposition (i.e., an action against a public authority) on the grounds that the plaintiff was likely to suffer considerable harm from an absence of a certain disposition (i.e., special permission to stay) and had no other appropriate means to avoid such harm. Because a foreign national is not supposed to have the right to make an application for review against an administrative agency in immigration administration, the plaintiff had no other way but to file this case in the form of a mandamus action.

The Tokyo District Court Second Civil Division (hereafter referred to as the 'Tokyo District Court') assessed the case from the same standpoint and stated that the action had to satisfy the following requirements:

(1) a mandamus action may be filed only when serious harm is likely to be caused if a certain original administrative disposition is not made; and (2) there are no other appropriate means to avoid that harm (Article 37-2(1) of the Administrative Case Litigation Act). In judging whether or not any serious harm would be caused as stipulated in the preceding paragraph, the court is to consider the degree of difficulty in recovering from the harm and to take into consideration the nature and extent of the harm as well as the content and nature of the original administrative disposition.

The Tokyo District Court then stated that the plaintiff 'is biologically male but identifies herself as female; following the original determination on her case, she started a relationship with a Japanese man from around March 2016 and went into cohabitation from around May of the same year and has been deepening the relationship. [...] [The plaintiff] took part in the Yokohama Wakaba-chō Tabunka Eigasai [multicultural film festival] in Naka ward, Yokohama city, as a guest speaker and made a presentation about Brazilian culture; following the said determination, she has been volunteering as a fashion model for kimono-fabric dresses at the request of a local designer in Yokohama'. The court acknowledged that 'If deported, the relationship which the plaintiff has been developing with her Japanese partner following the said determination would be harmed and also the connection she has been building with the local community would be lost. Accordingly, the court found, without needing to examine any other points, that the plaintiff "would likely suffer serious harm" if the original determination was not revoked and she was deported from Japan'.

The Tokyo District Court ruled that the relationship between C and her Japanese partner 'merits only a lower level of protection as it has been formed under a legal status that is subject to deportation, but even so, it is difficult to deny that it requires a certain degree of protection in light of the substantiality of the relationship etc'. The court also accepted that the plaintiff was likely to suffer serious harm and had no means other than to bring the matter to court by stating, 'On the basis of the new circumstances that evidently arose after the said determination, this court is of the opinion that the plaintiff has no appropriate means other than to take a mandamus action for the revocation of the said determination in order to avoid that harm. Accordingly, this mandamus action for the revocation of the disposition satisfies the requirement of "there are no other appropriate means to avoid the harm".

Despite recognizing (1) the satisfaction of the requirements for a mandamus action and the existence of substantive communal living that involved mutual cooperation and assistance between C and her Japanese partner as well as her involvement in the local community, the Tokyo District Court concluded that (2) it could not find sufficient grounds to order the revocation of the original determination. I present below my argument that there were 'sufficient grounds to order the revocation of the original determination' contrary to this court decision.

## The Tokyo District Court judgment and the McLean judgment

The Tokyo District Court judgment held that the immigration authority's refusal to revoke the determination against C could not be considered an overstepping or abuse of its discretionary power for the following two reasons. First,

> The Constitution guarantees freedom to choose and change residence within Japan (Article 22-1) but stipulates nothing about foreign nationals entering and residing in Japan and imposes no duty on the immigration authority to permit foreign nationals to enter or reside in Japan. It is this court's understanding that this is compatible with the concept, as an international custom, that a nation is under no obligation to admit foreign nationals into the country, absent a special treaty, and hence, whether or not foreign nationals are admitted into the country and, if admitted, on what conditions, is to be determined at the discretion of the subject nation. Consequently, under the Constitution, it is not only that foreign nationals are not guaranteed freedom to enter Japan but also that they are not guaranteed a right to residence or a right to demand a continuous residence; they are given a status enabling

them to reside in Japan only within the scope of the residence system for foreigners under the immigration law.

Second,

> The Act provides that special permission to stay may be granted when "the Minister of Justice finds that circumstances exist that warrant the granting of special permission to stay" without specifying requirements for it, nor does it have a provision on matters to be considered by the Minister of Justice for the purpose of constraining the Minister's decision-making; hence, the immigration control of foreign nationals should be administered from the standpoint of the protection of national interests, such as the preservation of domestic public peace and public order and morals, the preservation of health and hygiene, and the stability of the labor market, and by its nature, a timely decision needs to be made after extensive information gathering and consideration of various factors. Consequently, a decision to grant special permission to stay or not pursuant to Article 50-1(iv) of the Immigration Control Act is left to the very broad discretion of the Minister of Justice et al. and the only time their decision on whether or not to grant special permission to stay under the said paragraph becomes illegal is limited to situations in which they are found to have exceeded the scope of or abused the discretionary power vested in the Minister of Justice, such as completely failing to grasp the facts, or significantly falling short of general social norms in their decision-making.

In any case, the court reached the conclusion that 'the portion of this action seeking an order to grant the plaintiff special permission to stay is dismissed' by reference to the decision-making framework established in the McLean case.

Nevertheless, there have been divergent opinions about the discretionary control found in the McLean judgment in recent years. In the 'Appellate case in an action for the revocation of an approval of undertakings for public interest and for the revocation of a decision' (Tokyo High Court judgment of July 19, 2012; hereafter referred to as the 'Ken-Ō Expressway land expropriation case'), the court expressed self-criticism of the state of judicial ruling and control of administrative discretion by stating as follows:

> The original judgment accepted the broad discretion of administrative organs with regard to decision-making on the requirement of approval for an undertaking for public interest provided for by Article 20-3 of the Expropriation of Land Act, namely, "the undertaking for public interest plan contributes to appropriate and reasonable use of land" on grounds that such a decision "entails specialized, technical and policy-related considerations"; and upon ruling that such a decision becomes illegal only when there is a "departure from the scope of or abuse of the discretionary power", it limited the scope of the judicial review to an excess or abuse of the discretionary power, which is an exceptional error, and in applying that rule, cursorily dismissed the appellant's argument and accepted the state's claim that there was no departure from or abuse of discretion. According to the administrative discretion argument in the original judgment, the scope of review by the court is very limited. The court defers to a decision made by an administrative organ except in very unusual cases of a departure from or an abuse of discretionary authority where the decision was "not based on material facts" or "falling short of social norms" and consequently preserves the administrative organ's discretionary decision as it is. *This means that the judiciary merely performs the role of confirming an administrative organ's discretionary decision in almost all cases. In this situation, it must be said that the judiciary fails to function as a check on the power of administrative organs, that the principle of administration by law becomes hollowed out, and that the judiciary falls into a state of dysfunction.* (emphasis added)

The following general opinion on the current state of administrative discretion was also given in the Ken-Ō Expressway land expropriation case:

> The basis for precedents and theory of administrative discretion at present can be condensed into the following points. (1) Discretion control is deployed around the application of the abuse of discretion standard provided for in Article 30 of the Administrative Case Litigation Act. (2)

The traditional argument of discretion as to requirements and that as to effects are becoming relativized. (3) The general rule is that the scope of discretion is determined depending on cases and is not predetermined. (4) It is accepted that the scope for discretion in specialized and technical or policy-related decision-making is larger than usual. (5) However, it is not the case that the presence of a specialized and technical or policy-related element necessarily and totally permits administrative agencies to act as they see fit to the exclusion of judicial review. (6) There is a consensus that a judicial remedy should be applied in determining whether or not the requirement of Article 20-3 of the Expropriation of Land Act is satisfied, and there is no precedent or theory adopting the view that cases pertaining to the foregoing determination preclude a judicial review when they involve specialized and technical or policy-related consideration. (7) In general, a ministerial decision can be substituted by a judicial decision. (8) In the foregoing determination, treating the non-examination of an alternative for the undertaking in question as a problem is regarded as the setting forth of an appropriate point of consideration and not as a substitution for the agency's judgment, and it has been accepted that a judicial remedy may find it to be a reason for illegality, and therefore this non-examination of an alternative alone can be the sole factor for the finding of an abuse of the discretionary power. (https://www.courts.go.jp/app/files/hanrei_jp/937/082937_hanrei.pdf)

Also, the McLean judgment contains the following view, which is no different from the state of administrative discretion sharply criticized in the Ken-Ō Expressway land expropriation case:

> However, since the reason, purpose, and scope of discretion granted by law to an administrative agency differ, and circumstances in which the decision is found unlawful for excess or abuse of discretion vary, each kind of decision has to be examined individually. As far as the decision of the Minister of Justice concerning the existence of a "reasonable ground to acknowledge that the renewal of the period of sojourn is appropriate" [under Article 21, para. 3 of the Cabinet Order

on Immigration Control] is concerned, in the light of the nature of the discretionary power of the Minister as referred to above, it should be regarded as unlawful as excess or abuse of discretion only when it totally lacks factual basis or when it is evident that it significantly lacks appropriateness in the light of socially accepted views. (https://www.courts.go.jp/app/hanrei_en/detail?id=56)

Actually, in a majority of cases involving violation of the Immigration Control Act that resulted in a judgment against the state, the court found that the Minister of Justice et al. made a decision by 'not considering matters that should be considered and considering matters that should not be considered'. This logic came to be used widely for administrative discretion control when the 'Appellate action for the revocation of approval of an undertaking, public notice of land details and a decision for land expropriation' case (Tokyo High Court judgment of July 13, 1973; hereafter referred to as 'Nikkō Tarōsugi case') became final and binding.[1] Today, the case is often quoted in discussions about the nascent stage of environmental rights litigation. The logic of not considering matters that should be considered is universally employed regardless of the object for administration particularly in the administrative area where a decision is made as part of a unified procedural sequence under such statutes as the Expropriation of Land Act and the Immigration Control Act.

Incidentally, the realm of government policy pertaining to legislated restrictions on economic activities is where the logic of not considering matters that should be considered finds acceptance. Under the principle of separation of powers, decisions made by the political branches in the area of socioeconomic freedom are respected and the judiciary exhibits a lenient, rather than strict, attitude in reviewing administrative activities through legislative measures formulated by the representatives of the people. The prototype of this review approach was mentioned in Footnote 4 of the judgment on *Unites States v. Carolene Products Co.*, 304 U. S. 144 (1938).[2] As postwar Japan adopted the 'American-type concrete judicial review doctrine', it has been established through legal precedents that judicial reviews on economic regulatory matters are less stringent in Japan. Former Supreme Court Justice Katsumi Chiba states as follows.

Chapter 9

> Regarding the constitutional review standards, Japan began to adopt concepts such as the balancing of interests and the strict review standards modeled after doctrines created by the judiciary in the US from 1975. For reviewing a possible conflict with the equality requirement under Article 14 of the Constitution, whether or not a system giving rise to discrimination is reasonable became the decision criterion and the so-called 'reasonable relationship test' (whether the legislative purpose is justifiable and reasonable, and whether there is a reasonable relationship between the means to enforce the discriminating provision and the legislative purpose) came into use as a concrete index for assessment in the review. (Chiba 2019: 11–12)

In his own research official's report (Supreme Court Grand Bench judgment of July 1, 1992), Chiba explains the influence of US Supreme Court judgments on their Japanese counterparts as follows.

> The "clear and present danger" principle in Justice Holmes' ruling on the Schenck case in 1919 was originally formulated to determine whether it is appropriate to punish an expression of a particular idea or opinion under law rather than as a standard for determining the constitutionality of a law itself, but subsequently came to be used for the latter purpose by the US Federal Supreme Court. However, it is said that the 1951 judgment on the Dennis case led to a growing awareness that this principle was inadequate for the need to maintain protection for freedom of expression and lost general support in the US. […] The Douds case in 1950 was the catalyst for a broader application of the balancing of interests test by the US Supreme Court. The approach was used to carry out comparison and balancing under specific circumstances between the interest of the untrammeled maintenance of freedom of expression in question and the national and social interests to be maintained or restored by constraining that freedom. (Chiba 1995: 231)

The following passage in the McLean judgment signals the court's view that an administrative decision does not fall under the category for a strict judicial review as long as it remains within the scope of economic regulatory decisions made by the political branches:

> The Minister of Justice, when deciding whether the renewal of the period of sojourn should be allowed or not, must consider not only the appropriateness of the application by the foreign national in question, the entire behaviour of the foreign national, political, economic and social circumstances within Japan as well as the international situation, diplomatic relations, international comity and other circumstances from the viewpoint of the maintenance of public security and good morals in Japan, ensurance of health and hygiene, stability of the labour market and other interest of the state which are the purpose of immigration control and regulation of sojourn of foreign nationals, and make a timely and accurate decision. An appropriate result cannot be expected unless such a decision, due to its nature, is left to the discretion of the Minister of Justice who is responsible for the administration of immigration control. (https://www.courts.go.jp/app/hanrei_en/detail?id=56)

## Special permission to stay and the double standard of judicial review

It is understood that footnote 4 of the Carolene Products judgment mentioned in the previous section introduced the prototype of the 'double standard of judicial review'. While the court respects the legislative decisions made by the political branches in the realm of socioeconomic regulations, it adopts a stricter standard in reviewing laws related to the 14th Amendment to the US Constitution such as voting rights (citizenship rights), discrimination against ethnic minorities and civil liberties in the realm of thought and belief. The double standard of judicial review received a positive comment from Nobuyoshi Ashibe as follows and opened up the field of constitutional litigation in Japan as well.

> Where there is an error or inequity in restrictions on economic freedom […] injudicious laws can be amended or removed by resorting to the "ballot box and democratic process" but where a legislation results in

a violation of civil liberties or the rights of minorities, [...] the correct democratic process has to be restored by the active intervention of the court whose principal duty is to "protect the rights of minority groups not adequately represented in the political arena". (Ashibe 1973: 37–38)

In the 'violation of the Act on Special Measures for the Adjustment of Retail Business' case (Supreme Court Grand Bench judgment of November 22, 1972: hereafter referred to as the 'retail market location regulation case'), the court held that 'a judgment on the necessity and reasonableness of a regulatory measure in the socioeconomic area is primarily left to the discretion of the legislative branch, and such a regulatory measure is found to be unconstitutional only when the legislature overstepped the bounds of its discretionary power and the regulation is "clearly and grossly unreasonable"' (Ōishi and Ōsawa 2016: 218). The 'Action for the revocation of an administrative disposition' case (Supreme Court Grand Bench judgment of April 30, 1975; hereafter referred to as the 'pharmacy location regulation case') a few years later is known as a case about a negative-purpose regulation as opposed to the positive-purpose regulation in the aforementioned retail market location regulation case. The difference between the positive and negative purposes of regulations can be summarized as follows: '(1) the negative-purpose regulation is reviewed, on the basis of legislative facts, as to whether the regulation in question is a necessary and reasonable measure to serve important public interests and whether its purpose is unlikely to be achieved by a less restrictive alternative (this is called the "strict rationality standard"); and (2) the positive-purpose regulation is unconstitutional only when the restrictive measure in question is clearly unreasonable to a significant extent (the "clear unreasonableness" standard)' (Ōishi and Ōsawa 2016: 220). The different standards for unconstitutionality are applied depending on the regulatory purpose.

In immigration administration, special permission to stay is one of the areas where a double standard is used in reviewing a case. When any of the items listed under Article 24 of the Immigration Control Act (grounds for deportation) apply to a foreign national, the immigration authority (i.e., the Minister of Justice and authorized officials) investigates the suspected violation, receives an objection, if any, from the foreign national in a subsequent oral examination, and, even after determining that the objection is groundless, the immigration authority may grant the foreign national special permission to stay if it finds any reason to allow them to continue to reside in Japan.

Specifically, Article 50-1, 'Special case determinations by the Minister of Justice', provides that 'Even if the Minister of Justice finds that a filed objection is without reason [...] he/she may grant the suspect special permission to stay in Japan if the suspect falls under any of the following items: (i) he/she has obtained permission for permanent residence; (ii) he/she has had a registered domicile in Japan as a Japanese national in the past; (iii) he/she resides in Japan under the control of another due to human trafficking; and (iv) the Minister of Justice finds grounds to grant special permission to stay, other than the previous items'. While the first three items specify who qualifies for such determinations, item (iv) is more open-ended.

However, this provision is not completely without limit. For the Minister of Justice's act of granting permission to stay to a person who should otherwise be deported to be sanctioned as an act of state, the ministerial determination must be under certain constraints and not be based on their own interest or personal reason despite the openness of the provision. Because it has been enabled by the enforcement of a special law legislated in the Diet, the minister's determination is made by the exercise of discretionary power within the authorized bounds and does not constitute absolute discretion.

After the Protocol to Prevent, Suppress and Punish Trafficking in Persons, Especially Women and Children, Supplementing the United Nations Convention Against Transnational Organized Crime (hereafter referred to as the 'Trafficking Protocol') was adopted by the United Nations in November 2000, signed by Japan in December 2002, and approved in the Diet in June 2005, Article 50-1(iii) was added in the revision of the Immigration Control Act in July 2005. Prior to the 2005 revision, the current Article 50-1(iv) was Article 50-1(iii) (hereafter referred to 'former Article 50-1(iii)'). Permanent residents in item (i) and former Japanese nationals in item (ii) are stereotypically eligible for special permission to stay probably because they are typically found to have stable family and social relationships in Japan. Similarly, special permission to stay under former Article 50-1(iii) was actively granted to people who had stable family and social relationships in Japan.

This can be inferred from the presence of the following statement under the heading of 'III Major issues and guidelines on the immigration control administration service' in the Basic Plan for Immigration Control (2nd Edition):

> Upon judging the grant of this special permit to stay, Minister of Justice shall consider various aspects in each case comprehensively, such as the reason of application for the special permit to stay, the foreigner's family condition, living condition, behavior and other circumstances, necessity of humanitarian consideration for the foreign national and influence to other illegal residents. The special permit is granted basically when the foreign national has a deep connection with the Japanese community and when there arises a serious problem especially from the humanitarian point of view, if the said foreigner is deported. [...] On the other hand, *as for an illegal resident who is recognized to have a civil status or position with a Japanese national, a permanent resident or a special permanent resident and has close connection with the Japanese community, appropriate measures shall continue to be taken in individual cases with humanitarian consideration.* (https://www.isa.go.jp/en/policies/policies/nyukan_nyukan40.html, emphasis added)[3]

It can also be understood from various notices indicating criteria for granting special permission to stay, including Notice concerning Spouse or Child of Japanese National ('Spouse Notice') issued by the Ministry of Justice to the directors of regional immigration bureaus on April 8, 1992 and August 1, 1996, Notice concerning the Treatment of Foreign Nationals Who Support an Own Japanese Child ('Long-Term Resident Mother and Child Notice') of July 30, 1996, and a revised Spouse Notice ('Marriage Notice') of April 16, 1999.[4] In other words, special permission to stay has been granted to people who have a stable family relationship with a Japanese national or a long-term resident foreign national and maintain a social relationship demonstrating their assimilation into Japanese society since the time of former Article 50-1(iii).

The thinking behind former Article 50-1(iii) appears to live on today considering, firstly, that the Ministry of Justice has published the contents of these notices as the Guidelines on Special Permission to Stay in Japan on its website since October 2006. Second, the ministry changed the format of Permitted/Denied Cases after it started publishing them online in 2003 and divided the cases into four categories—(1) cases with a Japanese spouse, (2) cases with a non-Japanese spouse with legal residence status, (3) cases with a non-Japanese family, and (4) other—suggesting that the immigration authority uses the family relationship as an effective index to measure the degree of a foreign individual's stable assimilation into Japanese society in granting special permission to stay.

Then, why is it acceptable to grant special permission to stay and residence status to those who are supposed to be deported just because they are living a stable family life in Japan? It is not reasonable to conclude that it is an incidental consequence of the exercise of discretion on the part of the Minister of Justice and the authorized directors of regional immigration bureaus (renamed regional immigration services bureaus in 2019). *In the first instance, a decision made by the political branch is respected because the matter in question is seen as pertaining to the socioeconomic realm. If the foreign national affected by that decision is found to have a social existence, including family life, in Japan, however, decision-making is shifted to the 'mental realm' of the foreign individual in question as well as the Japanese nationals and foreign nationals with legal medium-to-long-term residence status who have family or social relationships with the foreign national in question. This shift compels a strict review. Then, the granting of special permission to stay is justified as it is considered that overruling the political branch's decision as a result of strict scrutiny does not make it illegal.*

## 'Foreigners' human rights' and the double standard of judicial review

There have been various arguments about foreigners' human rights in Japan. Junji Annen's '*Gaikokujin no jinken*' *saikō* (Rethinking 'foreigners' human rights') is unarguably a leading example of an argument that examines the conflict between the Constitution and the immigration law. He contends as follows.

> The system of dicing and slicing an individual and only permitting the undertaking of economic activities in a designated area seems to be premised on the line of thinking that entails a wholesale denial of freedom of economic activities to begin with and the subsequent granting of permission for selected economic activities as a privilege. It is difficult to think that this rule is acceptable under Article 22-1 of the Constitution no matter how broad the lawmaker's discretion over economic freedom may be. In this case, the restriction of foreigners' economic activities under the residence status system must be regarded as completely different in nature from that of Japanese nationals. (Annen 1993: 172)

In particular, he portrays foreigners' human rights as different from those of Japanese people because Japan continues to restrict them severely as if to defy international laws even after ratifying a series of international conventions, including the International Covenant on Civil and Political Rights.

It is common knowledge that the McLean judgment appears to persist in constraining foreigners' human rights while the International Covenant on Civil and Political Rights, the Convention relating to the Status of Refugees, the International Convention on the Elimination of All Forms of Discrimination against Women, and the Convention on the Rights of the Child subsequently came into operation in Japan. Criticisms such as Annen's are inevitable. Nonetheless, has Japan's ratification of these international conventions after the McLean judgment had any influence on foreigners' human rights at all? For example, following the ratification of the Convention relating to the Status of Refugees, membership of the national health insurance scheme and the national pension plan has been made available to resident foreign nationals even though they cannot demand it as their right. Since the ratification of the Convention on the Rights of the Child, non-Japanese children have been able to enroll in compulsory education if they wish, regardless of their residence status. These changes show that the availability of public services to resident foreign nationals has been broadened to a certain extent.[5] In the 197th session of the Diet, Prime Minister Shinzō Abe responded to House of Representatives member Akihiro Hatsushika's questions about public assistance for foreign nationals as follows:[6]

> For certain foreign nationals such as those who stay in Japan with residence statuses listed in the left-hand column of Appended Table II of the Immigration Control and Refugee Recognition Act (Cabinet Order No. 319 of 1951), protection under the Public Assistance Act (Act No. 144 of 1950) is offered from a humanitarian point of view if they fall into poverty. As the agencies need to ascertain the residence statuses of those who receive the said protection only for the purpose of confirming their eligibility to receive public assistance, the government has no plan to keep a tally of the number of recipients under each residence status category. [...] Many of the social security programs provide assistance to people who meet the requirements of each program, including foreign nationals.

This suggests that extending the coverage of the government's social security policy, including public assistance against poverty, to foreign nationals has become a normal practice in Japan today.

Under these conditions, the double standard found in decision-making on special permissions to stay can be observed in other areas concerning foreigners. In the 'A petition for a provisional disposition order prohibiting a hate speech demonstration' case (Yokohama District Court Kawasaki Branch decision of June 2, 2016), the court issued an order prohibiting hate speech and hate rallies against Zainichi Koreans based on the personal rights of individuals as well as corporations guaranteed under Article 13 of the Constitution as follows:

> *Every person attains personal values such as a high moral character, virtuous conduct, reputation and credibility from society while freely engaging in activity and developing their personality as they live peacefully in their place of residence as the basis of their livelihood, and the right to live in peace in their residence, the right to free activity and the right to*

*possess dignity and credibility are robustly protected as the personal rights derived from the provision of Article 13 of the Constitution and guaranteed for all legal residents in Japan equally. [...] The personal rights originate in the basic human rights guaranteed by the Constitution and it is construed that a juridical person engaging in activities as a social entity in Japan in a similar way to a natural person possesses the same rights* (Supreme Court Grand Bench judgment of June 24, 1970 in *Saikō saibansho minji hanreishū*, vol. 24, no. 6: 625). In other words, a juridical person attains social recognition of its value, including its reputation and credibility, by conducting its purported business freely and in peace in its place of business (including facilities under its management; the same applies hereinafter) as the basis for its social activity by setting forth the purpose of its business in the articles of incorporation and constituting legal personality by combining its officers, staff and employees, and *the right to conduct business in peace at the place of business, the right to conduct business activity freely, and the right to possess dignity and credibility are robustly protected as the personal rights derived from Article 13 of the Constitution.* (emphasis added)

While the aforementioned Yokohama District Court Kawasaki Branch decision of 2016 held that the foreigners' right to peaceful living in the community is guaranteed under Article 13 of the Constitution, another court squarely denied the right to receive public assistance requested by an eighty-two-year-old woman with Chinese nationality in the 'A mandamus action for an order to commence public assistance' case (Supreme Court Second Petty Bench judgment of July 18, 2014) for the following reason:

While the old Public Assistance Act did not make a distinction between "Japanese citizens" and others in relation to its coverage, Articles 1 and 2 of the current Public Assistance Act specify that the law applies to "citizens", which is construed as Japanese citizens excluding foreign nationals. Between the enactment of the current Public Assistance Act and the present time, no law or ordinance has been passed to extend the scope of the said act's application to certain types of foreign nationals. Accordingly, the court finds no grounds in the existing laws and regulations, including the current Public Assistance Act, to accept the application of the said act, mutatis mutandis, to certain types of foreign nationals. (*Shōmu geppō*, vol. 61, no. 2: 356–391)

In light of these examples, *foreign nationals, even permanent residents, are denied their rights where they are originally excluded from the social policy realm in which the relevant law is legislated, because of the judiciary's respect for the decision made by the political branches in the legislative process, even from the standpoint of the double standard. However, the court determines that protection under Article 13 of the Constitution extends to foreign nationals in the case of violations in the mental realm (i.e., the personal/moral realm) beyond the realm of economic liberties, as the Yokohama District Court Kawasaki Branch did in issuing a prohibitive order against hate rallies.* Clearly, these decisions were governed by the same way of thinking as that underlying the double standard in judicial review.

In his *Taikei kenpō soshō ron* (Theory of constitutional litigation), Kazuyuki Takahashi (2017) schematizes Japan's legal order as a hierarchical structure of laws and the separation of powers under a system of concrete constitutional review. According to the separation of powers, the legislative branch makes laws using the procedures stipulated in the Constitution while the administrative branch enforces the laws made by the legislative branch under the Constitution. The judicial branch adjudicates on any conflict between the outcome of administrative enforcement and the rights of Japanese citizens. Because the judicial branch adopts the concrete review approach in trials, it conducts a constitutional review only as individual disputes arise and does not abstractly nullify a law enacted by the legislature and administered by the executive branch. Special laws take precedence over general laws but they cannot escape the demands of constitutional provisions as long as they are legislated under the Constitution.

Based on the understanding suggested by Takahashi that the court determines 'compatibility between superior laws and inferior laws' within the 'hierarchical structure with the Constitution as the nation's supreme law', 'foreigners' human rights' are not effected in the way depicted by Annen in Japan. Annen does not deny the hierarchical structure that places the Constitution at the top. However, his thinking is dictated by the view that 'no matter how powerful the legislators' discretion regarding economic freedom may be, it is hard to imagine that this is acceptable under Article 22-1 of the Constitution of Japan'. That is to say, it is impossible to legislate an immigration law that is compatible with constitutional values.

However, it appears that the Immigration Control Act has never been what Annen describes it to be since the time of its legislation. At the foreign affairs and judicial affairs joint committee of the House of Councilors in the 13th session of the Diet on April 15, 1952, where the Immigration Control Order was discussed, committee member Osamu Itō posed the following question:

> In my view, human rights provisions in the Constitution, at the least, apply universally to not only Japanese citizens but also people from foreign countries entering or residing in Japan. On the other hand, this law represents the view that goes so far as to override the constitutional provisions guaranteeing various basic human rights. On this point, I would like to ask the proposer's opinion, first of all, about whether the Constitution basically applies here or not.

Hajime Suzuki, director of the immigration control agency, replied,

> There is no doubt that we respected the Constitution in formulating the Immigration Control Order and it was promulgated under the Constitution. This ordinance is actually a Potsdam Order and was scheduled to go into operation from November last year. We made international custom a primary consideration in drafting the law as it dealt with foreign nationals and with the view of making it acceptable anywhere in the international community. Of course, we fully respected human rights and formulated it as an ordinance to control immigration of foreign nationals in line with international custom.

It is possible to glean from this exchange the legislators' intent to align the immigration law with the guaranteed values of the new Constitution such as 'respect for individuals' and 'equality of sexes'.

## Discovering Justification for Special Permission to Stay

In my view, the administration of foreign nationals in Japan can be duly positioned if the immigration law is approached according to Takahashi's logic. *In other words, it is not the distinction between Japanese and foreigners that differentiates their human rights. The Immigration Control Act, which is a special law legislated by the representatives of the people in the Diet and enforced by the administrative branch, can be regarded as an economic regulatory legislation just like the Act on Special Measures for the Adjustment of Retail Business in the 'retail market location regulation case' and the Pharmaceutical Affairs Act in the 'pharmacy location regulation case'. For foreigners' human rights, the double standard is applied to reviews of the Immigration Control Act as an economic regulatory law and this becomes clear when we explain that special permission to stay is granted in certain cases when they are shifted to the realm that requires strict scrutiny. This interpretation makes it possible to sort the past court rulings on foreigner cases and the permitted/declined cases of special permission to stay according to a consistent logic.*

This means that,

> The Minister of Justice, when deciding whether the renewal of the period of sojourn should be allowed or not, must consider not only the appropriateness of the application by the foreign national in question, the entire behaviour of the foreign national, political, economic and social circumstances within Japan as well as the international situation, diplomatic relations, international comity and other circumstances from the viewpoint of the maintenance of public security and good morals in Japan, ensurance of health and hygiene, stability of the labour market and other interest of the state which are the purpose of immigration control and regulation of sojourn of foreign nationals, and make a timely and accurate decision. (https://www.courts.go.jp/app/hanrei_en/detail?id=56)

This is because the immigration law is an economic regulatory law for maintaining economic and social order in Japan and the Minister of Justice is required to exercise the discretionary power within the bounds of that law (i.e., discretion within the scope of the social and economic regulatory legislation).

# Conclusion

So, how should the case of C be treated? The Tokyo District Court acknowledged the following: (1) that there is a sincere relationship between C and her Japanese partner, by stating that the plaintiff '*is biologically male but identifies herself as female; following the original determination on her case, she started a relationship with a Japanese man from around March 2016 and went into cohabitation from around May of the same year and has been deepening the relationship*' (emphasis added); and (2) that C has been participating in the local community, by stating that 'in 2018 and 2019 the plaintiff took part in the Yokohama Wakaba-chō Tabunka Eigasai [multicultural film festival] in Naka ward, Yokohama city, as a guest speaker and made a presentation about Brazilian culture; following the determination on the case at hand, she has been volunteering as a fashion model for kimono-fabric dresses at the request of a local designer in Yokohama'. It is true that the relationship between C and her Japanese partner was formed while she was illegally staying in Japan as the defendant asserted. Even though it developed in unlawful residence conditions, the court ruled that the relationship between C and her Japanese partner 'merits only a lower level of protection as it has been formed under a legal status that is subject to deportation, but even so, it is difficult to deny that it requires a certain degree of protection in light of the substantiality of the relationship etc'.

*The Tokyo District Court recognized that the plaintiff had a domestic life with a Japanese male partner on the basis of her gender identity as a woman although she was born male, that their life was rooted in the local community, and that their life required a certain level of protection. Going so far as to acknowledge her gender identity in fact-finding means that the review of this case needed to step into the personality realm. The court should not stop at making a decision in deference to the political branches' decision in the realm of economic regulatory legislation. This case became a matter requiring a 'strict review'.* This case should have been subjected to strict scrutiny and resulted in the granting of special permission to stay in the first place. It should have been obvious through comparison and balancing with similar cases. *Consequently, the point of contention in this case should be whether or not determining that C's objection was groundless without conducting a strict review was illegal rather than whether or not there were sufficient grounds to overturn that determination.* As the court recognized, C's life with her partner was substantive and hence deserved protection, and therefore the case should have ended with a court order to revoke the disposition in question and grant special permission to stay.

## Notes

1 Hidekazu Hama (1974) reports on how this judgment was received at the time.
2 The judgment in the Carolene Products case can be accessed via the US Supreme Court website (https://supreme.justia.com/cases/federal/us/304/144/#F4).
3 This passage was retained in the Basic Plan for Immigration Control (3rd Edition). Although there was a minor wording change in the subsequent editions ('to have a civil status or position with a Japanese national, a permanent resident or a special permanent resident' was deleted), the passage still conveys the same message.
4 Notices concerning immigration administration are internal documents within the administrative agency and rarely published. However, the Long-Term Resident Mother and Child Notice was reported in *The Immigration Newsmagazine* published by the Immigration Association, *The Asahi Shimbun* and other national newspapers and *The Japan Times* English-language newspaper, publicizing the justice ministry's stance towards acceptance of foreigners. The relationship between the Spouse Notice, Long-Term Resident Mother and Child Notice and Marriage Notice was discussed in Chapter 3.
5 These changes are continually made based on the 'mutatis mutandis' concept and not regarded as being derived from the same 'rights' as those of Japanese. In any case, the practical application of the concept of citizenship also varies from one country to another and there is no universal rule dictating how it should be. In my view, welfare services that foreign nationals can receive in Japan may be provided under the 'citizenship' concept as a practical solution if many more people will be able to benefit from it.
6 Prime Minister Abe's response can be accessed via the House of Representatives website (http://www.shugiin.go.jp/internet/itdb_shitsumon_pdf_t.nsf/html/shitsumon/pdfT/b197078.pdf/$File/b197078.pdf).

# The Japanese System for Evaluating 'Foreigners' Human Rights': Shifting the Epistemological Perspective from 'Foreigners' Human Rights' to 'the Rights of Humans, Including Foreigners'

## Introduction

This chapter discusses how 'foreigners' human rights' are ultimately determined. The focus here is on the petition for reconsideration mechanism in reference to the second of my submissions to the Tokyo High Court. As in the previous chapter, I begin the discussion with an assessment of the original decision (the Toyo District Court judgment) based on the actual written opinion, but from a slightly different angle.

The term 'petition for reconsideration' is not found in the Immigration Control Act or the Regulation for Enforcement of the Immigration Control Act, which sets forth procedural rules. In other words, although the procedure of this petition is a known administrative act, it exists as such with no legal provisions whatsoever under the immigration law. So, how do we explain the legal basis of this special administrative act? How can this act under the immigration law be justified without any provisions in the law itself? As I discuss the petition for reconsideration in relation to these questions, I will present my conclusion on how the limits of foreigners' human rights are determined in Japan. This conclusion is the subject of my arguments throughout this book: 'the line drawn around foreigners' human rights'.

Chapter 10

# Why is a review needed?

With regard to the existence of cohabitation with mutual support and cooperation between C and her Japanese partner, the original judgment of the Tokyo District Court acknowledged the following: 'the plaintiff is biologically male but identifies herself as female; following the original determination on her case, she started a relationship with a Japanese man from around March 2016 and went into cohabitation from around May of the same year and has been deepening the relationship' and 'If deported, the relationship which the plaintiff has been developing with her Japanese partner following the said determination would be damaged and also the connection she has been building with the local community would be lost'. Accordingly, the court found, without needing to examine any other points, that the plaintiff '"would likely suffer a serious damage" if the original determination is not revoked and she is deported from Japan'. The court thus confirmed the plaintiff's 'assimilation into Japanese society'.

However, the Tokyo District Court ruled that the determination made by the director of the Tokyo Regional Immigration Bureau was not unlawful because it 'does not fall under the category where a significant circumstance warranting a review of the decision not to grant special permission to stay arose after the said determination and for the director of the Tokyo Regional Immigration Bureau to uphold the decision not to grant special permission to stay would be grossly unreasonable according to socially accepted ideas', which is the same logic as that used in the McLean judgment (Supreme Court Grand Bench judgment of October 4, 1978) (*Saikō saibansho minji hanreishū*, vol. 32, no. 7: 1223–1331). The court cited the following reasons: (i) 'Given the egregious nature of the record of the plaintiff's stay, although the relationship between the plaintiff and the Japanese partner may be equivalent to a marital relationship, it cannot be regarded as a significant circumstance that arose after the determination warranting a review of the decision not to grant special permission to stay'; (ii) 'There is no evidence supporting the plaintiff's claim that she would be subjected to crimes if deported to Brazil'; (iii) 'The expiration of the suspended sentence in the plaintiff's criminal case does not extinguish the substantive reason for the deportation order'; and (iv) 'The spread of the COVID-19 infection etc. are merely factors to consider in deciding the timing of the plaintiff's deportation'.

This line of reasoning was merely a rehash of the already concluded 'appellate case for the revocation of the deportation disposition' (Tokyo High Court judgment of August 26, 2015, discussed in chapters 3 and 4; hereafter referred to as 'prior action'. The addition of [iv] about the COVID-19 situation in the deportation destination was the only difference). The court conducted this review practically without reviewing the prior action on the same case. Yet, it found the following:

> The likelihood of serious damage is based on a new circumstance that evidently arose after the determination in question, and the plaintiff has no appropriate means other than a mandamus action for the revocation of the aforementioned determination in order to avoid such damage. Accordingly, this mandamus action for the revocation of the aforementioned determination satisfies the requirement of "no other appropriate means for avoiding damage" [...]. This mandamus action for the revocation of the aforementioned determination satisfies the requirement under Article 37-2 (i) of the Administrative Case Litigation Act and is therefore legal.

The court found that C's circumstance had changed since the prior action based on facts, recognized the plaintiff's 'assimilation into Japanese society' and determined that the case satisfied the requirements for a mandamus action.

In the case at hand, the plaintiff's standing to sue was newly recognized and the requirements for the action were satisfied. Yet, without annulling the prior action, the court drew the same conclusion for the same reason as that given in the first instance. Given the satisfaction of the requirements and the confirmed 'assimilation into Japanese society' as acknowledged in the original judgment, the failure to review the case from an angle different to one involved in the prior action in reaching a conclusion must amount to a transgression on the grounds of inconsistencies in the judgement's reasoning.

As the existence of life based on cohabitation and mutual aid and cooperation between C and her Japanese partner was confirmed and determined as being worthy of legal protection, reconsideration of this case must be conducted in the form of a strict review, as I argued in Chapter 9. Arriving at the conclusion, through inertia, that the case 'does not fall under the category where for the director of the Tokyo Regional Immigration Bureau to uphold the decision not to grant special permission to stay is grossly unreasonable according to socially accepted ideas' fails to explain how this case relates to the prior action.

## The acts of the disposing agency officials and the petition for reconsideration

It is said that when a foreign national who is found to fall under Article 24 (grounds for deportation) of the Immigration Control Act subsequently requests an oral examination, and if their claim of a special circumstance is rejected at the oral examination, they may file an objection, and if the objection is accepted by the Minister of Justice or the director of a regional immigration bureau authorized by the Minister of Justice, then special permission to stay is granted. The special permission to stay defined in this way in the law is a series of legal procedures to be followed when a certain special circumstance already exists at the time the foreign national is found to fall under Article 24.

In the case at hand, the plaintiff did not claim that a special circumstance (that merits reconsideration) existed when she fell under Article 24 (this claim was made in the prior action). It sought the granting of special permission to stay on the basis that C's relationship with her Japanese partner worthy of protection (to be given favor) came into existence after the determination in question. It took the form of a 'petition for reconsideration' precisely because of this reason. While the prior action considered whether C's circumstances at the time of the said determination (point A) warranted the granting of special permission to stay, the action at hand sought the granting of special permission to stay for a circumstance arising after the said determination (point B). As the relationship between C and her Japanese partner was acknowledged as requiring protection in the original judgment, the existence of that circumstance at point B was accepted by the court.

However, the Immigration Control Act has no provisions for how to deal with circumstances that arise at point B. The handling of cases very similar to the case at hand is explained in *Ihan shinpan yōryō* (Guidelines on adjudication of violations, 2016 edition) as follows:

> In cases such as an action for the revocation of a deportation disposition, the Minister of Justice et al. may in some cases withdraw the determination in question and grant special permission to stay in response to a circumstance that changed or newly arose after the said determination. *It is also possible to withdraw the determination in question and grant special permission to stay if doing otherwise is considered to be extremely problematic from a humanitarian viewpoint in the light of a circumstance that arose after the deportation disposition was made.* (Hōmu-shō Nyūkoku kanri-kyoku 2016: 74; emphasis added)[1]

In the case at hand, a circumstance at point B (i.e., that which arose after the deportation disposition was made) should be treated as acknowledged in the original judgment—the existence of a life of cohabitation and mutual aid and cooperation between C and her Japanese partner is a fact and deserves legal protection. In recent years, there have been some court rulings supporting legal protection for the life of same-sex couples involving cohabitation and mutual aid and cooperation as shown by examples such as the case seeking damages for a partner's infidelity in a same-sex de facto couple ('An action for damages case', Utsunomiya District Court Mooka Branch judgment of September 18, 2019)[2] and the case in which the existing marriage system disallowing same-sex marriage was ruled unconstitutional ('An action for damages case', Sapporo District Court judgment of March 17, 2021).[3] The case at hand was premised on the fact that C and her Japanese partner had a life deserving protection and the plaintiff sought the granting of special permission to stay in her petition for reconsideration with the said life as the reason for reconsideration.

A petition for reconsideration is a de facto act and not a legally prescribed procedure, as Prime Minister Shinzō Abe stated in the 185th extraordinary Diet session (House of Councilors written reply No. 49, November 19, 2013)[4]: 'It is my understanding that *what is sometimes called "petition for reconsideration" is a de facto act by which foreign nationals who have received a deportation order*, including those whose application for refugee status has been rejected, *file a request to revoke the said disposition and to issue special permission to stay* and not a statutory procedure provided for by the Immigration Control and Refugee Recognition Act (Cabinet Order No. 319 of 1951)' (emphasis added). It exists as a 'de facto administrative act' and the case at hand sought consideration of this action as such. Therefore, irrespective of whether or not special permission to stay is ultimately granted to C in this case, the determination in question needs to be rescinded before the granting of special permission to stay is considered and determined afresh.

Doing otherwise would mean that another court action would be brought on essentially the same case even though the prior action has been finalized. As mentioned earlier, the case at hand was filed as a different type of action for the revocation of the determination in question because it satisfied the requirements for a mandamus action as acknowledged in the original judgment. Determination in the case at hand should have been made (on whether special permission to stay should be granted) by taking into account a circumstance at point B as distinct from the prior action. The case at hand was a mandamus action for the revocation of a determination because it was seeking a court order to rescind that determination in order to allow a fresh determination under circumstances at point B (i.e., when 'assimilation into Japanese society' was recognized). This is the focal point of my argument that the original judgment was unlawful due to inconsistent reasoning.

## The petition for reconsideration and the double standard of judicial review

As stated above, a petition for reconsideration is a 'de facto act' as it is not defined in the letter of the law. As this act is 'construed to be left to an even broader discretion than that for the determination on the granting of special permission to stay due to the nature of the act of retracting a lawfully made determination on the grounds of circumstances that arose subsequently' (Hōmu-shō Nyūkoku kanri-kyoku 2016: 74), it is considered that there is no need to refer to the Guidelines on Special Permission to Stay. This is not provided for in the Immigration Control Act while it entails the exercise of a discretionary power even broader than the broad discretion exercised in determinations on special permission to stay.

However, no matter how broad the officials' discretionary power is, the 'de facto act' is an administrative act performed by national government personnel and not just a private person's act. There is, and should be, no administrative act not based on law. The 'administrative act based on law' is an established legal doctrine in modern law-governed states along with similar doctrines such as the fair and equitable principle and the principle of proportional justice.

Accordingly, the petition for reconsideration, which is an administrative act performed as a 'de facto act', must be placed in the existing legal system—it is performed as an administrative act precisely because it actually has a place in the existing legal system. Because of its 'de facto' nature, there is no reference to the 'petition for reconsideration' in the Immigration Control Act or the Regulation for Enforcement, which is a Ministry of Justice order, or the Guidelines on Adjudication of Violations under them. Instead, it is given the following generalized explanation: 'There is no legal provision allowing, after the determination was made that the objection was groundless, the revocation of the said determination and the granting of special permission to stay in consideration of circumstances that arose subsequently' (Hōmushō Nyūkoku kanri-kyoku 2016: 74).

An administrative act is performed without any legal provision, and this is validated by the state. How can this contradiction be resolved? If there is no provision for this de facto administrative act in the Immigration Control Act, it must be placed in a legal system superior to the act. As the Immigration Control Act is a special law, the only law that is superior to it is the Constitution.

In his classic work on the subject of foreigners' human rights, Junji Annen states, 'Regarding the order of precedence of effect between different forms of law, this thesis assumes the so-called supremacy of the Constitution (over treaties) positing that the constitutional principles are not changed by human-rights treaties and conventions, and therefore I do not believe that these treaties (or the "international human rights theory" founded on them) will have particular influences on my understanding of the issues expressed in this thesis' (Annen 1993: 168). Former Supreme Court justice Tokuji Izumi also argues as follows:

> If the party claims "a violation of a treaty", the Supreme Court will dismiss it on the grounds that "the claim of a mere law violation does not clearly fall under the circumstance stipulated in Article 312, paragraph 1 or 2 of the Code of Civil Procedures. As Japan has not introduced an individual complaint mechanism and also "a violation of a treaty" is not dealt with in the final appeal court, the Japanese courts do not seriously consider the claims of violations of the international human rights treaties even in this age of globalization. (Izumi 2020: 144)[5]

Izumi's comment suggests that Annen's assumption still stands today. The petition for reconsideration should thus be understood as an administrative act positioned in the legal order with the Constitution as the supreme law rather than international treaties and laws.

In terms of the relationship with the constitutional order dictated by the Constitution, the petition for reconsideration can be positioned in the same way as the special permission to stay was positioned in Chapter 9. Let us review how the special permission to stay mechanism is justified. Where a foreign national is investigated on suspicion of falling under any of the conditions for deportation under Article 24 of the act and files an objection in the subsequent oral examination, even after the immigration authority determines that the objection is groundless, it can grant special permission to stay if it finds a reason for (giving the benefit of) allowing the person to stay in Japan. This mechanism appears to be distorting a law with a law but this is not the case. The immigration authority initially deals with the case in the economic realm by respecting the political branch's decision, but if the subject of the determination has proven the existence of social life, including family life, the matter becomes a 'question in the mental realm' concerning not only the foreign national in question but also Japanese nationals and foreign nationals with medium-to-long-term residence status in their family and social relationships and compels the authority to conduct a strict review. The granting of special permission to stay is justified because it is considered that overturning the political branch's decision as the result of a strict review does not make it illegal.

The idea behind the petition for reconsideration mechanism with a broader scope for administrative discretion than that for special permission to stay is a purer and stronger version of the aforementioned logic. This is why, unlike special permission to stay, which must be granted according to a procedure prescribed by law, there is no procedural rule for the petition for reconsideration as a 'de facto' administrative act. Because an administrative act with no legal grounds whatsoever is impossible, however, the 'de facto act' is performed solely on the basis of the concept of strict review required by the Constitution as it is rooted in the constitutional order.[6] Determination of whether to advance to the strict review stage depends solely on the existence of facts compelling the adjudicator to do so. For the granting of a stay of execution of a deportation order and special permission to stay, the decision is entirely dependent on the finding of 'assimilation into Japanese society'. In the case at hand, the original judgment acknowledged the existence of facts making it eligible for strict review. At that point, the court should have revoked the original determination and moved on to determine whether or not special permission to stay should be granted to the plaintiff.

## Foreigners' human rights and the Asahi case

The McLean judgment is still used as a precedent four decades after it was made, and not without reason. Jirō Tanaka made the following comment regarding foreigners' right to employment in the public service: 'There is the question of the appointment of foreigners to public service positions. In my view, it is reasonable to divide national and local public service jobs into two categories—one closed to foreigners (i.e., jobs involving the exercise of administrative authority) and one open to foreigners (i.e., research, advisory or educational positions)' (Tanaka 1957: 175).

This reasoning can be found in the original judgment made by the Tokyo District Court on November 26, 1997, in the 'Case to seek declaration of eligibility to become a candidate for an examination for selecting management level employees' (Supreme Court Grand Bench judgment of January 26, 2005):

In particular, local government employees in managerial posts are likely to be involved in performing governing functions of the local public body, by exercising the local public body's public authority or participating in public decision-making. For this reason, it would be inappropriate, in light of the principle of sovereignty of the people, to consider that foreign nationals appointed as local government employees are necessarily guaranteed, as Japanese employees, the right to be promoted to managerial posts. However, managerial employees are engaged in a broad range of duties, and they may be involved in performing governing functions of the local public body, especially in public decision-making, in different manners and on different levels. Also, some managerial employees may be not so deeply involved in performing governing functions of the local public body, because they do not exercise its public authority or they are less likely to participate in public decision-making. Therefore, it is necessary to distinguish between managerial posts that must not be open to foreign nationals and those that may be open to foreign nationals, depending on the contents of duties as well as how and to what extent the authority granted to each post is involved in performing governing functions. It is not against the principle of sovereignty of the people to appoint foreign nationals residing in Japan to the latter type of managerial posts. [...] It should be considered that foreign nationals residing in Japan shall also be guaranteed the right to be appointed to the latter type of managerial posts under Article 22, Para. 1 and Article 14, Para. 1 of the Constitution. (https://www.courts.go.jp/app/hanrei_en/detail?id=732)

While the Supreme Court dismissed this approach to foreigners' right to public service employment, justices Shigeo Takii and Tokuji Izumi submitted dissenting opinions reinforcing it.[7]

On the other hand, the following ruling was made about foreigners' voting rights in local elections in the 'Case for the revocation of a decision dismissing an objection against the disposition for non-registration of the pollbook' (Supreme Court Third Petty Bench judgment of February 28, 2005):

> Although it cannot be said that Article 93-2 of the Constitution guarantees the right of foreign nationals residing in Japan to vote in local government elections, *the provisions concerning local self-government under Chapter VIII of the Constitution are construed to express the intent to guarantee, as a constitutional institution, a form of government in which public administration closely related to local residents' day-to-day living is performed by the local government in the locality based on the will of its residents given the importance of local self-government in a democratic society. Accordingly, it is reasonable to construe that, for any foreign nationals residing in Japan who are permanent residents and found to have a particularly close connection with the local government in their place of residence, the Constitution does not prohibit measures to be implemented, by law, to grant them the right to vote in elections of the head of the local government and members of the local assembly in order to reflect their will in the public administration function of the local government that is closely relevant to their daily life.*[8] (emphasis added)

This reasoning echoes the view of foreigners' right to public service employment expressed by Tanaka in 1957. Needless to say, some precedents become deeply entrenched because precedents and doctrines are built by an accumulation of past legal decisions. The McLean judgment is just one of such precedents.

Incidentally, arguments in this written opinion are not new either. The basic framework around the Constitution and special laws has been constructed through various court cases, including the 'Case charged for violation of the Food Control Act' (Supreme Court Grand Bench judgment of September 29, 1948) and the 'Case for the revocation of a disposition against an objection concerning public assistance under the Public Assistance Act' (Supreme Court Grand Bench judgment of May 24, 1967; hereafter referred to as the 'Asahi case'). The main argument of this submission has been founded on these cases.

In the Food Control Act violation case, Justice Shigeru Kuriyama argued as follows:

The majority opinion, after interpreting the provisions of Article 25 of the Constitution, considered the Food Control Act and explained that "the Food Control Act aims to manage foodstuff, to regulate its supply, demand and prices, and to control its distribution, in order to secure food for the people and to stabilize the national economy" before concluding that "It must be said that the act is a law to stabilize the living conditions of the people in general as much as possible for their welfare and is hence a legislation that is perfectly compatible with the intent of Article 25 of the Constitution". Looking at the case, however, the defendant appealed against the imposition of a penalty for the reason in the original judgment that "the defendant's action falls under Articles 9 and 31 of the Food Control Act, Article 11-5 of the Order for Enforcement of the said act, and Article 23-7 of the Regulation for Enforcement of the said act". As the defendant stated in the gist of the appeal, the foregoing provisions were applied to "the fact of transporting, without authorization, the eighteen liters of white rice and 1.8 liters of brown rice the defendant purchased". In the trial for the appeal at hand, therefore, this court must evaluate the points of argument about the unconstitutionality of the foregoing provisions so applied. (*Saikō saibansho keiji hanreishū*, vol. 2, no. 10: 1247)

The case at hand did not seek the court's ruling on the question of the discretionary power of the Minister of Justice and authorized officials over the granting of special permission to stay in general. It sought the revocation of the determination in question and the granting of special permission to stay after the revocation in consideration of the true living condition of C and her Japanese partner which was the reason for the filing of the petition for reconsideration. Even though the McLean judgment may remain as a precedent, the point of this case is clearly different from the disposition over which the McLean case was fought (see Chapter 8 for details). Given that the court acknowledged the fact of the changed circumstances as being worthy of legal protection after the determination not to grant special permission to stay, the court needed to re-examine the determination in question in light of the new fact. It could not make a reasonable decision by simply applying the precedent to the case at hand.

In the aforementioned concurring opinion in the Food Control Act violation case, Kuriyama also argued that 'Although similarly aiming for public welfare, legal provisions restraining the individual's economic activity such as food control, price regulation and the prohibition of private monopoly are subject to the requirements provided for by Articles 29-2, 31 and others of the Constitution'. The same requirements apply to the Immigration Control Act restraining foreigners' economic activity by residence status and therefore the case at hand is also subject to the same requirements.

The Public Assistance Act is said to have been formulated 'with the intent to avoid the subjective judgment of individual officials administering public assistance so that the necessary public assistance according to the level of poverty is provided to a person requiring it, hence public assistance shall be administered according to the standard specified by the Minister of Health, Labor and Welfare' (*Saikō saibansho minji hanre shū*, vol. 21, no. 5: 1052). The Guidelines on Special Permission to Stay has been established for the same purpose. Where public services are administered to a large number of recipients—millions in the case of public assistance and over 1,000 in the case of special permission to stay—variation in decision-making between individual officials must be minimized as much as possible. Standards and guidelines are established as a device to maintain consistency in administration.[9] It was held that as these standards and guidelines were formulated by a responsible minister, taking into consideration various factors, 'it should be construed that a determination under them does not give rise to the issue of unlawfulness as long as it does not deviate from the intent and purpose of the law' (*Saikō saibansho minji hanreishū*, vol. 21, no. 5: 1063).

However, Justice Jirō Tanaka argued as follows in his dissenting opinion on the Asahi case:

> In order to keep pace with actual living conditions by promptly responding to specific situations, it is desirable to permit some discretion to take more appropriate measures quickly. While the public assistance system is to guarantee it as a right and not a mere benefaction system as mentioned above, if the perception of public assistance as people's

right leads to the loss of warmth and compassion on the part of the administrators of the system, then the original intent and purpose of the system will not be achieved. (*Saikō saibansho minji hanreishū*, vol. 21, no. 5: 1069)

This statement speaks for the practice of court trial as alternative justice in Japan. In fact, although the Asahi case ended in a judgment against the plaintiff, the operation of the public assistance system thereafter was gradually changed in the direction sought by the plaintiff. The petition for reconsideration needs to be placed in a similar position.

The petition for reconsideration, in the Japanese language, has an element of appealing to the beneficence of a superior authority, but in reality it has nothing to do with beneficence. To proceed to the reconsideration stage, the case must be examined closely in terms of whether or not it warrants a strict review (i.e., the existence of 'assimilation into Japanese society'). Foreign nationals have no right to petition for reconsideration. However, under the Postwar Constitution of Japan as well as accumulated precedents, it is self-evident that those who have shifted to the strict review realm under the double standard of judicial review must be dealt with within the system. Precisely because the petition for reconsideration is an administrative act in the form of a 'de facto act' with no procedural rules whatsoever, it must not be used arbitrarily. Therefore, in the case at hand, the determination in question has to be revoked first, and then the decision-making can proceed regarding whether or not special permission to stay should be granted under the condition of a stable communal life between C and her Japanese partner, which was actualized subsequent to the determination in question and acknowledged by the court as being worthy of legal protection. If warmth and compassion are lost on the part of those who administer the petition for reconsideration mechanism, its intent and purpose cannot be achieved.

## Understanding the difference between 'foreigners' human rights' and 'the rights of humans, including foreigners'

My inquiry into 'foreigners' human rights' in this book has arrived at the conclusion that 'foreigners' human rights' do not generally exist in Japan. This statement has a different meaning from that in Annen's argument. As each residence status category defines what people are permitted to do in reality, the Immigration Control Act is the positive law that prescribes 'human rights according to residence status'. However, the elements provided for in the Immigration Control Act are not necessarily referred to as foreigners' human rights. The release of the Guidelines on Special Permission to Stay has made public the factors that are considered by the immigration authority in assessing applicants. Yet, I was unable to find evidence that a close examination of the attributes of individual foreigners is conducted before the limits of their human rights are determined.

What is closely examined is not only a balance with precedents under immigration law but also compliance with past interpretations under economic regulatory legislation. *In this sense, the scope and limits of economic regulatory legislation are the limits of control under the Immigration Control Act and foreigners' human rights are bound within that scope.* This is the point of difference between my argument and Annen's. It is likely that this difference stems from the difference between my focus on the specific and narrow area of special permission to stay and Annen's focus on foreigners' human rights in general.

However, this narrow view enabled me to notice that the limits of foreigners' human rights are determined in their etic relationship with various regulatory laws restricting human rights legislated in the Diet (i.e., economic legislation such as the Food Control Act, the Public Assistance Act, the Pharmaceutical Affairs Act, the Act on Special Measures for the Adjustment of Retail Business and the Forest Act, as well as the City Planning Act and the Agricultural Land Act including land expropriation measures) rather than the emic principles directly concerning foreign nationals such as their nationality and marital status (based on individual attributes).[10] The logic behind the limits of foreigners' human rights is based on 'provisions in the special acts of the Diet' and not on their 'foreign nationality'.

When court cases involving foreigners' human rights have received favorable judgments, they have been considered within the framework of 'decision-making by comprehensive balancing' precisely because 'foreigners' human rights' are determined on the basis of 'the special acts of the Diet'. Due to the fact that special acts are legislated by the people's representatives in the Diet, the logic that the legislation in question was unlawful from its inception is not acceptable. A special act can be ruled unlawful only when the case is approached from the double standard and it is determined that it needs to proceed to strict review.

However, it is extremely difficult to establish that this is the reasoning behind the operation of the Immigration Control Act. Moreover, the petition for reconsideration and special permission to stay are the only areas of immigration law that give rise to the double standard of judicial review. Further, the incorporation of the double standard of judicial review into the assessment processes for the petition for reconsideration or special permission to stay is not stated in the letter of the immigration law; these acts are positioned as legitimate administrative acts by logical deduction from their relationship with the constitutional order (which is the only approach I can think of although there may be other ways). This becomes noticeable only in the process of detailed comparison and analysis of the contents of specific cases with the focus on why special permission to stay was granted in some cases and denied in others.

In my mind, the emergence of this awareness through comparative analysis of individual cases resembled the scientific knowledge discovery process. According to Yoshitaka Yamamoto, 'In Europe from the Late Middle Ages to the Renaissance, people sincerely believed that ancient and classical Greeks and Romans were superior to modern humans and that prophets in the pre-Deluge ages were even better humans, closer to gods in possession of truths revealed by gods' (Yamamoto 2003a: 338). The pursuit of closeness to gods began because eschatological beliefs compelled people to want to learn ancient wisdom out of nostalgia for the 'good old days'. However, humanism, which is 'the idea that humankind is capable of knowing all and governing all things or mastering and controlling nature as they desire, changed the medieval relationship between God and humankind fundamentally' and eventually 'allowed humans to perform miracles, which used to be an exclusive domain of God', and transitioned to something that 'involved the reinstatement of magic' (Yamamoto 2003a: 341).

In the Age of Discovery, simply based on the view that the past was superior to the present, knowledge in the production of the mariner's compass needed for navigation, navigational knowledge needed for using the compass, knowledge in civil engineering and metallurgy for mining and industry, and even medical knowledge were accumulated as practical knowledge through experimentation by craftworkers and technicians. Although such knowledge may have been regarded as magic (i.e., what was studied in experiments and practice) at the time, it formed the foundations for overriding that gained from non-empirical book-based doctrines (i.e., truths that exist as given conditions beyond criticism).[11]

Yamamoto also argues in his *Sekai no mikata no tenkan 2 Chidōsetsu no teishō to uchūron no sōkoku* (Revolutions in worldview 2: Conflict between heliocentrism and cosmology) that the importance of Copernicus' role in calendar reform during the Renaissance lies not in his proposition of heliocentrism but in his postulate of the cosmic system itself, including the solar system, within which he positioned the motions of the sun and Earth in explaining his theory (Yamamoto 2014: 369–377). In short, Yamamoto's comment that 'Borrowing from the *Posterior Analytics* by Aristotle, what was mere "knowledge of the fact (what it is)" in Ptolemy was converted to "knowledge of the reason of the fact (why it is)" in Copernicus' (Yamamoto 2014: 375–376) paraphrases my awareness of the problem.

In the past, I had 'knowledge of the fact' that special permission to stay and the petition for reconsideration are dealt with on a case-by-case basis and that cases involving a family tend to be more successful, but my thinking stopped there. Now I have been able to discover 'knowledge of the reason of the fact' that the 'double standard of judicial review' was at work in those successful cases. Those historical texts in scientific literature have inspired great awareness in me.

When a foreigner goes to court in present-day Japan, the McLean judgment is the 'knowledge gained from non-empirical book-based doctrines' and 'truth that exists as a given condition beyond criticism'. When reference is made to the McLean judgment in a decision, it is common that no explanation is provided. For instance, the Tokyo High Court judgment on the case discussed in chapters 3 and 4 was two pages long (or a single page considering that the second page contained little more than the judges' signatures), and that on the case in chapters 9 and 10 was three pages long. While the McLean judgment is referred to, the court is permitted to present its conclusion without offering any reason, akin to the production of knowledge in the Middle Ages. Nevertheless, special permission to stay has been granted to over 1,000 cases per year in recent times and a certain proportion of court judgments do offer detailed explanations as to why the McLean judgment applies to the case in question (as did the Tokyo District Court judgment—twenty-four pages long, excluding attachments—for which the written opinion in Chapter 8 was submitted). Naturally, more meticulous explanations are offered in judgments supporting the granting of special permission to stay or judgments/rulings ordering a stay of execution of a deportation disposition.

Yamamoto nominates Della Porta as the scientist who straddled the Renaissance and modernity. According to Yamamoto, Della Porta's most famous work, *Natural Magic* (1589), is an encyclopedic collection of experiments conducted by himself and his students, a compilation of discrete observations and experiences, although some segments show early signs of the systematization of knowledge (with measurement and theory of static electricity in particular displaying a nascent modern approach) (Yamamoto 2003a: Chapter 16).

In the same way, the present book feels somewhat like a compilation of some of the cases seeking special permission to stay on which relatively more detailed judgments were handed down. This is because cases involving violations of the Immigration Control Act are the results of case-by-case decision-making based on individual foreigners' personal circumstances, and the underlying principles or rules governing such decision-making can only be discovered through content analysis and 'experimentation'. It is at once an emic study to analyze the specificity of each case and an etic study to identify common elements from a list of emic specifics. However, the etic elements I discovered as a result were not common characteristics among the foreign nationals who were granted special permission to stay by the

Japanese government as I had imagined (and on this point, this book failed in its attempt to discover 'foreigners' human rights'). What I found was the very elusive manner in which the logic applicable to special laws in general (i.e., the double standard of review) operates in determining the limits of foreigners' human rights in cases concerning special permission to stay or the petition for reconsideration.

This book began its analysis on the supposition that 'the limits of foreigners' human rights' would be found somewhere between the permitted and rejected cases within the special permission to stay system. From this viewpoint, *cases are generally rejected if special permission to stay is topicalized as the problem for the foreign national in question as an individual. This approach leads to the conclusion that there are no foreigners' human rights in Japan (which was established by the McLean judgment). On the other hand, when the existence of the foreign national in question extends beyond the individual and forms part of relationships with Japanese society, especially a family relationship with a Japanese spouse or Japanese children or a similar relationship with a permanent resident, legal consideration for welfare is extended to the people around the foreign national beyond the individual. The condition for which Japanese authorities are compelled to make this type of consideration is expressed as 'assimilation into Japanese society' and the lens through which foreign nationals' assimilation is recognized determines 'the rights of humans, including foreigners'. This recognition activates the logic for granting special permission to stay (i.e., the double standard of review).*[12] The issue in this case is 'the rights of humans, including foreigners' rather than 'foreigners' human rights'.

## Conclusion: The discovery of a 'human rights structure' in Japan

The outcome of the same foreigner's case can be either of the following: (1) the foreign national is not permitted to stay in Japan if the case is approached from the angle of 'foreigners' human rights'; (2) the foreign national is permitted to stay in Japan if the case is approached from the angle of 'the rights of humans, including foreigners'; or, the logic of (2) is extended to (3), in which the foreign national is permitted to stay if the case is approached from the angle of community, including foreign residents, where the individual has the right to enjoy peaceful community life as in the hate speech rally injunction case (see Chapter 5). In other words, foreigners' human rights in Japan are not inherent in the individual foreign national; human rights worthy of protection are differentiated from those unworthy of protection on the basis of the social relationships, primarily the family relationship, that the (individual) foreign national has formed in Japan.[13]

Special permission to stay concerns the incorporation of foreigners into Japanese society. While immigration policy in Western countries evolved from the assimilation of immigrants in the early twentieth century to their social integration from the postwar period to the 1970s and to their social incorporation upon acceptance of ethnic diversity from the 1980s onward, it is often argued that Japan's immigration policy lacks a social integration element. However, Japan's special permission to stay mechanism was premised on social incorporation from the outset by circumventing the social integration stage and its decision criterion indicates the desired mode of incorporation.

Viewing the individual's relationship formation as the mode of incorporation is akin to Tetsurō Watsuji's understanding of 'the betweenness of persons' as the fundamental principle of human existence in society.[14] Instead of individual persons, Watsuji found importance in 'betweenness' formed between individuals or an individual and a group and shone a light on qualitative differences between multiple layers of betweenness.[15] From Watsuji's point of view, 'the rights of humans, including foreigners' constitutes the recognition of the 'betweenness' that a foreign person forms in Japan. Watsuji argued as follows:

> Individual material solids can never in themselves constitute betweenness. On the other hand, what we are seeking are individual persons who constitute betweenness. Thus, it is to be taken for granted that such persons cannot be found in material solids deprived of their capacity to produce betweenness. [...] At this point a conclusion is reached. Insofar as betweenness is constituted, one human body is connected with another. And insofar as this connection is completely destroyed, then either the human body is a material solid, unable to constitute

betweenness, or it terminates in absolute emptiness. (Watsuji 1996: 67–68)

In Watsuji's view, an individual who is not connected to others and hence not incorporated into society is a discrete object devoid of meaning. The value of a person's being is actualized only when the person is able to produce betweenness with others. It is possible to detect the logic for evaluating 'the rights of humans, including foreigners' in this more universal theory of the betweenness of socially incorporated persons.

'The rights of humans, including foreigners', or the betweenness of socially incorporated persons as its universalized form, share the same attributes with what Levi-Strauss describes as 'structure': 'a whole made up of components and relationships between them, and these relationships maintain universal properties throughout the process of transfiguration (transformation)' (Levi-Strauss 1979a: 37).[16] The method of giving Japanese nationality to a person who was born to and raised by a Japanese family exists as the basic pattern of citizenship while the granting of special permission to stay to a person who has a family relationship with Japanese nationals or permanent or semi-permanent residents (or who demonstrates a similar level of 'assimilation into Japanese society') exists as its variant. The latter is destined to undergo further transformation and comes into existence as the recognition of foreigners' right to pursue happiness as they live in a community with their family members, including Japanese nationals and permanent residents.

Where the granting of nationality is expressed as a proto-citizenship function $F = f(x)$, the granting of special permission to stay can be expressed as $G = g(f(x))$ where $f(x)$ is modified by function g (which is 'assimilation into Japanese society'). When it progresses to the hate speech rally ban, function $g(x)$ is further modified by function h and the process is expressed as $H = h(g(f(x)))$. Relations between elements in these functions are similar and the structure for the evaluation of their relationships (always incorporating the idea of 'family' current at the time) does not change. This is the very reason why it is possible to argue that the same thinking underlies the finding of the unconstitutionality of the Nationality Act and the court actions for the granting of special permission to stay, and it is also possible to identify the same thinking behind the hate speech rally injunction case. These court cases were fought over the universal question of what 'human rights' recognized by Japan are beyond the difference in nationality status between Japanese and non-Japanese. In other words, all of them were fought over the question of citizenship. This may be called the 'human rights structure' in Japan in the language of Levi-Strauss. In my mind, the approach that leads to this 'human rights structure' is the 'comparative sociology of human rights'.

Some Western European and North American countries implement general amnesties when the number of irregular migrants reaches a certain level to give legal status to those who meet certain conditions. A general amnesty that applies to anyone who meets certain conditions implies that individual rights are inherent in all persons (or 'inalienable rights'). Japan's special permission to stay mechanism also turns irregular migrants into regular migrants but the government does not recognize it as a form of amnesty. This is confirmed by the following statement in the aforementioned Second Basic Plan for Immigration Control: 'Japan does not adopt the Amnesty policy, which several other countries have tried to adopt against illegal residents. It uniformly legitimizes illegal residents under certain prerequisites, which is nothing but an exceptional measure to maintain law and order to the end'.[17] It is likely that the government has adopted this view because of its subjective understanding of Japan's 'human rights structure' in administering 'the rights of humans, including foreigners'.

As mentioned earlier, Japan's special permission to stay mechanism does not recognize the inherent rights of individuals. This is because discrete individuals are 'empty'. When an individual is found to have formed betweenness with others and such betweenness is found to confirm the individual's incorporation into Japanese society by the adjudicator, the individual is granted special permission to stay. Similarly, a petition for reconsideration is accepted when the adjudicator finds betweenness that warrants reconsideration. Only Ministry of Justice officials and court judges can act as adjudicators of special permissions to stay and petitions for reconsideration. Therefore, these measures can be regarded as the 'beneficence' of the state. This extremely Japanese-style system of evaluating 'foreigners' human rights' results in 'the rights of humans, including foreigners'.

In the end, 'the rights of humans, including foreigners' are determined not only by the relative position of the case in question among all other cases involving foreigners but also by the place it occupies in the whole of Japan's legal and social order as a semantic universe that includes cases involving foreigners. This awareness needed an epistemic shift of Copernican magnitude in the conceptualization of foreigners and also entailed the understanding of what can be called the discovery of a 'human rights structure' in Japan. The basis for the court's decision to accept that Seikyū-sha, a social welfare corporation, had standing to sue in the hate speech rally injunction case is found in the Supreme Court Grand Bench judgment of 1970 over the political donations made by the Yahata Steel Works to the Liberal Democratic Party.

As the article title 'Amorphization amid Fragmentation: Japanese Society 1990–2020' suggests, present-day Japan is characterized by a progressive fragmentation of the building blocks of Japanese society and the creation of amorphous and transient societies by the fragmented parts (Sugimoto 2021). Yet, no matter how fragmented Japanese society becomes, as far as foreigners' stay in Japan is concerned, the effect of the 'human rights structure' principle applies a force to contain the past, the present and the future within certain limits. When we recognize the 'human rights structure', and 'the rights of humans, including foreigners' as its manifestation, we are able to gain a concrete understanding of this dynamic.

I use the concept of 'structure' in 'human rights structure' here after the fashion of Levi-Strauss. This refers to the pattern of interrelations between the common elements (contents) found in the way nationality is recognized, the way special permission to stay is granted, the way the petition for reconsideration is accepted and the way the hate speech rally injunction is granted, and does not signify the foundation or basis of the concept of human rights itself in Japan.

# Notes

1 The passage immediately before the quotation states, 'the director of a regional immigration bureau has the delegated authority to make a determination on a filed objection under Article 69-2 of the act and to grant special permission to stay (which does not preclude the Minister of Justice from exercising it themselves under the proviso to Article 61-2 of the regulation), but there are no stipulations permitting the withdrawal of the determination that the objection was groundless and the granting of special permission to stay in consideration of circumstances that arose after the said determination was made', citing the absence of provisions for these procedures in the Immigration Control Act itself.

2 The court ruled as follows: 'These days, diversification of values and lifestyles has made it difficult to assert the necessity to limit marriage to opposite-sex couples. It is common knowledge that there are countries that have introduced a system to legally recognize same-sex marriage and a considerable number of countries have adopted a system to publicly recognize the same-sex relationship, if not marriage, while some local governments in Japan have introduced a similar system. In light of this social change, there is a strong need for providing a certain level of legal protection to same-sex couples, depending on their circumstances. (In comparison with de facto marriage cases where the couples choose not to marry legally even though they can, it is difficult to find any reasonable grounds for denying almost all kinds of legal protection in the cases of same-sex couples who cannot marry legally even if they want to.) And Article 24-1 of the Constitution provides that "Marriage shall be based only on the mutual consent of both sexes" merely because same-sex marriage was not anticipated at the time of its enactment and it cannot be construed that the intent of the provision was to deny same-sex marriage, and therefore the court finds that the aforementioned understanding contravenes the Constitution'.

3 The judgment on this case reasoned that 'The essence of marriage is for man and woman to lead a communal life with sincere intentions for the purpose of enduring mental and physical union; given the only difference between opposite-sex union and same-sex union is their sexual orientation, it is understood that homosexual people can lead a communal life echoing the essence of marriage with a same-sex partner of the same sexual orientation just as opposite-sex partners can. [...] In light of the fact that the provisions in question do not include same-sex marriage merely because it was considered at the time of the Civil Code revision in 1947 that homosexual people were unable to form a normal marital relationship conforming to socially accepted ideas because homosexuality was regarded as a mental disorder; given that such perception has come to be rejected completely today, it is unfair to construe the provisions in question as having the intent and purpose to deny all kinds

of legal protection to homosexual people who lead a communal life echoing the aforementioned essence of marriage just as opposite-sex couples do', and concluded that 'In light of the purposes of the provisions in question and the intent of Article 24 of the Constitution, these provisions are not supposed be taken as reasons for denying same-sex couples all manners of legal protection'. It also ruled that 'Although the legislature's legislative discretion is extensive, the fact that the provisions in question do not offer homosexual people any legal means to enjoy even part of the legal effects arising from marriage while providing opposite-sex couples an opportunity to use the institution of marriage demonstrates the exercise of the legislative discretion by the legislative branch beyond the bounds of its power, and this distinction in treatment is considered, to that extent, to be discriminatory treatment lacking reasonable grounds. It is therefore appropriate to find that the provisions in question contravene Article 14-1 of the Constitution to the extent of the foregoing'.

4   Prime Minister Abe's reply can be accessed on the House of Councilors website (https://www.sangiin.go.jp/japanese/joho1/kousei/syuisyo/185/touh/t185049.htm).

5   The final appeal on the case at hand was dismissed by the Supreme Court Second Petty Bench on November 12, 2021, for exactly the reasons pointed out by Izumi: '1 Final appeal: A final appeal on a civil case may be filed with the Supreme Court only when it falls under the circumstance prescribed in Article 312, para. 1 or 2 of the Code of Civil Procedures; although the appeal on the case at hand raises the unconstitutionality and erroneous/inconsistent reasoning of the original judgment as the grounds, its substance is a claim of errors of fact or mere law violations and does not clearly fit any of the aforementioned circumstances. 2 Petition for the acceptance of the final appeal: Based on the reasons stated in the petition, the court has decided not to accept the appeal pursuant to Article 318, para. 1 of the Code of Civil Procedures'.

6   Tokuji Izumi argues, 'As you can see from precedents on the constitutionality question such as the judgment on the constitutionality of the Nationality Act, those who have worked in the Cabinet Legislation Bureau or in the legislative areas of the Ministry of Justice etc. tend to show stiff resistance to judging a law as unconstitutional. Court judges in general are extremely reluctant to derive the citizens' rights and liberties directly from the Constitution itself when asked to protect the individual's human rights [...] However, the Constitution is the undeniably codified supreme law of Japan and hence the courts must examine seriously whether the claimant's right or freedom is actually guaranteed under the Constitution. Yet, the courts often make a decision by interpreting a law subordinate to the Constitution first, considering whether the right or freedom in question is specifically provided for by the said law and whether a restriction

on such right or freedom is permitted by the said law, and concluding that such restriction cannot be a violation of the Constitution if it conforms to the said law' (Izumi, Nakagawa, Mizuno and Saitō 2017: 59–60). Nonetheless, this can mean that where an administrative act not established by a law is permitted in the enforcement of the law, the administrative act in question must be an act directly provided for by the Constitution, because otherwise it cannot be a lawful administrative act.

7   Shigeo Takii says in his dissenting opinion, 'However, in the case of a local public body in which many people are engaged in various duties, such as the jōkoku appellant, no reasonable grounds can be found if such local public body requires all its employees in managerial posts to have Japanese nationality, irrespective of the nature of their duties. Consequently, I consider that the measure taken by the jōkoku appellant to require Japanese nationality as a qualification for the Examinations for Management Selection closes the door on its employees who are foreign residents being promoted to managerial posts only by reason of nationality, and therefore it is in violation of Article 3 of the Labor Standards Law that prohibits discriminatory treatment by reason of nationality under Article 14 of the Constitution. [...] In other words, under Japanese positive laws, only Japanese nationals are eligible to elect and to be elected as public officials in particular posts, but this does not necessarily mean that as a natural consequence from the principle of sovereignty of the people, only Japanese nationals are guaranteed all rights relating to the right to participate in politics. [...] In my opinion, considering that the people's involvement in the foundation of governance differs between local administration and national administration, it should be considered that, in local administrative bodies, posts for which Japanese nationality is required as a natural consequence from the principle of sovereignty of the people should be limited only to principals of local public bodies, such as the heads of the bodies and there are no constitutional restrictions on appointment as government employees in other posts. If so, even though a legislative limit may be imposed, there are no grounds to construe that such other posts should be assigned only to Japanese nationals as a natural consequence from the nature of the posts, without any legislation to that effect' (https://www.courts.go.jp/app/hanrei_en/detail?id=73).

Tokuji Izumi later made the following comment on his dissenting opinion in this case: 'There was no mention of "foreign nationality" in the selection outline. The deputy director of the public health service noticed and declined to accept the application. In other words, it was the deputy director's decision. The personnel committee later approved the deputy director's action. The local assembly and the governor did not know about it. Foreign nationality was added to the selection outline as a reason for ineligibility from the following year. Even that was a decision made by the personnel committee, not approved by the local assembly. That seemed to be another problem in my eyes'.

8   However, it went on to say that 'Nevertheless, whether or not to institute such measures is entirely a matter for the state's legislative policy and not instituting such measures does not in itself give rise to the issue of constitutionality'.

9   In recent years, public assistance was provided to 1,638,944 households and 2,141,881 individuals in 2017, 1,635,280 households and 2,103,066 individuals in 2018, and 1,637,009 households and 2,070,253 individuals in 2019. Special permission to stay was granted to 1,255 cases in 2017, 1,371 cases in 2018, and 1,448 cases in 2019. Prior to the release of the Guidelines on Special Permission to Stay, permission was granted to 13,239 cases in 2004, 10,834 cases in 2005, and 9,360 cases in 2006. In view of these large numbers, I surmise that the guidelines were formulated at the time with the intention of minimizing variation between individual officers as well as making the process easier to understand for foreign nationals.

10  Makoto Oda argues that 'The aspect of Levi-Strauss' analysis of myths using bricolage to analyze a myth made by bricolage is evident in the characteristic of "deconstructing" the narrative of a myth. Levi-Strauss assumed that the full meaning of a myth cannot be gleaned from a single myth instead of seeing a myth as a self-contained structure' (Oda 2000: 162). By substituting 'myth' with 'precedent' and 'Levi-Strauss' with 'the author', the sentence reads: 'The aspect of the author's analysis of precedents using bricolage to analyze a precedent made by bricolage is evident in the characteristic of "deconstructing" the narrative of the precedent. *The author assumed that the full meaning of a precedent cannot be gleaned from a single precedent (judgment) instead of seeing a precedent as a self-contained structure*'. This highlights the assumption I used in arriving at the conclusion in this book and the adoption of the bricolage or myth analysis technique as my intellectual approach.

11  This understanding has a shared viewpoint in social science. *The Book that Changed Europe: Picart & Bernard's Religious Ceremonies of the World* by Lynn Hunt and others based on *Cérémonies et coutumes religieuses de tous les peuples du monde* published between 1723 and 1737 was written from a similar viewpoint. Very knowledgeable printmakers, Picart and Bernard, provided a lucid explanation of religions of the world, which became known through a growing body of travel books brought by Christian missionaries and explorers in the Age of Discovery, by objectively comparing their elements such as ceremonies and costumes using words and exquisite illustrations. As they were Huguenot refugees in the Netherlands who had escaped oppression in Catholic France, they published their non-judgmental accounts of religions while critically examining the relationship between religion and society. Hunt

and others highlight the effect of the activities of people like Picart and Bernard on the increasing religious relativization and secularization. They seek the source of the change in the expanding activity of knowledgeable craftworkers and technicians across national borders more than the philosophers of the time such as Rousseau and Montesquieu (Hunt, Jacob and Mijnhardt 2010).

12  In my view, the shifting of logic occurs not only in special permission to stay cases but also in cases seeking affirmation of nationality. For instance, the 'unconstitutionality of the Nationality Act' case (Supreme Court Grand Bench judgment of June 4, 2008) frequently mentioned in this book involved the Tokyo District Court judgment of unconstitutionality (victory for the plaintiff), the Tokyo High Court judgment of constitutionality (loss for the plaintiff), and the Supreme Court judgment of unconstitutionality (victory for the plaintiff). Yet, the Tokyo District Court and the Supreme Court gave different reasons for their findings of unconstitutionality. On the said case, when the child in question was seen through the lens of 'this child may be Japanese', it was perceived that a wide range of matters not accessible to a foreign national would need to be made accessible in the manner of a domino effect (as in the judgments of the Tokyo District Court and the Supreme Court) whereas when the child was seen through the lens of 'this child is not Japanese', then it would end in the conclusion that the plaintiff did not have the claimed right because of his foreign nationality (the Tokyo High Court judgment was underpinned by this viewpoint).

13  Emplacement of the individual's rights in social relationships by constitutional law from the Taishō era onward appears to have been built into the bedrock of Japanese legal interpretation, in conjunction with Tetsuo Najita's comment that 'Minobe's ideas rested on a denial of the natural-right theory, and in this respect he fell within the tradition of political ideology shaped by Katō Hiroyuki and others a generation earlier. The source of law in this view was neither natural nor metaphysical but social and historical. Rights, therefore, did not inhere in human nature but, like sovereignty, were an extension of constitutional law and of contract' (Najita 1974: 110).

14  In particular, a systematic description of this point can be found in Watsuji (1996: 101–179).

15  In *Ie no seido* (The household system), a collection of lectures on the meaning of the new Constitution that Sakae Wagatsuma gave in various locations in Japan after its surrender in World War II, he made reference to the idea of community and family in Watsuji's *Rinrigaku* (Ethics) before presenting his argument on the significance of gender equality in the new Civil Code under the new Constitution. This suggests that emphasis on 'betweenness' was already an unspoken premise in postwar Japan's family law (Wagatsuma 1948: 9–31).

16  Levi-Strauss elaborates as follows: 'This definition has three noteworthy points or three aspects. First, the definition places components and their interrelations on the same plane. In other words, something that looks like form from one viewpoint can appear as its content from another viewpoint and what looks like content can appear as its form. It all depends on the level on which you stand. Therefore, a constant relationship exists between form and content. That is one way to explain it. The second aspect is the concept of "invariance", which is a vitally important concept. For we are investigating something that remains unchanged when all else is changing. The third aspect is the concept of "transfiguration (transformation)" by which, I think, the difference between what is called "structure" and what is called "system" can be understood. System can also be defined as a whole comprised of components and their interrelations but it cannot transfigure. When modified, a system disintegrates and falls apart. On the other hand, structure characteristically transforms into a different system when some change is applied to its state of equilibrium' (Levi-Strauss 1979a: 37–38).

17  This statement was revised in the Third Basic Plan for Immigration Control: 'Japan has not adopted any amnesty policy which would encourage an inflow of new illegal foreign residents or extension of illegal residence, but special permission to stay has been granted to illegal foreign residents who have close links with Japanese society or who, from a humanitarian standpoint, would suffer from deportation'.

# Bibliography

## Japanese

Abe, Yasutaka (2008), *Gyōsei hō kaishakugaku I—Jissituteki hōchi kokka wo sōzōsuru henkaku no hō riron* (Interpreting administrative law I: Legal theory for reform to create a state governed by substantive law), Tokyo: Yūhikaku.

Annen, Junji (1993), '"Gaikokujin no jinken" saikō' (Rethinking 'foreigners' human rights'). In: *Gendai rikken shugi no tenkai (jō) Ashibe Nobuyoshi sensei koki shukuga* (The evolution of contemporary constitutionalism Part 1, commemorating the 70th birthday of Professor Nobuyoshi Ashibe), Tokyo: Yūhikaku, pp. 163–181.

Aoki, Masahiko (2001), *Hikaku seido bunseki ni mukete* (Toward a comparative institutional analysis), Tokyo: NTT Shuppan.

Aoki, Masahiko and Donald Dore (eds.) (1995), *Kokusai gakusai kenkyū Shisutemu toshite no Nihon kigyō* (The Japanese firm: The sources of competitive strength), Tokyo: NTT Shuppan.

Aoki, Masahiko and Masahiro Okuno (eds.) (1996), *Keizai shisutemu no hikaku seido bunseki* (Comparative institutional analysis: A new approach to economic systems), Tokyo: Tokyo Daigaku Shuppan Kai.

Aoyagi, Kōichi (2009), 'Sabetsu no chokusetsuteki kyūsai to shihō no shimei—Kokuseki hō 3 jō 1 kō iken hanketsu' (Direct remedies for discrimination and the mission of the judiciary: The Nationality Act Article 3-1 unconstitutionality judgment), *Tsukuba Law Journal*, no. 5, pp. 1–28.

Arikawa, Tsunemasa (2016), *Songen to mibun—Kenpōteki shii to 'Nihon' toiu mondai* (Dignity and status: Constitutional thoughts and the 'Japan' problem), Tokyo: Iwanami Shoten.

Asanuma, Banri (1997), *Nihon no kigyō soshiki no kakushinteki tekiō no mekanizumu—Chōki torihiki kankei no kōzō to kinō* (Mechanism for innovative adaptation in Japanese corporate organizations: The structure and function of long-term transaction relationships), Tokyo: Toyō Keizai Shimpō Sha.

Ashibe, Nobuyoshi (1973), *Kenpō soshō no riron* (Constitutional litigation theory), Tokyo: Yūhikaku.

Ashibe, Nobuyoshi (2015), *Kenpō dai 6 han* (Constitution, the 6th edition), revised by Kazuyuki Takahashi, Tokyo: Iwanami Shoten.

Awano, Masao and Shōko Okuda (2005), 'Hiroshima joji satsugai jiken, Perūjin taiho! "Akuma ga yatta"' (The Hiroshima girl murder case, a Peruvian arrested, claims 'The devil did it'), *Yomiuri Weekly*, December 18 issue, pp. 26–28.

Baba, Hiroji (1992), 'Gendai shakai to Nihon kaishashugi' (The modern world and Japanese companyism). In: Tokyo Daigaku Shakai Kagaku Kenkyūjo (ed.), *Gendai Nihon shakai 1 Kadai to shikaku* (Modern Japanese society 1: Issues and viewpoints), Tokyo: Tokyo Daigaku Shuppan Kai, pp. 29–83.

Chiba, Katsumi (1995), 'Shin Tokyo Kokusai Kūkō no anzen kakuho ni kansuru kinkyū sochi hō (shōwa 59 nen hōritsu dai 87 gō ni yoru kaisei mae no mono) 3 jō 1 kō 1 gō to Kenpō 21 jō 1 kō sonota' (The Act on Emergency Measures concerning Security Control of Narita International Airport [before amendment act No. 87 of 1984] Article 3-1-1 and the Constitution Article 21-1 and others). In: *Saikō saibansho hanrei kaisetu minjihen heisei 4 nen ban* (Commentary on the decisions of the Supreme Court: Civil cases [the 1992 edition]), Tokyo: Hōsō Kai.

Chiba, Katsumi (2017), *Iken shinsa—Sono shōten no sadame kata* (Constitutionality review: How to set focus), Tokyo: Yūhikaku.

Chiba, Katsumi (2019), *Kenpō hanrei to saibankan no shisen—Sono saki ni miteita sekai* (Constitutional precedents and the judge's gaze: A world beyond the horizon), Tokyo: Yūhikaku.

Doi, Takeo (1971), *'Amae' no kōzō* (Anatomy of dependence), Tokyo: Kōbundō.

Fujita, Tokiyasu (2012), *Saikōsai kaisō roku—Gakusha hanji no 7 nen han* (Memoirs of a Supreme Court justice: A former scholar's seven and a half years), Tokyo: Yūhikaku.

Fujita, Tokiyasu (2016), *Saiban to hōritsugaku—'Saikōsai kaikoroku' hoi* (Trials and jurisprudence: Supplementary volume to 'Memoirs of a Supreme Court justice'), Tokyo: Yūhikaku.

Gaikokujin kenshūsei mondai Nettowāku (ed.) (2000), *Mayakashi no gaikokujin kenshū seido* (Deceptions of the foreign trainee program), Tokyo: Gendai Jinbun Sha.

Gaikokujin kenshūsei mondai Nettowāku (ed.) (2006), *Gaikokujin kenshūsei jikyū 300 yen no rōdōsha—Kowareru jinken to rōdō kijun* (Foreign trainee workers on 300 yen per hour: Broken human rights and labor standards), Tokyo: Akashi Shoten.

Gaikokujin rōdōsha Bengo dan (ed.) (1992), *Gaikokujin rōdōsha to kenri kyūsai* (Foreign workers and human rights redress), Tokyo: Gendai Shokan.

Hama, Hidekazu (1974), 'Nikkō tarō sugi jiken—Dōro ni yoru kankyō hakai to jigyō nintei no tekihi' (The Nikkō tarō sugi case: Environmental destruction by road construction and the propriety of the approval of the undertaking), *Bessatsu Jurisuto* (Jurist supplementary volume), no. 43, pp. 181–183.

Hamamatsu-shi Kikakuchōsei-bu Kokusai-ka (2014), *Hamamatsu shi ni okeru Nihonjin shimin oyobi gaikokujin shimin no ishiki jittai chōsa hōkokusho* (Report on the attitude survey of Japanese and non-Japanese residents in Hamamatsu city), Hamamatsu: Hamamatsu-shi Kikakuchōsei-bu Kokusai-ka.

Hasebe, Yasuo (2006), *Kenpō no genkai* (The limitations of the constitution), Tokyo: Tokyo Daigaku Shuppan Kai.

Hatano, Isamu, Kenji Kurashima, Shinya Tanaka, Kazutaka Shigemi and Yūichi Ishizaki (2000), *Gaikokujin no hōteki chii—Kokusaika jidai to hō seido no arikata* (Foreigners' legal status: Globalization and the legal system), Tokyo: Shinzan Sha.

Hiraga, Kenta (1950), *Kokuseki hō jō kan* (The Nationality Act vol. 1), Tokyo: Teikoku Hanrei Hōki Shuppan Sha.

Hiraga, Kenta (1951), *Kokuseki hō ge kan* (The Nationality Act vol. 2), Tokyo: Teikoku Hanrei Hōki Shuppan Sha.

Hironaka, Toshio (2006), *Shin ban Minpō kōyō dai 1 kan sōron* (New edition outline of the Civil Code vol. 1 introduction), Tokyo: Sōbun Sha.

Hōmu-shō Nyūkoku kanri-kyoku (2016), *Ihan shinpan yōryō* (Guidelines on adjudication of violations), Tokyo: Hōmu Shō Nyūkoku Kanri Kyoku.

Hōmu-shō Nyūkoku kanri-kyoku Nyūkoku zairyū-ka (1992), 'Shin tetsuzuki zemināru No. 24 Zairyū shikaku nintei shōmeisho seido ni tsuite' (Information on a new procedure no. 24: The certificate of eligibility system), *Kokusai jinryū* (The immigration newsmagazine), no. 59, pp. 60–75.

Hosokawa, Kiyoshi (1984), 'Kaisei kokuseki hō no gaiyō' (An overview of the Nationality Act revision), *Minji geppō—Kokuseki hō, Koseki hō kaisei tokushū* (Monthly bulletin on civil cases: Special feature on the revision of the Nationality Act and the Family Registration Act), pp. 1–40.

Ishida, Shin'ichirō (2011), 'Alternative justice toha nanika' (What is alternative justice?). In: Shin'ichirō Ishida (ed.), *Alternative justice—Atarashii 'hō to shakai' heno hihanteki kōsatsu* (Alternative justice: A critical study of new 'law and society'), Osaka: Osaka Daigaku Shuppan Kai, pp. 7–37.

Ishida, Takeomi, Hironori Kondō, Emiko Miki and Kazuyuki Azusawa (1999), *Gaikokujin mondai bengo nōto—Bengoshi ga kataru kokusaika shakai Nihon de kurasu gaikokujintachi no kattō* (Notes on advocacy on the foreigners issue: Attorneys' accounts of the struggles of foreign residents in the globalized society of Japan), Tokyo: ALC Press.

Iwata, Kazumasa and Nihon Keizai Kenkyū Sentā (eds.) (2016), *Jinkō kaifuku—Shussei ritsu 1.8 wo jitsugensuru senryaku shinario* (Population recovery: A strategic scenario to achieve the target birthrate of 1.8), Tokyo: Nihon Keizai Shimbun Sha.

Izumi, Tokuji (1983), 'Torikeshi soshō no genkoku tekikaku, uttae no rieki' (Standing to sue and legal interest in actions for revocation). In: Chūichi Suzuki and Akira Mikazuki (eds.), *Shin jitsumu minji soshō kōza 9 Gyōsei soshō I* (New series on civil litigation practice 9: Administrative litigation I), Tokyo: Nihon Hyōron Sha, pp. 53–80.

Izumi, Tokuji (2013), *Watashi no Saikō Saibansho—Kenpō no motomeru shihō no yakuwari* (My Supreme Court: The role of the judiciary under the Constitution), Tokyo: Nihon Hyōron Sha.

Izumi, Tokuji (2019), 'Saikōsai no "sōgōteki kōryō ni yoru gōrisei handan no wakugumi" no mondaiten' (Problems with the 'framework for determination of reasonableness by comprehensive balancing'). In: Kenji Ishikawa, Tatsuhiko Yamamoto and Tokuji Izumi (eds.), *Kenpō soshō no jūjiro* (Constitutional litigation at a crossroad), Tokyo: Kōbundō, pp. 335–388.

Izumi, Tokuji (2020), 'Tōchi kōzō ni oite shihōken ga hatasubeki yakuwari Dai 2 bu (6)—Makurīn hanketsu no machigai kasho' (The role of the judiciary in the governing system part 2 (6): Errors in the McLean judgment), *Hanrei jihō* (Case report), no. 2434, pp. 133–145.

Izumi, Tokuji, Takehisa Nakagawa, Takeo Mizuno and Hiroshi Saitō (2017), 'Zadankai Shihō kaikaku no keizoku to gyōsei soshō kappatsuka heno michi' (Panel discussion on the path of ongoing judicial reform and revitalizing administrative litigation). In: Kōji Satō and Tokuji Izumi (eds.), *Takii Shigeo sensei tsuitō ronshū Gyōsei soshō no kappatsuka to kokumin no kenri jūshi no gyōsei he* (A collection of essays in memory of Shigeo Takii: Toward the revitalization of administrative litigation and more emphasis on citizens' rights in administration), Tokyo: Nihon Hyōron Sha, pp. 39–84.

Izumi, Tokuji, Yasuyuki Watanabe, Hajime Yamamoto and Towa Niimura (2017), *Ippo mae ni deru shihō—Izumi Tokuji moto Saikōsai hanji ni kiku* (Progressive justice: An interview with former Supreme Court Justice Tokuji Izumi), Tokyo: Nihon Hyōron Sha.

Jōzuka, Makoto (2016), 'Gaikokujin no taikyo kyōsei, zairyū shikaku tō wo meguru funsō' (Disputes involving the deportation, residence status etc. of foreign nationals). In: Makoto Jōzuka (ed.), *Gyōsei kankei soshō no jitsumu* (The practice of administrative litigation), Tokyo: Shōji Hōmu, pp. 1–19.

Kajita, Takamichi, Kiyoto Tanno and Naoto Higuchi (2005), *Kao no mienai teijūka—Nikkei Burajirujin to kokka, shijō, imin nettowāku* (Invisible residents: Japanese Brazilians vis-à-vis the state, the market and the immigrant network), Nagoya: Nagoya Daigaku Shuppan Kai.

Kamata, Satoshi (1979), *Shitsugyō—Fukyō to gōrika no saizensen kara* (Unemployment: On the front line of recession and rationalization), Tokyo: Chikuma Shobō.

Kanagawa Shimbun 'Jidai no shōtai' Shuzai Han (ed.) (2016), *Heito demo wo tometa machi Kawasaki Sakuramoto no hitobito—Sabetsu ha hito wo korosu* (The town that stopped hate rallies, the people of Sakuramoto, Kawasaki: Discrimination kills people), Tokyo: Gendai Shichō Shin Sha.

Kantō bengoshi Rengōkai (2012), *Gaikokujin no jinken—Gaikokujin no chokumensuru konnan no kaiketsu wo mezashite* (Foreigners' human rights: To resolve difficulties facing foreigners), Tokyo: Akashi Shoten.

Kawasaki no Zainichi Kōreisha to musubu 2000-nin Nettowāku (ed.) (2017), *Ichiji ichiji ni omoi wo komete—6 nin no Zainichi kōreisha ga mizukara tsuzutta jibun shi* (Each word with feelings: Autobiographies of six elderly Zainichi Koreans), Kawasaki: Kawasaki no Zainichi Kōreisha to musubu 2000-nin Nettowāku.

Kim, Sang-gyun (2014), 'Heito supīchi kisei no igi to tokushusei' (The significance and particularity of hate speech regulation). In: Sang-gyun Kim (ed.), *Heito supīchi no hōteki kenkyū* (Legal study of hate speech), Kyoto: Hōritsu Bunka Sha, pp. 150–165.

Koike, Kazuo (1990), *Shigoto no keizaigaku* (The economics of work in Japan), Tokyo: Tōyō Keizai Shinpō Sha.

Koshiyama, Yasuhisa (1983), 'Kōkoku soshō no taishō' (Subject of actions for the judicial review). In: Chūichi Suzuki and Akira Mikazuki (eds.), *Shin jitsumu minji soshō kōza 9 Gyōsei soshō I* (New series on civil litigation practice 9: Administrative litigation I), Tokyo: Nihon Hyōron Sha, pp. 27–52.

Kuwahara, Yasuo (ed.) (2001), *Gurōbaru jidai no gaikokujin rōdōsha—Doko kara kite doko he* (Foreign laborers in the era of globalization: Where are they from and where are they going?), Tokyo: Tōyō Keizai Shinpō Sha.

Kyōtani, Eiji (2016), 'Book review: Nobuhiko Nibe, Tetsuya Okamura and Hiroshi Yamaguchi (eds.) *Toyota to Toyota*', *Shakaigaku Hyōron* (Japanese sociological review), vol. 67, no. 3, pp. 338–340.

Levi-Strauss, Claude and Yasuo Ōhashi (ed.) (1979), *Kōzō, shinwa, rōdō—Claude Levi-Strauss Nihon kōen shū* (Structure, myth, labor—Claude Levi-Strauss lectures in Japan), Tokyo: Misuzu Shobō.

Machado, Daniel (2018), *Burajiru no dōseikon hō—Hanrei ni yoru hō seisei to kazoku gainen no tenkan* (Same-sex marriage in Brazil: Judicial law-making and the shifting concept of family), Tokyo: Shinzan Sha.

Miki, Emiko (2017), 'NO PASARAN "Sakuramoto wo fuminijiranaide"' (They shall not pass 'Don't trample on Sakuramoto'). In: Heito Supīchi wo Yurusanai Kawasaki Shimin Nettowāku (ed.), *Konzetsu! Heito tono tatakai—Kyōsei no machi Kawasaki kara* (Eradicate! Fighting hate: From the harmonious community of Kawasaki), Tokyo: Ryokufū Shuppan, pp. 93–103.

Monden, Yasuhiro (1989), *Toyota shisutemu—Toyota shiki seisan kanri shisutemu* (Toyota system: Toyota-style production control system), Tokyo: Kōdan Sha Bunko.

Mori, Chikako (2014), 'Heito supīchi to reishizumu no kankeisei—Naze ima sore wo towaneba naranainoka' (The relationship between hate speech and racism: Why does this question need to be asked now?). In: Sang-gyun Kim (ed.), *Heito supīchi no hōteki kenkyū* (Legal study of hate speech), Kyoto: Hōritsu Bunka Sha, pp. 3–17.

Mori, Hideaki (2011), 'Kokuseki hō 3 jō 1 kō ga, Nihon kokumin dearu chichi to nihon kokumin denai haha tono aidani shusseishita atoni chichi kara ninchisareta ko ni tsuki, fubo no kon'in ni yori chakushutsu shi taru mibun wo shutokushita (junsei no atta) baai ni kagiri Nihon kokuseki no shutoku wo mitometeiru koto ni yotte kokusekino shutoku ni kansuru kubetsu wo shōjisaseteiru koto to kenpō 14 jō 1 kō; Nihon kokumin dearu chichi to Nihon kokumin denai haha tono aidani shusseishita ato ni chichi kara ninchisareta ko ha, Nihon kokuseki no shutoku ni kanshite kenpō 14 jō 1 kō ni ihansuru kubetsu wo shōjisaseteiru, fubo no kon'in ni yori chakushutsu shi taru mibun wo shutokushita to iu bubun (junsei yōken) wo nozoita kokuseki hō 3 jō 1 kō shotei no kokuseki shutoku no yōken ga mitasareru toki ha, Nihon kokuseki wo shutokusuru ka' (The relationship between a distinction in granting Japanese nationality caused by Article 3, para.1 of the Nationality Act which provides that a child born out of wedlock to a Japanese father and a non-Japanese mother and acknowledged by the father after birth may acquire Japanese nationality only if the child has acquired the status of a child born in wedlock as a result of the marriage of the parents [legitimation], and Article 14, para.1 of the Constitution; shall a child born out of wedlock to a Japanese father and a non-Japanese mother and acknowledged by the father after birth acquire Japanese nationality if the child satisfies the requirements for acquisition of Japanese nationality prescribed in Article 3, para.1 of the Nationality Act, except for the requirement of acquiring the status of a child born in wedlock as a result of the marriage of the parents [legitimation requirement]?), *Saikō saibansho hanrei kaisetsu minji hen heisei 20 nendo* (Commentary on the decisions of the Supreme Court, civil cases, 2008), Tokyo: Hōsō Kai, pp. 267–325.

Mōri, Tōru (2017), 'Kenpō soshō no jissen to riron (dai 1 kai)—Heito demo kinshi kari shobun meirei jiken' (Constitutional litigation practice and theory [no. 1]: The hate rally provisional injunction order case), *Hanrei jihō* (Case report), no. 2321, pp. 3–9.

Nagano, Hitomi (2015), 'Hanrei kenkyū shakai hoshō hō hanrei' (A study of legal cases in social security law), *Kikan shakai hoshō kenkyū* (Journal of social security research), vol. 50, no. 4, pp. 464–472.

Nakamura, Il-song (2014), *Rupo Kyoto Chōsen gakkō shūgeki jiken—'Heito kuraimu' ni kōshite* (Report on the attack on the Kyoto Korean school: Standing against 'hate crime'), Tokyo: Iwanami Shoten.

Nakane, Chie (1967), *Tate shakai no ningen Kankei* (Japanese Soceity), Tokyo: Kōdansha.

Nema, Genshin (1995), 'Nyūshoku 40 shūnen kinen shi ni yosete' (For the special publication commemorating the 40th anniversary of the settlement). In: Koronia Okinawa Nyūshoku 40-shūnen Kinen Shi Hensan Iinkai, *Uruma kara no tabidachi* (Departing Uruma), Santa Cruz: Koronia Okinawa Nyūshoku 40-shūnen Kinen Shi Hensan Iinkai, pp. xiv–xv.

# Bibliography

Nema, Genshin (2000), 'Boribia ni okeru Nikkei shakai no tenbō' (An outlook for Nikkei society in Bolivia). In: Boribia Nihonjin Ijū 100-shūnen Ijū Shi Hensan Iinkai (ed.), *Nihonjin ijū 100-nen shi Boribia ni ikiru* (The centenary of Japanese migration: Life in Bolivia), Santa Cruz: Boribia Nikkei Kyōkai Rengōkai, pp. 26–29.

Nibe, Nobuhiko, Tetsuya Okamura and Hiroshi Yamaguchi (eds.), *Toyota to Toyota— Sangyō gurōbaruka senshin chiiki no genzai* (Toyota city and Toyota Motor: The current state of an advanced area of industrial globalization), Tokyo: Tōshindō.

Ninomiya, Masato (1983), *Kokuseki hō ni okeru danjo byōdō* (Gender equality in nationality law), Tokyo: Yūhikaku.

Nohara, Hikari and Eishi Fujita (1988), *Jidōsha sangyō to rōdōsha—Rōdōsha kanri no kōzō to rōdōsha zō* (The automotive industry and its workers: Labor management structure and worker profile), Kyoto: Hōritsu Bunka Sha.

Noma, Yasumichi (2015), *'Zainichi tokken' no kyokō—Netto kūkan ga umidashita heito supīchi* (zōho ban) ('Zainichi privilege' is fiction: Hate speech created in cyberspace [augmented edition]), Tokyo: Kawade Shobō Shinsho.

Nomura, Masami (1993), *Jukuren to bungyō—Nihon kigyō to Teirā shugi* (Skill and the division of labor: Taylorism and the Japanese enterprise), Tokyo: Ochanomizu Shobō.

Oda, Makoto (2000), *Levi-Strauss nyūmon* (Introduction to Levi-Strauss), Tokyo: Chikuma Shinsho.

Ōishi, Makoto and Hideyuki Ōsawa (eds.) (2016), *Hanrei kenpō* (dai 3 han) (Constitutional law: Selected cases 3rd edition), Tokyo: Yūhikaku.

Okuda, Yasuhiro (2010), *Kokuseki hō, kokusai kazoku hō no saiban ikensho shū Nihon Hikaku Hō Kenkyūjo shiryō sōsho 9* (Written opinions to court cases in nationality law and family law: Institute of Comparative Law in Japan resource series 9), Tokyo: Chūō Daigaku Shuppan Kai.

Ōmura, Atsushi (2018), 'Jobun' (Foreword). In: Daniel Machado, *Burajiru no dōseikon hō—Hanrei ni yoru hō seisei to kazoku gainen no tenkan* (Same-sex marriage in Brazil: Judicial law-making and the shifting concept of family), Tokyo: Shinzan Sha, pp. v–x.

Ōno, Taiichi (1978), *Toyota seisan hōshiki—Datsu kibo no keiei wo mezashite* (Toyota production system: Beyond large-scale production), Tokyo: Daiyamondo Sha.

Ōnuma, Yasuaki (1978), 'Shutsunyūkoku kanri hōsei no seiritsu katei—1952 nen Taisei no zenshi' (The legislative process for the immigration law: Circumstances leading up to the 1952 system). In: Hajime Terasawa, Sōji Yamamoto, Ribō Hatano, Wakamizu Tsutsui and Yasuaki Ōnuma (eds.), *Kokusai hōgaku no saikōchiku ge* (Rebuilding international law part 2), Tokyo: Tokyo Daigaku Shuppan Kai.

Ōnuma, Yasuaki (1993), *Shinban Tan'itsu minzoku shakai no shinwa wo koete—Zainichi Kankoku Chōsenjin to shutsunyūkoku kanri taisei* (New edition, Beyond the myth of monoracial society: Zainichi Koreans and Japan's immigration control system), Tokyo: Tōshindō.

Oyama, Yōichi (ed.) (1985), *Kyodai kigyō taisei to rōdōsha—Toyota no jirei* (The giant corporation and its workers: The case of Toyota), Tokyo: Ochanomizu Shobō.

Saikō saibansho Jimu-sōkyoku Shōgai-ka (1950a), *Saikōsai shōgai shiryō dai 7 gō Taiwanjin ni kansuru hōken mondai* (Supreme Court external affairs resource no. 7: Jurisdiction issue concerning Taiwanese), Tokyo: Saikō saibansho Jimu-sōkyoku.

Saikō saibansho Jimu-sōkyoku Shōgai-ka (1950b), *Saikōsai shōgai shiryō dai 9 gō Shutsunyūkoku kankei hōrei shū* (Supreme Court external affairs resource no. 9: Immigration laws and regulations), Tokyo: Saikō saibansho Jimu-sōkyoku.

Sakanaka, Hidenori and Shigeru Takaya (1991), *Kaiseinyūkanhō no kaisetsu* (Commentary on the revised immigration law), Tokyo: Nihon Kajo Shuppan.

Sakanaka, Hidenori and Toshio Saitō (2007), *Shutsunyūkoku kanri oyobi nanmin nintei hō chikujō kaisetu (dai 3 han)* (Clause-by-clause commentary on the Immigration Control and Refugee Recognition Act [the 3rd edition]), Tokyo: Nihon Kajo Shuppan.

Satō, Kōji (1990), *Kenpō* (shinban) (The Constitution [new edition]), Tokyo: Seirin Shoin.

Segi, Hiroshi (2014), *Zetsubō no saibansho* (Courts of despair), Tokyo: Kōdan Sha Gendai Shinsho.

Segi, Hiroshi (2015), *Nippon no saiban* (Justice in Japan), Tokyo: Kōdan Sha Gendai Shinsho.

Shiono, Hiroshi (2005), *Gyōsei hō* (Administrative law), Tokyo: Yūhikaku.

Shutsunyūkoku kanri hōrei Kenkyū kai (2011), *Chūkai hanrei Shutsunyūkoku kanri gaikokujin tōroku Jitsumu roppō* (heisei 24 nen ban) (Annotated case reports for immigration control, alien registration: Immigration law and practice [the 2012 edition]), Tokyo: Nihon Kajo Shuppan.

Sonobe, Itsuo (1983), 'Gyōsei soshō to minji soshō tono kankei' (The relationship between administrative litigation and civil litigation). In: Chūichi Suzuki and Akira Mikazuki (eds.), *Shin jitsumu minji soshō kōza 9 Gyōsei soshō I* (New series on civil litigation practice 9: Administrative case litigation I), Tokyo: Nihon Hyōron Sha, pp. 3–26.

## Bibliography

Suzuki, Eriko (2007), 'Senbetsuka ga susumu gaikokujin rōdōsha—Hiseiki taizaisha no haijo to gōhō taizaisha no kanri kyōka' (Increasing selectiveness in the employment of foreign laborers: Exclusion of irregular stayers and tighter control of legal residents). In: Ichirō Watado, Eriko Suzuki and A. P. F. S. (eds.), *Zairyū tokubetsu kyoka to Nihon no imin seisaku—'Imin senbetsu' jidai no tōrai* (Special permission to stay and Japan's immigration policy: The age of 'selective immigration'), Tokyo: Akashi Shoten, pp. 10–24.

Tagaya, Kazuteru (2016), *Jitsumu saiban rei Shutsunyūkoku kanri oyobi nanmin nintei hō* (Practical case examples: The Immigration Control and Refugee Recognition Act), Tokyo: Nihon Kajo Shuppan.

Takahashi, Kazuyuki (2005), *Rikken shugi to Nihonkoku kenpō* (Constitutionalism and the Constitution of Japan), Tokyo: Yūhikaku.

Takahashi, Kazuyuki (2006), 'Dai 8 shō Jinshin no jiyū oyobi keiji tetsuzuki jō no sho kenri' (Chapter 8: Rights in criminal proceedings and personal freedom). In: Toshihiko Nonaka, Mutsuo Nakamura, Kazuyuki Takahashi and Katsutoshi Takami, *Kenpō I* (dai 4 han) (The Constitution I [the 4th edition]), Tokyo: Yūhikaku, pp. 387–433.

Takahashi, Kazuyuki (2013), *Rikken shugi to Nihonkoku kenpō* (dai 3 han) (Constitutionalism and the Constitution of Japan [the 3rd edition]), Tokyo: Yūhikaku.

Takahashi, Kazuyuki (2017), *Taikei kenpō soshō* (Theory of constitutional litigation), Tokyo: Iwanami Shoten.

Takami, Katsutoshi (2006), 'Dai 2 shō Nihon kenpō shi' (Chapter 2: History of the Japanese Constitution). In: Toshihiko Nonaka, Mutsuo Nakamura, Kazuyuki Takahashi and Katsutoshi Takami, *Kenpō I* (dai 4 han) (The Constitution I [the 4th edition]), Tokyo: Yūhikaku, pp. 45–80.

Takii, Shigeo (2009), *Saikō saibansho ha kawatta ka—Ichi saibankan no jiko kenshō* (Has the Supreme Court changed: Self-examination by a judge), Tokyo: Iwanami Shoten.

Takii, Shigeo (2015), 'Saikōsai shinri to chōsa kan' (Supreme Court trials and judicial research officials). In: Masato Ichikawa, Shirō Ōkubo, Hiroshi Saitō and Chihara Watanabe (eds.), *Nihon no Saikō saibansho* (The Supreme Court of Japan), Tokyo: Nihon Hyōron Sha, pp. 234–244.

Takii, Shigeo (2017), 'Takii Shigeo sensei ni kiku, kikite Takehisa Nakagawa, Susumu Yamaguchi' (An interview with Shigeo Takii by Takehisa Nakagawa and Susumu Yamaguchi). In: Kōji Satō and Tokuji Izumi (eds.), *Takii Shigeo sensei tsuitō ronshū Gyōsei soshō no kappatsuka to kokumin no kenri jūshi no gyōsei he* (A collection of essays in memory of Shigeo Takii: Toward the revitalization of administrative litigation and more emphasis on citizens' rights in administration), Tokyo: Nihon Hyōron Sha, pp. 85–109.

Tanaka, Jirō (1957), *Gyōsei hō sōron Hōritsugaku zenshū 6* (General administrative law: Collected works in jurisprudence 6), Tokyo: Yūhikaku.

Tanno, Kiyoto (2016), '"Gyōsei kara no kao no mieru ka" to "kao no mienai teijūka" no heizon' (Coexistence of 'invisible residents' and the administration's attempt to make them visible). In: Yukihiko Kitagawa and Kiyoto Tanno, *Idō to teijū no shakaigaku* (Sociology of mobility and settlement), Tokyo: Hōsō Daigaku Kyōiku Shinkō Kai.

Tanno, Kiyoto (2020a), *Kokuseki no kyōkai wo kangaeru—Nihonjin, Nikkeijin, Zainichi wo hedateru hō to shakai no kabe* (zōho ban) (The boundary between nationalities: Legal and social barriers between Japanese, Nikkeijin and Zainichi Koreans [augmented edition]), Tokyo: Yoshida Shoten.

Tashiro, Aritsugu (1974), *Kokuseki hō chikujō kaisetsu* (Clause-by-clause commentary on the Nationality Act), Tokyo: Nihon Kajo Shuppan.

Tokyo bengoshi kai Gaikokujin no Kenri ni kansuru Iinkai Gyōsei soshō Kenkyū bukai (ed.) (2013), *Nyūkan soshō manyuaru* (Immigration litigation manual), Tokyo: Gendai Jinbun Sha.

Toyoda, Eiji (1985), *Ketsudan—Watashi no rireki sho* (Fifty years in motion), Tokyo: Nikkei Bunko.

Tsuneoka, Takayoshi (2012a), 'Gyōsei sairyō no tetsuzukiteki shinsa no jittai (jō)' (The reality of the procedural review of administrative discretion [part 1]), *Hanrei jihō* (Case report), no. 2133, pp. 148–157.

Tsuneoka, Takayoshi (2012b), 'Gyōsei sairyō no tetsuzukiteki shinsa no jittai (chū)' (The reality of the procedural review of administrative discretion [part 2]), *Hanrei jihō* (Case report), no. 2136, pp. 148–157.

Tsuneoka, Takayoshi (2012c), 'Gyōsei sairyō no tetsuzukiteki shinsa no jittai (ge)' (The reality of the procedural review of administrative discretion [part 3]), *Hanrei jihō* (Case report), no. 2139, pp. 148–159.

Uozumi, Yūichirō, Shōji Nishida, Katsuo Yakura, Shingo Miyake, Yoshifu Arita, Sōhei Nihi and Ryōko Tani (2016), *Heito supīchi kaishō hō—Seiritsu no keii to kihonteki na kangaekata* (The hate speech elimination act: Its enactment process and basic thinking), Tokyo: Daiichi Hōki.

Wagatsuma, Sakae (1948), *Ie no seido—Sono rinri to hōri* (The household system: Ethics and theory), Tokyo: Kantōsha.

Watanabe, Shōgo and Daisuke Sugimoto (eds.) (2015), *Nanmin shōso hanketsu 20 sen—Gyōsei handan to shihō handan no hikaku bunseki* (Twenty court judgments in favor of refugees: Comparative analysis of administrative decisions and judicial rulings), Tokyo: Shinzan Sha.

Yamaguchi, Gen'ichi (2007), 'Zairyū Tokubetsu kyoka ni okeru "sen hiki" wo kangaeru—Genzai no jitsumu wo zairyō to shite' ('Line drawing' for special permission to stay: The current practice). In: Ichirō Watado, Eriko Suzuki and A. P. F. S. (eds.), *Zairyū tokubetsu kyoka to Nihon no imin seisaku—'Imin senbetsu' jidai no tōrai* (Special permission to stay and Japan's immigration policy: The age of 'selective immigration'), Tokyo: Akashi Shoten, pp. 209–216.

Yamamoto, Kiyoshi (1981), *Jidōsha sangyō no rōshi kankei* (Management-labor relations in the automotive industry), Tokyo: Tokyo Daigaku Shuppan Kai.

Yamamoto, Yoshitaka (2003a), *Jiryōku to jūryoku no hakken 2 Runessansu* (The discovery of magnetism and gravitation 2: The Renaissance), Tokyo: Misuzu Shobō.

Yamamoto, Yoshitaka (2003b), *Jiryōku to jūryoku no hakken 3 Kindai no hajimari* (The discovery of magnetism and gravitation 3: Early modern times), Tokyo: Misuzu Shobō.

Yamamoto, Yoshitaka (2014), *Sekai no mikata no tenkan 2 Chidōsetsu no teishō to uchūron no sōkoku* (Revolutions in worldview 2: Conflict between heliocentrism and cosmology), Tokyo: Misuzu Shobō.

Yasuda, Kōichi (2012), *Netto to aikoku—Zaitokukai no 'yami' wo oikakete* (The Net and patriotism: Searching the "dark side" of the Zaitokukai), Tokyo: Kōdan Sha.

Yasui, Hidetoshi (2013), 'Genpatsu soshō ni okeru "shuchō risshō no hitsuyō" ni tsuite' (The need for 'allegations and proof' in nuclear power plant litigations), *Hōgaku ronsō* (Kyoto law review), vol. 57, no. 4, pp. 613–642.

Yoshioka, Masuo (ed.) (1978), *Zainichi Chōsenjin to shakai hoshō* (Zainichi Koreans and social security), Tokyo: Shakai Hyōron Sha.

Yoshioka, Masuo (ed.) (1980), *Zainichi Chōsenjin no seikatsu to jinken* (The life and human rights of Zainichi Koreans), Tokyo: Shakai Hyōron Sha.

Zainichi Chōsenjin no Jinken wo Mamoru kai (1968), *Zainichi Chosenjin no zairyū ken wo meguru saibanrei shū—Shutsunyūkoku kanri rei, gaikokujin tōroku hō ni kansuru saiban tōsō no kiroku* (Court cases on Zainichi Koreans' right to residence: Records of court battles over the Immigration Control Order and the Alien Registration Act), Zainichi Chōsenjin no Jinken wo Mamoru Kai.

Zainichi Kōreisha Kōryū kurabu Torajinokai (2015) '*Yukkuri ippo, hassuru hitokoe ni kometa omoi' halmeoni (obāchan) to issho! Sakuramoto shōtengai 800m demo kōshin hōkoku shū* ('Thoughts and feelings in one slow step, one voice' together with halmeonis (grandmothers)! A collection of reports on the Sakuramoto community 800-meter-march), Kawasaki: Kasawaki-shi Fureai Kan.

# Other

Aoki, Masahiko (1988), *Information, Incentive, Bargaining in the Japanese Economy*, Cambridge: Cambridge University Press.

Bloch, Marc (1953), *The Historian's Craft: Reflections on the Nature and Uses of History and the Techniques and Methods of Those Who Write it*, Peter Putnam (trans.), New York: Vintage Books. Translated from the Original French book *Apologie pour L'histoire ou Metier d'historien*, published in Paris by Armand Colin Editeur in 1949.

Caldeira, Teresa P. R. (2001), *City of Walls: Crime, Segregation, and Citizenship in Sao Paulo*, Berkeley: University of California Press.

Fernandes, Florestan (1968), *Sociedade de Class e Subdesenvolvimento*, Rio de Janeiro: Difel.

Ginzburg, Carlo (2002), *The Judge and the Historian: Marginal Notes on a Late-Twentieth-Century Miscarriage of Justice*, Antony Shugaar (trans.), London: Verso. Translated from the original Italian book *Il Giudice e Lo Storico: Considerazioni in margine al processo Sofri*, published by Giulio Einaudi editore S.p.A. in 1991.

Horie, Takashi, Hikaru Tanaka and Kiyoto Tanno (eds.) (2020), *Amorphous Dissent: Post-Fukushima Social Movements in Japan*, Tokyo: Trans Pacific Press.

Hunt, Lynn, Margaret C. Jacob and Wijnand Mijnhardt (2010), *The Book that Changed Europe: Picart & Bernard's Religious Ceremonies of the World*, Cambridge: The Belknap Press of Harvard University Press.

Imai, Masaaki (1986), *Kaizen: The Key to Japan's Competitive Success*, New York: McGraw-Hill Education.

Kamata, Satoshi (1982), *Japan in the Passing Lane: Insider's Account of Life in a Japanese Auto Factory*, Tatsuru Akimoto (trans.), New York: Pantheon Books.

Kenny, Martin and Richard Florida (1993a), *Beyond Mass Production: The Japanese System and Its Transfer to the US*, New York: Oxford University Press.

Kenny, Martin and Richard Florida (1993b), 'Beyond Mass Production: Production and the Labor Process in Japan'. In: Tetsuro Katō and Rob Steven (eds.), *An International Debate: Is Japanese Management Post-Fordism?*, Tokyo: Mado-Sha, pp. 19–68.

Marshall, T. H. and Tom Bottomore (1987), *Citizenship and Social Class*, London: Pluto Press.

Montero, Alfred P. (2006), *Brazilian Politics: Reforming a Democratic State in a Changing World*, Cambridge: Polity Press.

Najita, Tetsuo (1974), *Japan: The Intellectual Foundation of Modern Japanese Politics*, Chicago: The University of Chicago Press.

# Bibliography

Pike, Kenneth Lee (1954), *Language in Relation to a Unified Theory of the Structure of Human Behavior Part 1*, Glendale California: Summer Institute of Linguistics.

Smith, Adam (1937), *An Inquiry into the Nature and Causes of the Wealth of Nations*, Edwin Canan (ed.), New York: Modern Library.

Smith, Adam (1976), *The Theory of Moral Sentiments*, D. D. Raphael and A. L. Macfie (eds.), Oxford: Oxford University Press.

Sugimoto, Yoshio (2014), *An Introduction to Japanese Society* (4th edition), Cambridge: Cambridge University Press.

Sugimoto, Yoshio (2021), 'Amorphization amid Fragmentation: Japanese Society 1990–2020'. In: Johann Pall Arnason (ed.), *Historika Sochiogogie*, Prague: Charles University-Karokunum Press.

Tanno, Kiyoto (2013), *Migrant Workers in Contemporary Japan: An Institutional Perspective on Transnational Employment*, Teresa Castelvetere (trans.), Melbourne: Trans Pacific Press.

Tanno, Kiyoto (2020b), 'Opposing Hate Speech in Japan: Valuing Differences and Breaking a New Ground for Human Rights'. In: Takashi Horie, Hikaru Tanaka and Kiyoto Tanno (eds.), *Amorphous Dissent: Post-Fukushima Social Movements in Japan*, Tokyo: Trans Pacific Press, pp. 167–189.

United Nations Convention on the Elimination of All Forms of Discrimination against Women (2010), *General Recommendation No.27 on Older Women and Protection of Their Human Rights* (CEDAW/ C/ GC/ 27).

United Nations Economic and Social Council (2009), *General Comment No.20: Non-discrimination in Economic, Social and Cultural Rights* (art.2, para.2, of the International Covenant on Economic, Social and Cultural Rights) (E/C.12/gc/20).

United Nations General Assembly (2001), *Question of Torture and Other Cruel, Inhuman or Degrading Treatment or Punishment* (A/56/156).

United Nations Human Rights Office of the High Commissioner (2012), *Born Free and Equal: Sexual Orientation and Gender Identity in International Human Rights Law*, New York and Geneva: United Nations.

Vogel, Ezra (1979), *Japan as Number One: Lessons for America*, Cambridge: Harvard University Press.

Waldron, Jeremy (2012a), *The Harm in Hate Speech*, Cambridge: Harvard University Press.

Waldron, Jeremy (2012b), *Dignity, Rank, and Rights*, New York: Oxford University Press.

Watsuji, Tetsurō (1996), *Watsuji Tetsurō's Rinrigaku: Ethics in Japan*, Seisaku Yamamoto and Robert E. Carter (trans.), Albany: State University of New York Press.

Womac, James P., Daniel T. Jones and Daniel Roos (1990), *The Machine That Changed the World: The Story of Lean Production—How Japan's Secret Weapon in the Global Auto Wars Will Revolutionize Western Industry*, New York: Rawson Associates.

# Index

## Terms

Abenomics, 24, 142, 145–146, 149
abuse of the Minister of Justice's discretionary authority, 56 See also Minister of Justice
Act on
    Access to Information, 121
    Proper Technical Intern Training and Protection of Technical Intern Trainees, 142
    the Partial Revision of the Special Measures Act Concerning the Immigration Act, 76
    the Promotion of Efforts to Eliminate Unfair Discriminatory Speech and Behavior against Persons with Countries of Origin other than Japan, 12, 110 See also Anti-Hate Speech Act
action against a public authority, 207
Administrative Case Litigation Act, 46, 121, 208, 211, 231
Administrative Complaint Review Act, 121
Administrative Procedure Act, 154
Alien Registration Order, 12, 21, 183–185, 198
alternative dispute resolution, 14
alternative justice, 13–15, 168–169, 242
American-type concrete judicial review doctrine, 213
Amnesty International, 102, 108
Ansei Five-Power Treaties, 176
Anti-Hate Speech Act, 12, 110, 118–119, 121–122, 124, 126–127, 166–167, 169 See also hate speech (hate speech rally)
Appended Table I, 182, 189
Appended Table II, 29, 154, 182–183, 186–187, 189, 221
Article See also Constitution of Japan
    13 of the Constitution, 56, 120, 124–126, 166–167, 221–223
    29-3 of the Constitution, 45
    39 of the Constitution, 58–59

Asahi case, 167, 237, 239, 241–242
assimilation into Japanese society, 91, 185, 218–219, 230–231, 234, 237, 242, 247, 249

balance between crime and punishment, 57, 97
*bandeirantes*, 101
Basic Plan for Immigration Control, 188, 218, 227, 250, 257
beneficence of the state, 250
betweenness of (socially incorporated) persons, 248–249

Carolene Products judgment, 215
*casamento de fato*, 195
child born out of wedlock, 201, 203
clear and present danger, 214
clear unreasonableness standard, 216
Committee for Japan's Future, 23
company-first person, 132
companyism, 132, 133, 149
company-specific skills, 133
comparative sociology of human rights, 1, 250
comprehensively balancing various factors, 202
compulsory-execution-type, 180
*concubinato*, 194, 195
Constitution of Japan, 1, 21, 56, 76, 91, 97, 181, 196, 224, 242
Constitution of the Empire of Japan, 165, 168 See also Meiji Constitution
'Control of entry and exit of individuals, cargo, aircraft, and surface vessels into and from Japan' (GHQ/SCAP-3), 179
Convention on the Elimination of All Forms of Discrimination against Women, 89, 191, 197, 220

Convention on the Rights of the Child, 75, 93, 191, 197, 200, 220
Convention relating to the Status of Refugees, 75, 93, 191, 197, 220
cross-border employment system, 144, 145
cross-trained workers, 133, 134
cumulative penalties, 57

de facto administrative act, 234–235
de facto relationship, 68, 189
dependent (former 4-1-15), 182, 186, 191
deportee's family and social ties, 198
designated activities (former 4-1-16-3), 182
dignity of the person subjected to law, 173
director of the Tokyo Regional Immigration Bureau, 34–39, 45, 71, 73, 78, 207, 230, 232
discretion within the scope of the social and economic regulatory legislation, 225
district courts' and attorneys' logic, 161
double standard of judicial review, 17, 215, 219, 234, 242, 244–245
dual criteria for evaluation, 17

economic regulatory law for maintaining economic and social order, 225
emic approach, 3, 108, 154–155
enterprise unionism, 131–132
equality of all genders (equality of the sexes), 1, 92, 224
establishment of discretionary disposition standards, 159
Establishment of Immigration Service, 179 *See also* SCAPIN
etic approach, 2–3, 107
exercise of bare power, 18
exercise of discretionary authority, 158, 160

factor against, 74, 78
fake Nikkei, 12, 24–25, 28–29, 33, 36, 38, 40, 42, 48, 107, 151–153, 171
family formation in Japan, 89, 107
Family Register Law, 50, 175

Federación National de Asociaciones Boliviano-Japonesas, 26
Food Control Act, 239–241, 243
foreigners' human rights, 2, 9, 15–16, 18–19, 120, 122, 126, 151–152, 155–156, 161, 163, 165–168, 170, 204, 219–220, 223, 225, 229, 235, 243–244, 247–248, 250 *See also* human rights (*jinken*)
foreign labor as an institution, 136–137, 145–146
former 4-1-14, -15, -16-1 and -16-3, 182, 186, 191
framework of rational decision-making by comprehensive balancing, 202
freedom of expression, 76, 119, 125, 214

gay pride parade, 103, 108
gender identity, 75, 89, 92, 226
GHQ, 13, 21, 177–179
GHQ/SCAP-3, 179
good conduct, 68, 96, 154, 187
Great East Japan Earthquake, 143, 146
Guidelines on Special Permission to Stay, 2, 85, 154, 219, 234, 241, 243, 255

*haken-giri* (laying off temp workers), 23
*halmeonis*, 111
hate demonstration, 122, 221 *See also* hate speech
hate speech (hate speech rally), 109–122, 124–127, 151, 166–167, 170, 221, 248–251
hierarchical structure with the Constitution as the nation's supreme law, 223
Himeji Juvenile Prison, 54, 64
homosexuality, 75, 252 *See also* sexual orientation, gender identity
horizontal relationship, 123–124
human rights (*jinken*), 92
human rights of sexual minorities, 76

*ie*, 92
*Ihan shinpan yōryō*, 14, 154, 233
Ikata Nuclear Power Plant case, 47, 50, 159

# Index

immediate execution type, 180, 205
Immigration, 179 *See also* SCAPIN
Immigration Control and Refugee Recognition Act, 8, 12–13, 18, 29, 69, 83, 90, 154–155, 187, 196, 221, 234
Immigration Control Order, 12–13, 180–182, 185, 196–197, 224
immigration inspector, 8, 35, 69, 71, 86, 191–192, 196
immigration officer, 8, 21, 27, 30
Imperial Ordinance on Orders Issued Incidental to Acceptance of the Potsdam Declaration, 181, 186
incomplete contracts, 131
information economics, 130
International Bill of Human Rights, 190, 197
International Covenant on Civil and Political Rights, 56, 75–76, 93, 191, 200, 220
International Covenant on Economic, Social and Cultural Rights, 75, 99, 191
International Human Rights Laws of Sexual Orientation and Gender Identity, 89
invisible hand, 13, 21
invisible residents, 134, 147–149

Japan Federation of Economic Organizations, 143
Japanese family system (*ie*), 92
Japanese-style management, 129–130, 133–134, 136
Japanese-style system of evaluating 'foreigners' human rights, 250
Jefatura Departamental, 26
*jinken* (human rights), 92
jus sanguinis, 199, 201, 205

*kaisha ningen* (company-first person), 132
*kaishashugi* (companyism), 132
*kaizen*, 131, 134
Kawasaki municipal Fureaikan hall, 111, 117
Kawasaki Network of Citizens Against Hate Speech, 112

Ken-Ō Expressway land expropriation case, 211–212
knowledge of the fact, 245
Kurihama Reform School in Yokosuka, Kanagawa, 53, 65–66

law and economics, 130
laying off temp workers, 23
LGBT, 11–12, 69, 76, 97–98, 104, 108, 151–152, 168, 175, 190
lifelong employment, 131, 135
limitations of discretion as an exercise of administrative authority, 160
limits on directives, 159
lodging notification and other matters, 177
logic for allowing foreigners' human rights, 161
logic for foreigner control, 157, 161
logic of subjects' rights, 165
long-term contracts in intra-group transactions, 131
Long-Term Resident Mother and Child Notice, 80–81, 88, 218, 227
Long-Term Resident Notice, 51, 83, 154, 187–188

making residents visible from above, 148
Marriage Notice, 80–81, 88, 218, 227
matters concerning foreigners' entry, 177
matters concerning the Qing subjects residing in the Empire of Japan, 205
McLean judgment, 10, 17, 154, 157, 164, 170, 175, 190, 193, 197, 204, 209–210, 212, 214, 220, 230, 237, 239–240, 245–247
Meiji Civil Code, 92, 177
Meiji Constitution, 92, 164, 205 *See also* Constitution of the Empire of Japan
Memorandum for registration of Chinese nationals, 21
military service book issued by Bolivia's Ministry of Defense, 31, 44
Mining Regulations, 176

Minister of Justice, 2, 8–9, 14–17, 20–21, 30, 34–35, 49, 56, 69, 71–74, 76–83, 96, 152–153, 168, 175, 182–183, 186–188, 190–191, 193, 202–203, 210, 212–213, 215–219, 225, 232–233, 240, 252
Ministry of Justice Human Rights Bureau, 126, 166
Ministry of Justice Public Notice No. 132 issued on May 24, 1990, 29, 51, 154, 187
modern slavery, 2
*monozukuri*, 135

Nakaharaheiwa Park, 109–110, 118
*narai* process, 135
Nationality Act, 7, 93–94, 156–157, 161, 163, 172, 181, 183, 199–204, 206, 249, 253, 256
negative-purpose regulation, 216
new institutional economics, 131
Nikkei contract workers, 131
Nikkō Tarōsugi case, 213
Notice of 1999, 80–81
Notice on 'residence status for same-sex spouse', 195, 206

Office of the Supreme Commander for the Allied Powers (GHQ), 177
Office of the United Nations High Commissioner for Human Rights, 75
other factors, 74–75, 77, 85
owner-driver taxi case, 157–158

pachinko ball game machine case, 159
permanent resident (former 4-1-14), 182, 186, 191
permanent residents' personal rights, 122, 124
personal use of stimulant drugs, 71, 87, 92
petition for reconsideration, 15, 17–18, 194, 207, 229, 232–237, 240, 242, 244–245, 247, 250–251
positive-purpose regulation, 216
postwar Nationality Act, 181
Press Regulations, 176
principle of equality, 70, 84–86, 153, 160, 193

principle of good faith, and so on, 160
principle of proportionality, 84–86, 160, 193
production contracting service division (or company), 138
proto-citizenship function, 249
prototype of today's special permission to stay, 185
Public Assistance Act, 121, 221–223, 239, 241, 243
public notice on long-term residence, 7, 29, 36–37, 66, 68

quality control circles, 131, 134
question in the mental realm, 236

Regulation of National Banks, 176
repatriation support program, 23, 67
requirement of good conduct, 154
residence status system, 155–156, 180, 183, 193, 204, 220
residence statuses in Table II, 186–187
respect for individuals, 1, 224
retail market location regulation case, 216, 225
'Revision of the Alien Registration Order and its Enforcement Regulations', 183, 185, 198
revision of the Immigration Act in 1990, 24, 51
rights of foreign-national sexual minorities in Japan, 70 *See also* human rights of sexual minorities
rights of humans, including foreigners, 19, 243, 247–251
Road Traffic Act, 54
routinized decision-making under directives and notices, 193

same-sex de facto couple, 233
same-sex marriage, 12, 88, 97–98, 102, 175, 194–195, 206, 233, 252
*São Paulo Shimbun*, 103, 104
SCAPIN, 178–179, 205
Seikyū-sha, 111, 118, 125, 251

seniority-based (salary) system, 131, 133
sexual orientation, 75, 89, 92
Ship Act, 176
social death, 85–86, 95, 169
Social Welfare Act, 118, 166
Special Act on Immigration Control, 185–186
special inquiry officer, 8, 21, 64, 95
special permission to stay, 2–7, 9, 11, 14–15, 17–18, 20–21, 31, 36, 39, 45–46, 49, 56, 60–66, 69–74, 76–89, 91, 94, 97, 104–108, 124, 152–153, 162–165, 168–169, 171–172, 175, 185, 188, 190, 192–194, 198–199, 201–202, 204, 207, 210, 216–219, 225–227, 230, 232–237, 240–252, 255–257
Spouse Notice, 79, 80, 88, 218, 227
spouse or child of Japanese national (former 4-1-16-1), 182
standards for discretionary decision-making, 159–160
standpoint of the judicial branch, 206
State Redress Act, 31–32, 40, 44
status of the subject people, 164
status of their residence, 164
stay of execution of a deportation order, 7, 9, 20–21, 98, 161–163, 237
stay of execution of the deportation disposition, 152
Stimulant Drugs Control Act, 54–56, 61, 70–71, 74–75, 84–87, 89, 97, 104, 153
strict rationality standard, 216
structure, 8, 51, 95, 102, 130, 134–135, 138, 156–157, 169, 179, 223, 247, 249–251, 255, 257
suicidal judgment, 15
supervising immigration inspector's discretion, 192
Supreme Commander for the Allied Powers Index Numbers (SCAPIN), 205
Supreme Court's logic, 161

technical intern trainee, 2, 137–139, 141–143, 146–147, 150
Toyota Production System, 129–131, 136
Toyotism, 129, 131, 134, 136
Trafficking Protocol, 217
transfiguration (transformation), 101, 249, 257
transgender, 21, 69–72, 75, 87–88, 91, 97, 103, 153, 163, 194
Treaty of Amity and Commerce between the US and Japan, 176
Treaty of Peace with Japan, 182, 185, 191

unconstitutionality of the Nationality Act, 163, 199, 249, 256
unequal treaties, 176
*uniao estavel*, 195
United Nations Human Rights Commission, 75, 77
Universal Declaration of Human Rights, 75

*vara de familia*, 195
vertical relationship, 123

written deportation order, 8, 25, 191, 197

Yokohama District Court Kawasaki Branch, 114, 118, 120, 122–126, 166, 221–223

Zainichi Tokken wo Yurusanai Shimin no Kai (Zaitokukai), 109, 117

# Personal Names

Abe, Shinzo, 17, 24, 221, 227, 233, 253
Abegglen, James, 150
Annen, Junji, 120, 152, 155–157, 161–162, 164, 166, 219–220, 223–236, 243

Aoki, Masahiko, 130–131
Aoyagi, Kōichi, 163
Arikawa, Tsunemasa, 168, 172
Asanuma, Banri, 130–131

Ashibe, Nobuyoshi, 17, 215
Awano, Masao, 171
Baba, Hiroji, 132–133, 149
Bellah, Robert, 150
Benedict, Ruth, 150
Bloch, Marc, 8, 13, 20

Chiba, Katsumi, 201, 206, 213–214
Choe, Gangija, 170
Coarse, Ronald, 131

Doi, Takeo, 130

Fernandes, Florestan, 100
Fujita, Eishi, 131–132, 134–136
Fujita, Tokiyasu, 169, 171, 201
Fujiyama, Masayuki, 192
Furuta, Yūki, 202

Ginzburg, Carlo, 6–7, 13, 15

Hama, Hidekazu, 227
Hasebe, Yasuo, 152, 155
Higuchi, Naoto, 134, 147–148
Hosokawa, Kiyoshi, 200

Ishida, Shinichirō, 14
Iwata, Kazumasa, 49
Izumi, Tokuji, 46, 201–202, 236, 238, 253–254

Jōzuka, Makoto, 8, 10–11, 160

Kajita, Takamichi, 134, 147
Kamata, Satoshi, 150
Kim, Sang-gyun, 123
Koike, Kazuo, 130, 134
Kuriyama, Shigeru, 239, 241
Kuwahara, Yasuo, 150

Levi-Strauss, Claude, 249–251, 255, 257

Machado, Daniel, 194–195
Majima, Madoka, 172
Marshall, T. H., 1
Maruyama, Yuki, 172
Miki, Emiko, 7, 172
Miura, Tomohito, 111, 117
Monden, Yasuhiro, 130
Mori, Hideaki, 200, 203

Najita, Tetsuo, 256
Nakane, Chie, 130
Nema, Guillermo, 26, 39, 49
Newton, Isaac, 19
Nohara, Hikari, 134–135

Oda, Makoto, 255
Okuda, Shōko, 171
Okuda, Yasuhiro, 94
Ōno, Taiichi, 130, 150
Oyama, Yōichi, 134–135

Pike, Kenneth, 2

Saitō, Toshio, 58, 181
Sakanaka, Hidenori, 58, 181, 183
Segi, Hiroshi, 162
Shiono, Hiroshi, 171
Smith, Adam, 13, 21
Sonobe, Itsuo, 45
Sugimoto, Yoshio, 129–130
Suzuki, Hajime, 224

Takahashi, Kazuyuki, 58–59, 196, 223, 225
Takami, Katsutoshi, 164, 165
Takii, Shigeo, 201, 238, 254
Tanaka, Jirō, 237, 239, 241
Tashiro, Aritsugu, 205
Toyoda, Eiji, 150
Tsuneoka, Takayoshi, 157–162
Tsuno, Osamu, 202

# Index

Vogel, Ezra, 130

Wagatsuma, Sakae, 256
Waldron, Jeremy, 116, 168, 172
Watsuji, Tetsurō, 248–249, 256
Williamson, Oliver E., 131

Yamaguchi, Genichi, 15, 162, 172
Yamamoto, Yoshitaka, 19, 244–246
Yokoo, Kazuko, 202